Sheela na gig

Sheela na gig

THE DARK GODDESS
OF SACRED POWER

Starr Goode

Inner Traditions
Rochester, Vermont • Toronto, Canada

Inner Traditions
One Park Street
Rochester, Vermont 05767
www.InnerTraditions.com

Library of Congress Cataloging-in-Publication Data
Names: Goode, Starr, author.
Title: Sheela na gig : the dark goddess of sacred power / Starr Goode.
Description: Rochester, Vermont : Inner Traditions, 2016. | Includes bibliographical
    references and index.
Identifiers: LCCN 2016014972 (print) | LCCN 2016016267 (e-book) |
    ISBN 9781620555958 (hardback) | ISBN 9781620555965 (e-book)
Subjects: LCSH: Sheela-na-gigs. | Vulva—Religious aspects. | Goddess religion. |
    BISAC: BODY, MIND & SPIRIT / Spirituality / Divine Mother, The Goddess, Quan
    Yin. | BODY, MIND & SPIRIT / Spirituality / Celtic. | SOCIAL SCIENCE / Women's
    Studies.
Classification: LCC BL458 .G649 2016 (print) | LCC BL458 (e-book) |
    DDC 203/.7--dc23
LC record available at https://lccn.loc.gov/2016014972

Printed and bound in India by Replika Press Pvt. Ltd.

10 9 8 7 6 5 4 3 2 1

Text design and layout by Virginia Scott Bowman
This book was typeset in Garamond Premier Pro and Trade Gothic with Gothic Ultra used as
    the display typeface
Photographs by Starr Goode unless otherwise noted
Illustrations by Ruth Ann Anderson unless otherwise noted

To send correspondence to the author of this book, mail a first-class letter to the author
c/o Inner Traditions • Bear & Company, One Park Street, Rochester, VT 05767, and we will
forward the communication, or contact the author directly at **www.starrgoode.com**.

To my mother's brother,
Adam Gifford

To my friend of a lifetime,
Chetana Karel

To my goddess daughters,
Xochi and Marka Maberry Gaulke

Contents

Invitation In

It is haunting to stand before the ruins of an Irish church and look up above the rounded doorway to discover the stone Sheela na gig half-hidden in a cartouche of ivy. She has reigned from her perch on the south wall for over eight hundred years, the guardian of the entrance and sovereign of all the land she surveys. Her inescapable presence overwhelmed me when at long last I finally made it to Ireland to see before me what I had previously only read about.

The first time I saw an image of a Sheela was over twenty-five years ago. A friend showed me a photocopy of a book by a Danish art historian, Jørgen Andersen, titled *The Witch on the Wall: Medieval Erotic Sculpture in the British Isles*. She turned to a picture of the Kilpeck Sheela and said to me, "You'll be interested in this." From her copy of the book I made my own, and thus began a journey.

I was stunned by this image—clearly a female, yet clearly not human, displaying her large pudendum with no shame on a Christian church. How could this be? How could such a figure exist at such a time and in such a place? The medieval masons, the artists who created these sculptures, left no texts of explanation. Her image would have to carry me where no words could.

Over the ensuing years it was my sacred pleasure to make many voyages to the British Isles, and to Ireland, to see more of her kind. I used the taxonomy of all the known Sheelas in Ireland, England, Wales, and Scotland from Andersen's research. This list was my guide to the Sheelas of those northern isles, as I searched for them on rural churches, through fields of grazing cattle, on remote islands, and in graveyards. A whole day could be spent tracking down one Sheela.

Killinaboy Church Sheela,
County Clare, Ireland.

Nothing represents the necessity of reimagining the female in Western culture more than the startling Sheela na gig. The power of her image signifies a wholeness that can never be completely understood. But standing in the green countryside among the gray stones, meeting her *in person,* was a beginning...

PART I

History

1
Historical Overview
Agreements and Disagreements

The image of a Sheela na gig is astonishing to behold. In her time she has been called "whore," "hag," "witch," "evil-eye stone," "devil," "healer," and "goddess." She embraces a conundrum of opposites: She clearly offers up her ripe sex, yet she emanates a repelling menace from the upper half of her body. Her hips tilt in open invitation, yet she can be a monstrous hag with a skull of death. Most figures are carved in high or low relief from limestone, but they also may be of gray, red, or white sandstone, or granite, often in contrast to the stones surrounding her[1]—all the better to accent her quintessential feature: her private parts being pulled open by her hands. One almost winces, so spirited is this spreading open of her vulva. Only this one feature makes a Sheela a Sheela—she must be exposing her genitals. Through their display, all Sheela na gigs assert the powers of the female sex.

Despite centuries of debate about their meaning, the Sheela na gigs remain a mystery. Arguments began in the nineteenth century when antiquarians, those early archaeologists stirred by a romantic passion for things of the past, started to catalog antiquities in the countryside, including the medieval figure of the Sheela. Puzzled by these strange images, they questioned why stone carvings of naked females in bold sexual exhibition of themselves appeared on Christian churches throughout the islands of Ireland and Great Britain. Questions continue to this day. Are the Sheelas incarnations of the devil used to warn against the evils of the flesh, or are they part of the undying legacy of the ancient Great Goddess? Why should a nude woman with genitals half the size of her body have been so popular in the misogynistic Middle Ages, and why does she continue to fascinate us today?

Each Sheela na gig has a unique appearance or, one might say, personality. She comes in different shapes and sizes, in height measuring anywhere from one to three feet. She may have the shrunken dugs of a hag or full, pendulous breasts hanging from the sides of her body. She may be a fierce crone with bony ribs or possess a pregnant-looking belly. A Sheela na gig more times than not is as bald as the stone from which she is carved, but she may have plaits flying out from either side of her head. The countenance of the Sheela na gig conveys a wide range of expressions: the mouth pursed in an *O* of fright or ecstasy, or an ominous display of teeth (see figure 1.1). The thick lips of her face can echo her swollen sexual labia (see figure 1.2). Clearly, the

Figure 1.1. Chloran Sheela, County Westmeath, Ireland. This figure has a singularly large head, with the most prominent teeth of any Sheela. It was found in a field in 1859 and probably came from a nearby church. *(Image © The Trustees of the British Museum)*

Figure 1.2. Cavan Sheela, County Cavan, Ireland. This formidable Sheela once adorned a church. She has a protruding tongue and a large vulva reaching down past her knees. *(Courtesy of Cavan County Museum; photograph by Starr Goode)*

Sheela na gig is no ordinary woman. One glance at her exaggerated vulva tells us that she is, literally, female; but figuratively, what meaning does she embody?

The Written Record

During the era of the Sheela na gigs, between the twelfth and the early seventeenth centuries, no written commentary on their purpose exists. The first recorded account of a Sheela occurs in 1840. In his Ordnance Survey Letters, John O'Donovan, a prominent surveyor hired to record antiquities throughout Ireland, writes of his memorable encounter with a Sheela na gig on the Kiltinan Church, County Tipperary (see figure 1.3). He cites Thomas O'Conor, also doing field work in Tipperary, who had visited this same Sheela two weeks earlier. O'Conor had described a female sculpture "whose attitude and expression conspire to impress the grossest idea of immorality and licentiousness" and found it "a complete mystery why such a figure should be placed at a house of public worship."[2] O'Conor goes on to wonder about its ill effects on the minds of the Christian congregation.

Both men's Victorian sensibilities seem to have been quite undone by the blatant sexuality of the Sheela na gig. O'Donovan found it to be in "very bad taste to exhibit such a figure on a Christian chapel" and claimed that its presence there must "owe its origins to the wantonness of some loose mind."[3] O'Donovan traveled around Ireland for thirteen years in the course of his duties as a surveyor, yet he allotted more time to his comments on this Sheela than to any other single artifact.[4] Disgusted though he may have claimed to be, he was certainly mesmerized by the striking figure, and like so many others he could not stop looking. Nevertheless, many Sheelas did not get recorded, purposely ignored by shocked researchers who considered them to be "hideous historical oddities."[5]

With the discovery of new figures, new articles appeared periodically in various journals.[6] In 1894, "Figures Known as Hags of the Castle, Sheelas, or Sheela na gigs" tabulated a list of all known Sheelas. Published in the *Journal of the Royal Society of Antiquaries of Ireland,* the article describes

Figure 1.3. Kiltinan Church Sheela, County Tipperary, Ireland. Nineteenth-century surveyors of Irish antiquities found this dancing Sheela obscene. *(Photograph courtesy of Joe Kenny, www.fethard.com)*

thirty-two Irish and three English figures. The paper claims that during the fourteenth and fifteenth centuries, Sheelas were called Hags of the Castle and placed on building walls "either for ornament, or under the idea of their possessing some occult and sacred influence, such as conferring good fortune or additional safety on the owner."[7] At last, a purpose is ascribed to the Sheela! The lords of the castle may have believed her sexual display to be sacred, possessing apotropaic, or protective, powers.

Moving on to the twentieth century, Edith M. Guest, a pioneering scholar, traveled extensively in the Irish countryside conducting a field survey of the Sheelas. This work resulted in her seminal "Irish Sheela-na-gigs in 1935," which updated and enlarged the 1894 list and identified sixty-five Sheelas. She describes variations in their appearances and cites all the available data on each figure, with accompanying photographs. Guest opens her taxonomy with the dry observation that there has "lately been a revival of interest" in the Sheelas; she sees an ancient female lineage for the Sheelas as "being probably symbols of a pre-historic cult."[8]

Modern interest in the Sheelas was revived in 1977 with the first comprehensive study of the subject, Jørgen Andersen's masterwork *The Witch on the Wall: Medieval Erotic Sculpture in the British Isles.* Expanding interest in the study of the Sheelas continues into the present, with several books by Irish and English authors (more on this later), while the discovery of more Sheela na gigs continues to this day. The dedicated Sheela seeker can still find her on many structures in the countryside and in museums, especially in Ireland, a land possessing the greatest concentration of Sheelas. A scientific database compiled in 2007 finds that one hundred and twenty-one Sheelas exist in Ireland, forty-seven in England, six in Scotland, and four in Wales.[9]

The Puzzle of Her Name

The name Sheela na gig is not from any one language but is a blend of English and Gaelic. The Irish behind the half-anglicized name is difficult to trace.[10] The exact meaning of her name, like so many of her qualities, perplexes us. O'Donovan, in his 1840 letters, refers to the figure as Síle Ni Ghig and Sheela ni Ghig.[11] Around the same time, a member of the Royal Irish Academy reports that Shela na Gig is the name used by country people.[12] In fact, most Sheelas are found in rural settings. Possible translations of the name Sheela na gig from the Irish include Sighle na gCíoch, meaning "old hag of the breasts," or Síle-ina-Giob, in all the scholarly literature, meaning "Sheela [a name for an old woman] on her hunkers," which well describes the froglike squat of the figure.[13] Or, getting to the gist of the matter, Síle-na-gigh, "Sheela of the vagina"; *gigh* is slang, not a standard Gaelic term.[14]

Foclóir Gaedilge agus Béarla, a 1904 Irish-English dictionary, gives several definitions of Síle ní Gadra. One general meaning is "wanton or inappropriate sexuality"; another is "a personification of Ireland." So her meanings can range from that of a loose woman to a goddess.[15] In the late nineteenth century, the anglicized form, Sheela na Guira, was attributed to the Sheela on Cullahill Castle (see figure 1.4).[16] Local folklore holds that the figure was "a former head of the O'Hare family."[17] Such attributions affirm the Sheela's power as a Hag of the Castle guarding clan territories and connect her to the Celtic goddess of sovereignty, who not only protects the land but is the land itself (more on this in chapter 3).

The earliest form of the name dates to 1781, when oddly enough there was a British Royal Navy ship with the name HMS *Sheilah-nagig* active in the West Indies. The name was explained as Síle na Guig, which translates as "Irish Female Sprite."[18] One scholar connects *gig* with *jig* (a lively dance) with her discovery of country folk dances called Sheela na giggs.[19] Certainly some Sheelas stand on one foot, which hints at a possible shaman's function, as if they dance between the worlds (see figure 1.5). In the end, one can despair like H. C. Lawlor did when he writes in the journal *Man,* "The term 'sheela-na-gig' has no etymological meaning and is an absurd name."[20]

Agreements and Disagreements

Arguments over the origins of the elusive Sheela na gig abound in several recently published books. Might she be a regenerative symbol for the cycle of life, representing fecundity, decay, and renewal? Does she embody the power of Celtic goddesses first conjured on pagan soil but linking back to Stone Age divinities of ancient Europe? Or did she originate on the European continent as a decorative motif on medieval Romanesque churches, depicting the sin of lust?

Art historians Anthony Weir and James Jerman, in *Images of Lust: Sexual*

Figure 1.4. Cullahill Castle Sheela, County Laois, Ireland. With a concentrated gaze, she surveys the land from forty feet up on the south wall of a peel tower; she has a massive upper body, but the lower half is missing. *(Photograph courtesy of John Harding, www.sheelanagig.org)*

Figure 1.5. Ballynahinch Castle Sheela, County Tipperary, Ireland. One must walk through the atmospheric ruins of a church to find a Sheela performing a jig over a door on the east wall of a peel tower.

Carvings on Medieval Churches, contend that the Sheela's open display functions strictly as a Christian image to warn against lust. The image first appears in the twelfth century as an architectural design on Romanesque churches in northern Europe. In *The Witch on the Wall,* Jørgen Andersen also sees the Sheelas' beginnings as a sexual exhibitionist appearing on churches, but he believes that, over the centuries, they transformed into more powerful, protective figures when later blended with indigenous Irish traditions.

Two more recent works, by Joanne McMahon and Jack Roberts (*The Sheela-na-Gigs of Ireland and Britain: The Divine Hag of the Christian Celts*) and by scholar Maureen Concannon (*The Sacred Whore: Sheela Goddess of the Celts*), hold that the image of the Sheela, rather than being a minatory one, was revered by country folk. Rural people saw the figure as a holdover from the earlier Celtic Christian era or an even earlier Celtic pagan period of powerful female figures. A carving of a familiar female divinity could entice the pagan country folk into the Christian churches. Thus the Catholic Church employed the Sheela figure as a means of converting the population to Christianity. These authors regard the Sheelas as being native to Ireland, present long before the coming of Christianity, with antecedents in Celtic sculpture and myth.

Another stance is that the true Sheelas only emerged in Ireland after the first English invasion of 1169. This Sheela mixes the traditions of the Anglo-Norman invaders with the existing Gaelic culture. The Irish artists saw in the female exhibitionist motif the duality of their goddesses who had powers over creation and destruction. Thus inspired, they combined the Romanesque figure with their lingering pagan beliefs to create the medieval Sheela. The Irish Sheelas morphed to become bigger and more wild and monstrous, with a menacing strength. They often appear on castles built by English lords who employed Gaelic masons.

Sociologist and author Barbara Freitag, in *Sheela-na-gigs: Unravelling an Enigma,* argues that these sculptures were seen by peasants in the countryside as magical birthing stones. They represented folk deities and were used to help women survive childbirth. In her 2009 doctoral dissertation *Lifting the Veil: A New Study of the Sheela-Na-Nigs of Britain and Ireland,* archaeologist Theresa Oakley also seeks to bring a new understanding to the meaning of the Sheela na gigs. In this academic study replete with spreadsheets, pie charts, and a gazetteer, the author eschews any theories except her own. She believes that the Sheelas are magical entities with apotropaic powers that manifest in their sexual display. And although she wants to lift the veil, Oakley concedes the figures are "representations of that which can never and is not meant to be seen."[21]

Others, like eminent archaeologist Marija Gimbutas, trace the image of the Sheelas back to the origins of art and religion in Neolithic and Upper Paleolithic Europe. Her prominent vulva links her to the Old European goddess of death and regeneration, who as a personification of nature and the cosmos ruled over all cycles of existence. The sacred display of the Sheelas connects her to the vulvas carved on prehistoric cave walls. This art is probably the oldest European representation of the powers of life, the stream of creation and dissolution that never stops.

The era of the Sheelas spanned over five centuries. They were set on churches, castles, tower houses, walls, bridges, holy wells, tombs, capitals, and standing stones. But times change, and with the more brutal English invasions, the growing power of Puritanism, and the resulting Counter-Reformation of the Catholic Church, the image of the Sheela na gig was no longer tolerated by the church.

No written records remain to unravel the mysteries of the Sheelas. No treatise from their time exists on the meaning behind the image, on what spiritual impulses or ideas inspired their creation. All interpretation is specu-lation, formed by the available evidence but also shaped by the bias of the observer. Many make claims that they cannot adequately back up. With the rise of feminist scholarship that deconstructs entrenched patriarchal con-cepts, a new analysis of the past shows the sexuality of the Sheelas in a more positive light. Scholar James H. Dunn notes that when writing about the Sheelas, "all theories may touch the truth in some way."[22] No one knows for sure. However, one can say with certainty that her image survives, and the fascination with the mysterious Sheela na gigs has only continued to grow.

2

The Sheela as Sin

For some art historians, there is no mystery about the origins of the Sheela na gig. She began as a carving of sexual exhibitionism on medieval churches; by openly displaying her female genitals she symbolizes the sin of carnal lust. Medieval religious dogma dictated that punishment in hell should fit the crime on earth. Fornicate in this life, and a woman might be burdened with a huge vulva in the next—the next being, presumably, in hell.[1] Her supposed grotesqueness mirrors a disgusting sexuality. She is a sermon in stone that terrorizes and thus protects the good folk from eternal damnation. The image also served as visual entertainment for an illiterate congregation. Such figures played out the great medieval drama of salvation or damnation. Thus the Sheela figure has been interpreted by some scholars as a tangible form of the devil emblazoned on a church wall. But is the Sheela an embodiment of sin? Did her image begin in the exhibitionist motif? What validity do such claims hold?

The Spread of Romanesque Architecture

Early in the twelfth century, the first dated female exhibitionist figures are found on Romanesque churches in France and Spain. This new style of architecture soon reached the shores of Great Britain and Ireland. It was a time of tremendous social upheaval. The date of 1000 CE had been a milestone in the history of western Europe. The millennial milestone passed, the age of the Viking raids had ended, and the world was still intact. Western Europe became a more peaceful place. Christianity spread, and a great building boom began. "It was as if the world had shaken itself, and, casting off its old garments, had dressed itself again in every part in a white robe of churches."[2] What emerged was the first truly European style of architecture, the Romanesque (although it was based on some elements of Roman buildings, such as rounded arches and barrel vaults).

These newly constructed Romanesque churches sprang up alongside well-traveled pilgrimage routes on the coasts of northern Spain and western France. To accommodate a growing number of pilgrims, larger churches were built on a crosslike floor plan, all the better to view newly enshrined religious relics. These religious edifices were immensely popular. On any given day the cathedral of Santiago de Compostela, in northern Spain (which claimed to possess the bones of St. James), could expect a thousand pilgrims to pass through.[3] However, pilgrims on the road to Santiago were not always known for their spiritual purity; on the way they indulged in secular joys as they shopped for souvenirs and enjoyed the wares of wine sellers and the attentions of the prostitutes who crowded the pilgrimage routes.[4] One can recall that that most famous of literary pilgrimages, Chaucer's *Canterbury Tales,* about a group of pilgrims on their way to visit the shrine of Saint Thomas à Becket at Canterbury Cathedral, certainly had its bawdy elements.

With this age of pilgrims, the Romanesque school of architecture extended through France and Spain, and then to the British Isles and Ireland. The frequency of travel made the transmigration of art forms rapid and easy.[5] Similarities of iconographic ideas propagated throughout the Romanesque world, often by means of itinerant masons, who traveled with their pattern books to various building sites.[6] Well-traveled English lords, Irish kings, aristocrats, and prominent churchmen also returned from visits to continental shrines to build their own churches.[7] Most important, it was on these sacred structures that the female exhibitionist figure made an early appearance.

Corbel Tables

A popular architectural feature of medieval Romanesque churches was the corbel table, which supported the cornice of the building with a ledge of small sculptures encircling the outside walls. These corbel tables displayed figures of fantastical stone carvings (see figure 2.1). Romanesque sculpture,

shunning a cool, classical balance, was wild and passionate. This art is characterized by words like *bizarre, grotesque,* and *dynamic,* and it still has the power to haunt us.[8] In carving individual corbel figures, the masons seem to have let their imaginations run free, creating a wide-ranging gallery of disturbing figures. The female exhibitionist motif in a shameless posture of display fits in well with her misshapen neighbors: foliage spewers (see figure 2.2), acrobats, entertainers, misers, clutching couples, tongue pullers, anus showers, and devouring beasts of every kind, as well as seductive mermaids (see figure 2.3) whose dangerous sexuality echoes that of the later Sheelas. Countless examples of these female exhibitionists can be found among the abundant corbel art of northern Europe. No one can say for sure how many of these figures exist because "it would take an age to scour all the corbel tables in France and Spain."[9]

Figure 2.1. A corbel table at Romsey Abbey, Hampshire, England, depicting a Sheela-like figure (the original Romanesque corbel was replaced in Victorian times) giving birth between two corbels of animal masks.

Figure 2.2. Foliage spewer and display figure, Melbourne Parish Church, Derbyshire, England. This catlike carving assumes a Sheela posture with a double V-shaped vulva below her breasts. Is this a figure of sin, or is the abundance of nature pouring from her mouth?

To what end are these females displaying themselves? In *Images of Lust,* Anthony Weir and James Jerman's exhaustive study of the corbel sculptures in Romanesque art, the authors see a Christian admonition against the sin of lust in the female figure's exhibitionistic pose. The medieval church, with its celibate clergy who had taken vows of perpetual chastity, was particularly obsessed with the lure of female sexuality. The corbel table figures, through their unholy images, act as a morality lesson on the ever-present dangers of human life as seen through the lens of a medieval worldview. Sins like fornication lead to an eternity in hell. The spirit of lust *is* a female exposing her sex in a gesture "ugly as sin."[10]

Across the Romanesque corbel tables, many a dramatic exhibitionist

Figure 2.3. Clonfert mermaid, chancel arch, Clonfert Abbey, County Galway, Ireland, 15th century. An enduring sexual motif, the split-tailed mermaid holds the traditional comb and mirror.

figure displays herself, her body distorted from the confining space of a corbel bracket. At times with an air of ridicule, these figures chronicle from beneath the eaves the temptations of humanity. A female exhibitionist can appear as a classic *acrobatiste* with a formidable flexibility. The Champagnolles acrobat is one such corbel figure, found on the church of Saint Pierre, built along the pilgrimage route to Spain (see figure 2.4). Her rude countenance shows a mouth pursed in surprise, caught up in a

Figure 2.4. Champagnolles exhibitionist, Saint-Pierre, parish church of Champagnolles, Charente Maritime, France, 12th century—one of many impudent corbel carvings on the church. *(Photograph courtesy of Tina Negus)*

sensation as she touches herself, pulling apart her lower lips. About her is a feeling of an entertaining earthiness, as if the mason just couldn't help himself as he rendered in stone her formidable flexibility. As such figures possess the primary quality of a Sheela na gig—the nude display—Jørgen Andersen thinks that in the exhibitionist motif, we have "found a model" for the Sheelas.[11]

English and Irish Romanesque Figures

Crossing the English Channel, we find the earliest recorded English Sheela at Kilpeck, Herefordshire, in the southwest of the country (see figure 2.5). She stands out among the eighty-five carvings on the corbel table surrounding the Church of St. Mary and St. David, one of the most perfect English Romanesque churches in England. Records show that church construction began around 1140 after builder Oliver de Merlemond, the seneschal for a wealthy Norman lord, returned from a pilgrimage to France, where he had undoubtedly been influenced by the corbel design patterns he saw there.[12] A series of figures at Kilpeck reveals the exact sequence of a French church that de Merlemond had visited: a clutching couple, a musician, an acrobat. To this day, the Sheela has a smile on her huge bald head as she pulls open a great pudendum the same size as her body. This image is reproduced in books and in statuettes more often than any other Sheela na gig, making her the most famous of her kind. Her corbel companions include animals, masks, musicians, debauched lovers, mythical creatures—all attesting to the unusual license given to artists to create these small sculptures that appear in a strange amalgamation of Celtic, Anglo-Saxon, Scandinavian, and French Romanesque themes.

A walk around this handsome church reveals a cornucopia of images: a Tree of Life tympanum (see figure 2.6), intricate Celtic scrollwork, a Green Man, a phoenix in a cocoon of frankincense and myrrh, an Agnus Dei, four rams, dragons above angels, beasts biting humans, a manticore, lions, an upside-down ibex, beak heads, Viking animal heads, a hound and a hare in harmony, a kissing couple, a pig, knights, a pair of doves, a basilisk that can kill with a look, and, of course, the famous Sheela na gig.

Figure 2.5. Kilpeck Sheela, Church of St. Mary and St. David, Herefordshire, England, 12th century. She has cheerfully displayed her femaleness for centuries.

Figure 2.6. Tree of Life tympanum, Church of St. Mary and St. David, Herefordshire, England, 12th century. Crowning the magnificent south door, the Tree of Life shows the influence of pagan symbols in the creation of this Christian church.

In Ireland, the earliest dated Sheela or acrobatic exhibitionist figure is found on the Nun's Church at Clonmacnoise, County Offaly, a well-known Irish center of learning in the Middle Ages. This figure brings up the question: At what point does the exhibitionist female earn the name of Sheela? Even though she lacks the characteristic hand gesture, she more than makes up for it with her wide display. At Clonmacnoise, about half a mile away from the main complex of buildings, a "veritable monk's town," sits the solitary Nun's Church, near the beautiful banks of the River Shannon (see figure 2.7).[13] Construction on this gem of Irish Romanesque architecture was completed in 1167, just two years before the first Anglo-Norman invasion of Ireland by Britain. Chronicles record "the church of the nuns at Cluain-mic-noise was finished by Dearvorgail, daughter of Morrogh O'Melaghline."[14]

Figure 2.7. Nun's Church at Clonmacnoise, County Offaly, Ireland, 12th century. At this spiritual site, women offered up their blessings.

The Clonmacnoise exhibitionist can be found as a carving on the third tier of the chancel arch at the back of the church near the altar. Part of a series of spandrel motifs set in a repeated pattern of chevrons, she is the outstanding figure of the design (see figure 2.8). Her peanut head displays a wide grin, and in a feat worthy of a French acrobatiste, her legs are so spread apart that her heels rest on her cheeks. Like the Kilpeck Sheela, she seems merry in the bold display of herself. Researchers Joanne McMahon and Jack Roberts note that Irish and British Romanesque decorations are more "tamed down" than those disturbing figures on the Continent because "there was a greater fear of hell and damnation amongst the people of medieval Europe than among the Saxons and Celts of Ireland and the British Isles."[15]

Figure 2.8. Exhibitionist figure, chancel arch, Nun's Church at Clonmacnoise, County Offaly, Ireland, 12th century. Half in shadow and half in light on the cold, wet Sunday of my visit, she has been in her original setting for over eight hundred years.

Concentration of Church Power and the Degradation of Women

At the time that the first female exhibitionists were carved out of stone by medieval masons, Christianity dominated Europe. The conquest of England by William, duke of Normandy, in 1066 brought with it many religious orders from the Continent. By the middle of the next century they "had built more than 1,000 religious houses," and subsequently English-trained bishops went to Ireland, seeking to wrest power from the old Celtic Christian Church.[16] The Roman Catholic Church began to tighten its political grip over Ireland with the goal of making Rome the center of religious authority. From the twelfth century onward, new monastic orders such as the Cistercians, Augustinians, and Dominicans were formed to consolidate papal dominion as well as for the Roman Catholic Church to establish canonical practices like appointing its own bishops.[17]

One of the Roman church's goals was to destroy the independence of the Celtic Christian Church and to accrue for itself the "vast lands and wealth" of the Irish monastic system, whereby the chieftain of a clan provided the land for the church or monastery.[18] In 1155, the English pope Adrian IV granted to King Henry II "the hereditary possession of Ireland," paving the way for England's first invasion of Ireland.[19] For the pope, it was intolerable that the Irish church, less repressive than the Roman Catholic Church on the Continent, still permitted married clergy, let alone the existence of the Brehon laws. These laws included the old Celtic custom of divorce and remarriage, thereby granting more freedom to women. Due to the legacy of powerful women in Celtic society, the Irish had a different worldview that did not share medieval Europe's fear of female sexuality.[20]

As a consequence of repressive twelfth-century "reforms" in Ireland by the English such as the Synod of Cashel and the Synod of Kells, the native Celtic monasteries were doomed.[21] Historical forces such as the first Anglo-Norman invasion of Ireland, in 1169, and the concentration of power in Rome effectively "cut the knot" of the Irish kinship system and its hereditary land laws, and it established a feudal structure based on the diocesan system, with all tithes and taxes essentially paid to Rome.[22]

So what does it mean that the female exhibitionist and then the Sheela na gigs began to appear on monasteries founded by foreign continental orders? Two Irish authors with works on the Sheela disagree. Eamonn Kelly, of the National Museum of Ireland, argues that this was a warning by the Anglo-Norman church to the Irish against the sin of lust.[23] In contrast, scholar Maureen Concannon draws on many disciplines, including history, archetypal psychology, and archaeology, in offering a feminist interpretation of the figures as the goddess of the land's sovereignty, and she contends that the presence of the Sheela figures reflects the earlier, enduring Gaelic belief in the Great Mother.[24] Irish customs had provided "substantial rights for women."[25] But as the "sheer power represented by the newly centralized papacy" took root, women, instead of being revered, would now be seen as objects of temptation.[26] Tragically, it became a time of intense misogyny.

The slaughter of the witch burnings would soon begin. In Rome it was debated whether women even had souls. There was no doubt, however, that women, via Eve, had brought about the downfall of "mankind." St. Jerome preached: "Woman is the gate of the devil, the path of wickedness, the sting of the serpent, in a word a perilous object."[27] And what better image on which church fathers could project their misogyny than the display of a big, rude vulva, regarding such a sexual display as the very embodiment of the mortal sin of *luxuria,* "lust," one of the seven deadly sins? The sin most attributed to men was *avaritia,* "avarice," represented by the figure of the miser clutching his bag of gold whose weight drags him down to hell (see figure 2.9).

The Minds of the Masons and the Pagan Past

We know that exhibitionist females appear on twelfth-century churches in the company of other figures in various stages of damnation. What intentions lie behind the creation of these figures? What was in the minds of the artist-masons? Were their imaginations influenced by their current environment, or was there an influence that reached back much further than medieval Europe?

Figure 2.9. Miser with money purse, Melbourne Parish Church, Derbyshire, England. Enter the church but be warned of a damning sin by the carving on the south doorway!

Jørgen Andersen says that it is not known from where the Sheela came, and that one can only hope to understand her within the medieval setting. He insists that she "crops up, a fully developed motif in the repertoire of the Norman carvers, from about the middle of the 12th century."[28] We know the mason worked in a milieu of misogyny; it was expected that he abhor the female body. Yet, admits Andersen, some carvers may have been given to "subtle thought" with "a belief in the power of the nude."[29] One cannot live without instincts. While no one can speak to the contents of the unconscious minds and motivations of others, we know that these stone masons weren't that far removed in time from thousands of years of worship of the female body of the Great Goddess. Who knows what atavistic themes might have been lingering in the minds of these artists?

Such figures of sexual display can be seen as part of the folk art of the Middle Ages. And this folk art, even Anthony Weir and James Jerman in *Images of Lust* concede, drew its inspiration from eclectic sources, including classical and heathen ones, while still insisting its morals were pure Christian. These authors point out that "many classical hybrid monsters found their way into Romanesque iconography, among them a fish-tailed human female."[30] Romanesque motifs were often adapted from images of classical divine figures such as Tellus Mater, Mother Earth. Other "inspiration can be pointed to, such as the Greek cult associated with the goddess Demeter and her daughter Persephone."[31]

Did the Sheela na gig originate from an exhibitionist motif imported from France and Spain? Jørgen Andersen confesses to some confusion in the conclusion of his chapter on the Sheela as a Romanesque motif: "The sheela shows a somewhat baffling development within the Western world. But there is nothing very mysterious about her existence. She belongs with the alluring shapes and monster combats in the strange sub-world of Romanesque art, where an erotic colouring of the troubles of mankind [*sic*] are always a possibility."[32]

Yes, it is baffling if one's analysis completely eschews any pagan traditions. She popped up out of nowhere, just like that?

3
Celtic Connection

The question arises: How can the Sheela na gig be only a medieval figure? Pagan goddesses from mythic literature and Celtic stone sculptures link the Sheela to times before the Middle Ages. The Irish adapted their Sheela na gigs from earlier images found in words and stone, making the figures the latest expression of Celtic beliefs that never died in Ireland. As art historian Françoise Henry notes in *Irish Art in the Early Christian Period,* "A remarkable continuity is one of the most striking aspects of Irish art."[1] Some Celtic sculptures date back to the Iron Age, possibly as early as 50 BCE, and into the early Christian era, ca. 400 to 800 CE. Tales and myths were only written down later by medieval Irish monks (roughly between the fifth and twelfth centuries). Even though the beliefs and old learning of the native Irish culture were recorded at these later dates, because of the Celtic fidelity to the art of oral recitation, we still get a "remarkably faithful picture of the Iron Age Celts."[2]

Pagan Ireland, Christian Ireland

The roots of the Sheela na gigs stretch back into pagan Ireland. Never occupied by the Romans, the Irish were able to keep their tribal Celtic culture alive well into the Christian era. Ireland lived in a "strange seclusion," on the fringes of the Roman Empire and outside its influence, so the pagan Irish were free to cultivate their ancient traditions and "preserve a prehistoric fluidity of mind."[3] Unlike those conquered people, the Celts never had to endure the shame of having their culture characterized as second-rate and primitive compared to the well-organized juggernaut of Roman civilization. Nevertheless, when the Roman Empire collapsed in the fifth century CE, Christianity spread across Europe all the way to Ireland, and in this way the pagan polytheistic beliefs of the Celts blended with Christianity. Françoise Henry believes this is why Celtic art did not disappear with the arrival of Saint Patrick, the Romano-British Christian missionary.[4]

This is not to say there were no conflicts; the legend of Saint Patrick driving out the snakes—of which there were in fact none in Ireland—became the familiar patriarchal trope of subduing the female monster. The Great Goddess of the old pagan religion was demonized as an evil serpent, with the new conquering hero/saint slaying the dragon of the once-powerful divine feminine. Miriam Robbins Dexter, a scholar of Indo-European and women's studies, in the opening chapter of her book *Whence the Goddesses,* delineates in substantive detail the origins of the dragon/serpent as a probable descendant of the Neolithic snake goddess found throughout Old Europe (ca. 7000 BCE to 3500 BCE).[5] She describes the fate of this female deity in many post-Neolithic societies of Europe, the Near East, and Egypt: "In the earliest myths of the hero and the dragon or serpent, the serpent was often a goddess: the Greek Python, the Sumerian Tiamat, and the Indic Danu may have been successors to the Neolithic European snake goddess. The new, young, warrior-hero (Zeus, Marduk, Baal, Indra, Yahweh, Horus) slew the serpent of darkness, thus killing off the old order of deities, the ancient dragons and serpents who were viewed as 'chaotic.'"[6] At the root of such slaughter lies a fear of the feminine.

In his masterwork *How to Kill a Dragon,** author Calvert Watkins, professor of linguistics and classics at Harvard University, identifies the standard formula of the central myth of the patriarchal Indo-European poetic traditions: the divine hero slays the dragon or serpent. This theme is fundamental to the symbolic culture of speakers of the proto-European language

---

*Special thanks to scholar Max Dashú who in 1970 founded the Suppressed Histories Archives (www.suppressedhistories.net), a collection of 15,000 slides and 20,000 digital images and has created 150 slideshows on female cultural heritages across human history. She pointed the way to Watkins's book.

and occurs in the same linguistic form in a wide range of sources and over millennia.[7] In a folktale about Saint Patrick, one such woman-demon-serpent was Caorthanach, who was said to have been drowned by Patrick in the sea.[8] In a connected story, the Sheela na gig on Taghmon Church (see figure 3.1), County Westmeath, is also sometimes known as Caorthanach. She was once a human woman, but Saint Patrick disapproved of her sexuality so he transformed her into a stone Sheela and placed her on a wall, where she must remain until Judgment Day.[9] Yet the deep-seated Celtic goddesses "could hardly be displaced overnight by a new creed," and in fact the church, in its efforts to convert the indigenous population, tolerated "what could be kept of the old beliefs and secular customs."[10]

Sculptural Representations

Examples of early Celtic and Celtic-Christian sculpture can be found along the shores and islands of Lower Lough Erne, County Fermanagh. At Killadeas, a figure known as the Bishop's Stone (see figure 3.2) feels almost as if it is planted in the ground of the church cemetery. The figure's thick lips can be seen in the later Cavan Sheela (figure 1.2), and the deliberate scarring of its cheek is echoed in the Kiltinan Church Sheela (figure 1.3). Jørgen Andersen says that the Bishop's Stone continues the imagery of earlier Celtic "idols," and he wonders if an awareness of these visual themes lasted long enough "so as to color the idea of a sheela, as medieval carvers saw it."[11]

In the iconography of the Bishop's Stone, pagan and Christian traditions overlap. The figure's big head reflects the Celtic belief that the prominent head is "the seat of the soul, the very center of being."[12] The figure's pillar-shaped body has a panel of carved interlaced ornamental designs characteristic of Irish art. The same techniques can be seen in illuminated manuscripts such as *The Book of Durrow,* one of the earliest books of the Christian gospels dating back to the seventh century CE.[13] The stone derives its ecclesiastical name from an additional carving on another of its sides—a clergyman with his bell and crozier, which bishops received when they were consecrated.[14]

The ancient Killadeas cemetery with its unmarked tombstones demonstrates a remarkable continuity in that the grounds are still used for

Figure 3.1. Taghmon Church Sheela, County Westmeath, Ireland, 15th century. A different interpretation for her presence on this semifortified manorial church: she guarded the territory from rival tribes by the force of her four eyes, menacing appearance, and knees clasped high to show her sex.

Figure 3.2. Bishop's Stone, County Fermanagh, Ireland—a forebear of the Sheelas.

interments. Among these graves stand several other timeworn stones. On one remarkable slab, thirteen (by my count) cup marks—carved holes on a stone's surface—collect rainwater like miniature holy wells, signifying the Celtic worship of life-giving water, a pagan testament to the stone's sacredness (see figure 3.3).[15] Later this Cup Stone was Christianized by the addition of a carving of a cross within a circle made on its back side. Hence, the Cup Stone bears the same incongruities as the Bishop's Stone—another example

Figure 3.3. Irish Cup Stone, near Loughcrew, Ballinvalley I, County Meath, Ireland, dating from around the end of the 4th century BCE. A tradition going back to the Irish Neolithic period, these cup marks at the center of concentric circles were engraved on a megalith. *(Courtesy of the Marija Gimbutas Archives at Opus Archives)*

of the Irish blending of imagery from different eras, which continued with the Sheela na gigs.

Traveling north along Lough Erne to Archdale Bay, we find more sculptures on White Island. A look at the history of the island reveals the complex past of Ireland. On this remote island during the early Christian era, a small monastery once existed. A workshop there produced stone sculptures devoted to Christian subjects (except for the anomaly of a Sheela-like figure). The site was probably chosen for its sense of peace and "mystical" silence.[16] This peace was shattered by Viking raids around the ninth century, and the church was left in ruins, the figures scattered in the fields.[17] A Romanesque church was later built in the twelfth century, and by the arch of the doorway the Sheela-like figure was inserted sideways like some Hags of the Castle (more on this in chapter 4; see "Guardian of Entrances").[18] There it remained for centuries, as attested to by a nineteenth-century drawing (see figure 3.4). In 1929, when the church was rebuilt, this figure, along with seven other sculptures, was embedded in the back wall of the church.

How does this earlier figure visually resemble a Sheela? It makes the essential Sheela gesture of reaching down below the abdomen as its body squats down. The sculpture has the big head of Celtic tradition, but with a strange grin, smiling like the Kilpeck, Buckland, and Oaksey Sheelas. However, unlike these Sheelas it is partially clothed in a short tunic, and even though its knees are widely parted, it shows no clear genital display.

The White Island stone figure is one of the best examples of a blending of pagan and Sheela features. Hunkered down like so many of the Sheela na gigs, it has a cross-legged stance similar to the Celtic horned god Cernunnos, a god of nature and prosperity. His "cult was sufficiently deep rooted and important enough to leave indelible traces in later Christian tradition."[19] The White Island sculpture also shares a primary function with the Sheelas: it is a guardian. Set sideways by the door, it watches over the entrance like some of the Irish Sheelas known as Hags of the Castle. This purposeful reuse on the twelfth-century church of the White Island Sheela-like figure shows a lingering belief in the power of this pagan image.[20]

Moving north once more, to the top of Lough Erne, we find Boa Island, named after the Badb, the Celtic warrior-goddess who sometimes fulfills the role of the goddess of sovereignty. Located at the Caldragh cemetery on the west end of the island are two of the most impressive of any Irish stone carvings—the Janus figure and the Lustymore Idol (see figure 3.5). As remote as this site is, the sculptures still generate great interest. In 2007, it was proposed that the figures be moved to the Belfast Museum to protect them from the elements, even though a sheltering canopy had recently been set

Figure 3.4. White Island Church, Lough Erne, County Fermanagh, Ireland. Based on a 19th-century illustration by the antiquarian W. F. Wakeman depicting the 12th-century church, with the 9th-century figure guarding the entrance.

Figure 3.5. Lustymore Idol and Janus figure, Caldragh Cemetery, Lough Erne, County Fermanagh, Ireland.

up. Locals fought this "tooth and nail," and a Fermanagh historian claimed that the iconic figures must remain in place, especially as the Janus figure has been featured "in almost every guide book to Ireland in any language and in almost every book on Celtic and Pre-Christian art."[21]

These two figures are over two thousand years old by Françoise Henry's dating. She contends that the statues are "obviously religious monuments" and most probably made around 50 BCE by Celtic refugees from Gaul who had fled Caesar's conquests.[22] While this date seems very early, others say they were created much later, between 400 and 900 CE, but they cite no evidence or criteria for attributing them to that later time period.[23] The two figures are clearly pagan, but who made them—Celtic people from the Continent, or early Christians who wished to include pagan traditions in their burial sites? The name of the site, Caldragh, adds another layer of meaning. *Cillíní* cemeteries, also known as *ceallúnach, callragh,* and *caldragh,* were unconsecrated grounds, places to bury pagans or unbaptized people.[24]

To this day the two figures stand isolated in the rough grass among the ruins of the atmospheric graveyard. Surrounded by trees and hedges and the uneven terrain of fallen headstones, the place radiates a palpable sense of antiquity. Both figures retain Iron Age pagan identities, dictated by their very un-christian appearance. Indeed, they have not, "like many other Irish monuments, been vaguely Christianized with fanciful saints' names."[25]

Both the Janus figure and the Lustymore Idol have big heads set on powerful shoulders and a typical squatting posture, confirming their Celtic origins. The double-faced Janus statue may be a hermaphrodite, with a penis on the east side of the body and, on the west side, parted lips with a protruding tongue, symbolic of the vulva.[26] Chevron designs tattooed on both sets of cheeks on this figure link the back-to-back faces. Tattooing is a frequent motif on the later Irish Sheelas such as those on the Fethard Wall, Killinaboy, and Moate, to name but a few.

The Lustymore Idol was transplanted in 1939 from nearby Lustymore Island, surviving centuries there "in spite of the inhabitation of Lustymore by monks."[27] I had frequently read that the Lustymore Idol was a male figure. However, on my visit to the island, upon close examination, I saw a faint inverted *V* that marks the top of her vulva (see figure 3.6). Also undeniable

Figure 3.6. Lustymore Idol, Caldragh Cemetery, Lough Erne, County Fermanagh, Ireland. There is nothing like one's own direct observation to notice what patriarchal bias cannot—her femaleness.

is the characteristic Sheela gesture of arms reaching down past the abdomen, grabbing at the vulva area. Anthony Weir further asserts her femaleness with his observation that she is blind in her left eye (not fully carved), making her a divine hag, the Cailleach.[28]

This quality of blindness can be an image of not just old age but inner vision, as in the Irish tale "Dá Choca's Hostel," wherein the goddess Badb appears as the hag "squinting with her left eye" and makes prophecies to her host.[29] Just before his death, the great Irish warrior Cú Chulainn encounters on the road "three Crones, blind of the left eye."[30] The Cailleach has well-known powers of destruction and creation. Such seemingly paradoxical forces also appear in the body of the Sheela, with her dried-up paps above a fertile vulva. All these traits make the Lustymore Idol a very Sheelaesque female and a strong example of the Celtic influences that helped to shape the medieval Sheelas.

Leaving the stone sculptures of Lough Erne and traveling back to Celtic Britain, a female figure was discovered in 1881 in the peat moss near Glencoe, in western Scotland. Dating back to between 725 and 525 BCE, the Ballachulish statue is a life-size figure, almost five feet high, standing on a flat base (see figure 3.7). The bog where she was found looks out to the entrance of a sea loch. In a Sheela-like gesture, both hands are placed on her abdomen above a swollen pubic area with a pronounced cleft to mark her labia. She is sculpted not from stone, but from wood. Because of the sacredness of trees to the Celts, they often fashioned their deities in wood. The Ballachulish figure, carved from oak, was found "with traces of a wickerwork structure" that suggest this site was originally a shrine or perhaps a burial mound.[31] The Celts viewed these mounds as entrances to the spirit world. Thus the Ballachulish "goddess," with her large vulva, can be regarded as a forebear of the Sheelas and a protectress of the boundaries between worlds. Many Sheelas guard the entrances of churches (themselves a place to cultivate other states of consciousness), and the vulva itself is literally a portal of transformation.

Figure 3.7. Ballachulish figure, Glencoe, western Scotland. Over two thousand years old, she is the oldest human figure from Scotland. (*Image © National Museums Scotland*)

Figure 3.8. South Tawton Sheela, St. Andrew's Church, Devonshire, England, 15th century. A wooden Sheela on a wooden ceiling placed high where two roof beams cross. Nearly two feet long, she appears to be surrounded by foliage, with feet looping back much like the Austerfield Sheela at the other end of the country, in Yorkshire. *(Photograph courtesy of John Harding, www.sheelanagig.org)*

Furthermore, not all Sheelas were made of stone. Eamonn Kelly, of the National Museum of Ireland, contends that "there may have been wooden sheela-na-gigs in existence."[32] To this day, in South Tawton, Devonshire, in England, a wooden Sheela can be found as one of the roof bosses of the fifteenth-century Church of St. Andrew (see figure 3.8).

Finally, one of the earliest Celtic prototypes for the Irish Sheela na gig dates back to the fourth century BCE and is found in Reinheim, Germany. A man digging gravel in a sandpit in 1954 uncovered one of the most impressive Celtic burial grounds yet to be discovered. Under a mound, an oak-lined chamber was found, the grave of a powerful queen or princess. She had been ceremoniously interred with "signs of great wealth including gold arm rings and a torc (necklace) and indeed, what may have been the entire contents of her jewel-box, about two hundred pieces made of gold, bronze, amber, coral and glass."[33]

One of the finest pieces of jewelry found in the burial chamber is a female figure carved on the terminus of a gold armlet (see figure 3.9). She displays her vulva in the fashion of a Sheela na gig, with hands pulling open her labia. Rich in iconography, a bird perches above her head, connecting her with an ancient bird goddess or perhaps to Celtic warrior goddesses who can shape-shift from bird to human form. She may also have an association with a snake goddess due to her "spiraling snake legs."[34] In any case, the Reinheim female is the only exhibitionist figure that predates the Middle Ages that is not from the classical world.

All of this art reveals a Celtic tradition of figures carved in stone, wood, and gold, some of which are a millennia older than the Romanesque exhibitionists. They are part of a long tradition of pagan imagery that was "never lost from sight in Ireland."[35]

Sheelas in Literature

The Sheela na gig shares certain attributes with earlier female supernatural figures found in Celtic epics and myths. Her image connects her to the divine hag of the Celts in particular, mirroring the paradox of Celtic goddesses in the duality of both a ripe sexuality and the withered features of a hag. Such duality is the basis of all Celtic thought. The sovereignty goddess can be both creatrix and destroyer, matchless beauty and terrifying hag, a source of bounty or doom.[36] The literary motif of the duality of the ugly hag shape-shifting into an alluring goddess "is seen most clearly in the stories of the conferring of the divine sovereignty of Ireland by such a deity on the king-elect."[37]

In Ireland, the sovereignty goddess is the personified living spirit of the land. To undergo the ritual of the sacred marriage to the Goddess, to mate with her, a mortal man must be courageous indeed to show the stuff that kings are made of. This Irish tradition of the mythic marriage between the land and the king lasted until the seventeenth century, when the English invasion, led by Oliver Cromwell, destroyed much of old Gaelic Ireland.[38]

Figure 3.9. Reinheim figure, near Saarbrüken, West Germany, 370–320 BCE—a grave companion to a Celtic queen. *(Courtesy of the Marija Gimbutas Archives at Opus Archives)*

Subsequently, in the eighteenth and nineteenth centuries, the old sacred marriage motif continues but is transformed into the *aisling,* or dream poetry, wherein Ireland, Éire, appears to the poet in a vision as a woman crying out for her lost spouse and decrying her degradation by foreign usurpers.*[39]

One of the most well-known accounts of the hag-goddess conferring sovereignty (an early redaction dates from the fifth century CE) concerns a legendary high king of early Ireland, Niall. The story of Niall and the Nine Hostages is "an origin-myth in which the dynasty of the Uí Neill, descendants of Niall, [was] founded."[40] The story goes like this: Niall and his four stepbrothers, thirsty from hunting, come upon a well guarded by a loathsome hag whose considerable mouth echoes the exaggerated labia of the Sheelas:

> *She had a mouth in which there was room for a hound.*
> *She had a tooth-fence around her head.*
> *She was an ugly horror of Ireland.*
> (*Book of Leinster,* lines 4580–83)[41]

Aggressively sexual, the hag demands a kiss from the brothers in order that they may drink from her waters. They all flee in terror except for Niall. He is willing not only to kiss the hag but to sleep with her: "As the two embraced, the hag was transformed into a lovely maiden and Niall acceded to the throne."[42]

In the Irish tale "The Destruction of Da Derga's Hostel" (Togail Bruidne Dá Derga), possibly written down as early as the eighth or ninth century,[43] a different fate befalls a young king when he loses his sovereignty by failing to embrace another very Sheela-like hag.[44] In this story, King Conair's refusal of the crone causes the disintegration of his rulership. An ominous portent for the king appears when he enters Da Derga's hostel: "A woman of huge mouth, big, dark, a trouble, ugly, came after him.

---

*A well-known example of this is the play by William Butler Yeats and Lady Gregory, *Cathleen ni Houlihan,* the heroine of which is a personification of an independent Ireland.

Thereafter, even if her snout were thrown upon a branch it would remain sticking to it. Her lower lip [i.e., her labia] extended to her knee."[45] This unnatural vulva is the essence of the Sheelas, many of whose "lower lips" almost touch the ground.

Later in the story, another hag, the Celtic war goddess Badb in her guise as a sovereignty goddess, appears at the hostel after sunset and asks to be admitted to the house: "Each of her two shins was as long as a weaver's beam. They were as black as a beetle's back. A dusky, very wooly cloak about her. Her lower [pubic] hair extended to her knee. Her lips [were] upon the side of her head."[46] She stands alone in the hostel door, a liminal space, just as many Sheelas guard the doors and windows of Irish churches, their vulvas a threshold of transforming energy, the symbol of life and death.[47] In the case of the story of Da Derga's hostel, the goddess Badb foreshadows King Conaire's death. From the door, assuming a magical posture, she stands on one leg with a hand up in the air and utters prophecies to the inhabitants of the hostel.[48] This female has a striking resemblance to the Kiltinan Sheela (figure 1.3), who strikes the exact same stance. Conaire refuses to allow her to enter the hostel, and maintaining her posture, the goddess curses him. Because she remains in her form as a hag, his reign is not legitimatized.[49] When Conaire sexually rejects the goddess, he soon loses his kingdom, then his very life.[50]

The provinces of the Celtic goddesses range from warrior to hag to bestower of sovereignty and protectress of the land to which a goddess remains bound.[51] In the Irish tales of goddesses of war or territorial sovereignty, a strong sexual element is present. Celtic scholar and author Anne Ross maintains that these goddesses are described "in a way which is an almost exact parallel to the imagery of these enigmatic Sheela figures."[52]

From Goddess to Saint

Over the centuries, Christianity eventually absorbed what it could of the old pagan ways, but it could not completely do away with the pagan goddesses. As scholar James H. Dunn points out in his far-ranging essay on the Sheelas: "A central image with which Christianity would have to contend in Ireland is that of the woman who is historically the locus of power and the seat of sovereignty."[53] Aspects of their powers were still manifesting in local territorial deities. With the advent of the new Christian creed, however, a problem arose because of the vacuum created by replacing the numerous Celtic gods and goddesses with one male God. This conundrum was partially solved by the Catholic Church, which turned the Celtic pantheon into an array of saints.[54] Brigit made "several transitions in her route" from Mother Goddess to saint.[55] Another well-known conversion shows the endurance of the ancient religion: Gobnait, once a local goddess, had sovereignty over her particular territory. With her trio of sisters, she ruled over the holy well. In the way of Irish history, the pagan goddess Gobnait is transformed into a saint—Saint Gobnait.

The Abbey of St. Gobnait is located in the village of Ballyvourney, County Cork.[56] It is one of the more popular pilgrimage sites in Ireland. Replete with a modern statue of the saint and the ancient holy well, the ruins of the abbey also house a Sheela na gig. The new image of Saint Gobnait is rendered in stone: She wears a nun's habit; rosary beads drape her wrists; her palms press together in prayer; and her eyes close to outer reality (see figure 3.10). She stands on a hive-shaped plinth encircled by bees, a reference to her attunement with nature, as the bees obeyed her call. In earlier customs recorded in the seventeenth century, a wooden statue of Saint Gobnait was carried around. Hardly seeming very Christian, dancing revels took place under a beam of flowers, with apples and cakes. The couple who could dance the longest into the night at the crossroads won the prize of flowers. In another testimony to Gobnait's powers, the statue was carried "round to sick people, and so it is said, to assist in childbirth."[57]

To this day, on February 11, the saint's feast day, pilgrims come to worship at Ballyvourney. They make their rounds, or *turas,* from the holy well to the Sheela na gig, placed above a window on the south wall of the abbey. While earlier parts of the ritual have been banned by priests, pilgrims continue to recite prayers, to drink from the curative waters of the well, and to touch the Sheela na gig (see figure 3.11). But only hands covered over with handkerchiefs can touch the Sheela, and then one enters the church via the

Figure 3.10. Saint Gobnait, Abbey of St. Gobnait, Ballyvourney, County Cork, Ireland. Goddess and saint, Gobnait could command the forces of nature and presided over rituals of pleasure and healing.

window under the Sheela.[58] Is this an act of respect, an acknowledgment of divine powers that no human may directly contact? In any case, belief in the powers of the Sheela abides.[59]

While we may never know all the original uses of the Sheelas, breaking the surface of her medieval patina reveals a depth of connection to early Irish sculptural art and to mystical tales. And there is one simple fact about the Sheela na gigs: more exist in Ireland than in any other place in the world.

Figure 3.11. Ballyvourney Sheela, Abbey of St. Gobnait, Ballyvourney, County Cork, Ireland. Rites to call on her power continue to this day. Her lower half has been hacked away, a malefic fate that has befallen some of the Sheelas.

4
Medieval Mindset on Pagan Soil

The Christian religion was not a tabula rasa springing up pristine during the medieval period. In fact, it took the Roman Catholic Church centuries of concentrated warfare to conquer the ancient traditions of pagan Europe. Taking the longest view, Christianity is a veneer, the last coat of varnish on the surface of a religious history that began in the Upper Paleolithic period with the pervasive worship of the Great Goddess. The artistic soil of Europe was first pagan. As the archaeological record shows, the earliest evidence of the art of sculpture begins tens of thousands of years ago, when across ancient Europe artists created the so-called Venus figurines. Among the hundreds discovered, not one male figure exists—a testimony to the primacy of the Mother Goddess.

Goddess Religion in Early Britain and Ireland

In Ireland and Britain, enduring traditions testify to the Celtic and Neolithic roots of the Sheela na gigs. Scholar Frank Battaglia attests to "the firmest evidence of goddess religion in the ancient British Isles," beginning with the Neolithic peoples who built great stone monuments such as Stonehenge, to the Roman presence in Britain, and including the Picts, the Anglo-Saxons, and the Celts.[1] Author of several books on the Celts, Miranda Green traces the origins of their beliefs back to "the 'very clear evidence' for the cult of the Mother Goddess in Europe between circa 7500 BC and 3000 BC."[2] Green claims that goddesses "were central to Celtic perceptions of the world" and that "they may have dominated the religion of the Celtic world."[3] In *Pagan Celtic Britain,* Anne Ross, a scholar who writes from wide experience of living in Celtic-speaking communities, where she has traced vernacular tradition, affirms that in the Celtic world-view there was "a mother goddess who presided over mortals," and that the gods themselves belonged to and were controlled "by a great divine mother, nurturer of the gods and of the land."[4]

Perhaps the most magnificent monuments of Neolithic art reflecting the Goddess religion in Ireland and Britain are the great passage grave tombs like Newgrange, in the Boyne Valley of Ireland, and that most famous of all Neolithic sites, Stonehenge, in County Wiltshire, England. Built around five thousand years ago, Newgrange is aligned to the rising sun on the winter solstice. The morning rays enter the main entrance and shine down the long passage of nineteen meters to an altar at the end of the inner chamber (see figure 4.1). This enactment symbolizes the tomb of the winter death goddess being regenerated to become the womb that brings new life in the spring. Furthermore, engravings on the entrance stone (double and triple snake coils) and on the back curbstone (multiple arcs with a triangle inside) represent the ever-creative vulva of the Goddess.[5]

Stonehenge has been described—almost as a cliché—as a place that must be the burial site for some big, important (male) chief. However, as Battaglia points out, "R. J. C. Atkinson, a principle excavator of Stonehenge, discovered on stone 57, one of the huge trilithons erected about 1500 B.C., what he *reluctantly acknowledged* [emphasis mine] to be the 'probable . . . representation of a mother-goddess.'"[6] The monument, like Newgrange, has alignments with the winter solstice sunrise. Its construction continued for over a thousand years, between 3000 and 1500 BCE, thus demonstrating an astonishing endurance of the peoples' belief in the sacredness of the site.[7] Battaglia adds that the clustering of homes within walking distance of one another around Stonehenge is characteristic of "matrilocal residence associated with matrilineal kinship," and that this social organization descends from the practice of the Neolithic Goddess religion.[8]

Figure 4.1. Triple spiral at Newgrange, Boyne River Valley, County Meath, Ireland, ca. 3200 BCE. View from the back chamber looking outward to the passage where the sunlight enters and illumines the carving. *(Courtesy of the Marija Gimbutas Archives at Opus Archives)*

A recent article, "Stonehenge: A View from Medicine," in the July 2009 issue of Britain's *Journal of the Royal Society of Medicine,* has even more startling news: the arrangement of the stones depicts female genitalia. Anthony Perks, a doctor of obstetrics and gynecology at the University of British Columbia, claims that from an aerial view "Stonehenge's inner bluestone circle represents the labia minora and the giant outer sarsen stone circle is the labia majora. The altar stone is the clitoris and the open center is the birth canal."[9] Perks contends that the worldview held by ancient people of a Great Creatrix who generates and sustains life means that "Stonehenge could represent, symbolically, the opening by which Earth Mother gave birth."[10] Thus the whole monument honors her life-giving powers.

One of the most ancient depictions of a humanlike divinity in Britain is the Dagenham Idol. Carved from Scotch pine, it measures about nineteen inches (see figure 4.2). Discovered in 1922, it is now housed in the Colchester Castle Museum in eastern England. The museum inscription describes the figure as being 4,500 years old, "the second oldest human depiction in this country, found twenty feet down in an area of marsh at Dagenham on the north bank of the Thames." Several other wooden figures have been recovered from bogs at various sites in Ireland and Britain, such as the Ballachulish figure mentioned in chapter 3. The Ralaghan effigy was found during peat-cutting in County Cavan (see figure 4.3). On display at the National Museum in Dublin, she is sculpted from yew and is over three feet high. She dates back to between 1100 and 1000 BCE.[11] Both carvings have remarkably similar holes in the pubic area, even though the Dagenham Idol is three thousand years older.

Here the question arises: Are these two figures female, male, or hermaphroditic? Are the holes there to insert a phallus, or is it a vulva? Gender ambiguity remains. However, no phallus was found near either site. The Dagenham Idol certainly has the rounded hips of a female, and the Ralaghan figure has a pronounced female pubic triangle. Archaeologist Bryony Coles, in her study "Anthropomorphic Wooden Figures from Britain and Ireland," reports that upon putting a finger inside the hole of the Ralagan figure, she discovered it "actually widens with the body, and on the floor of the hole there is a small patch of white granular material, possibly quartz."[12] Because of these factors, and that the hole in the Dagenham Idol has a female oval shape, both openings are "ill-designed" to hold a phallus.[13] All in all, such figures suggest a rich thread of tradition that has survived down through the creation of the Sheelas.

The Emergence of the Sheela na gig

For tens of thousands of years, the human imagination has been devoted to the Goddess. Hence it can hardly come as a surprise to find on the same soil of Europe images of supernatural females like Sheelas adorning sacred and secular architecture. Like all living images—those that retain their

Figure 4.2. Dagenham Idol, Dagenham, England—a late Neolithic figure at least as old as Stonehenge. *(Courtesy of Colchester and Ipswich Museum Service; photograph by Starr Goode)*

Figure 4.3. Ralaghan figure, County Cavan, Ireland. She bears the ancient female image of the downward-pointing triangle. *(Image © Heritage Images)*

vital energy—there are surfaces and depths beneath. When the figure of the medieval female exhibitionist meets with indigenous Celtic traditions, the image evolves into the Irish Sheela. Nevertheless, some scholars, such as Jørgen Andersen, still deny any pagan origins on the grounds that "it is less easily proved" than the Sheela being a "medieval Christian conception."[14] However, as scholar Frank Battaglia argues, Andersen "would have us understand Sheelas as arising spontaneously in the minds of medieval church artists rather than as an expression of folk religious practice which can be traced back for millennia in most of the areas where Sheelas appear."[15] Finally, says Battaglia, the idea that the Sheela is just a twelfth-century French exhibitionist motif on churches cannot account "for why so many Irish Sheelas are found on castles or in locations like a medieval town wall in Tipperary."[16]

What then does account for it? We have laid out the case for the spread of Romanesque architecture, which brought the female exhibitionist figures over to Britain and Ireland from the Continent, and for the pagan background providing a fertile foundation for the creation of the Irish Sheela na gig. We have also touched on other historical events that helped shape the milieu of the Sheelas: the 1169 Norman invasion of Ireland, and the Roman Catholic Church destroying the Celtic Christian Church.

After the twelfth-century colonization of Ireland by the Norman barons, the Romanesque architecture, a transitional style, faded, and in time the English Gothic style of the invaders evolved into Irish Late Gothic. On the walls of medieval buildings, between the thirteenth and the seventeenth centuries, the independent Irish Sheela na gigs emerged.[17] The indigenous Irish sculptural and mythic traditions transformed the Romanesque motif. Sheela na gigs are most concentrated in the center of the country, on churches and then on castles that were built on their newly gained land by Anglo-Norman lords who used Gaelic masons.[18] Deeply influenced by Irish culture—its laws, language, and literature—the barons became, as the saying goes, "more Irish than the Irish." They intermarried with Irish families and made alliances with Irish kings. This assimilation helped foster a Gaelic resurgence in the arts from the late thirteenth to the sixteenth centuries.[19]

Much like the earlier Romanesque explosion of churches along pilgrim routes in Spain and France, Ireland, after the Norman invasion, "began to be covered with castles, with keeps, and fortified places" as the new lords established themselves on the land.[20] The greater proportion of Sheela na gigs in Ireland "either originate from or are found on buildings" erected during this massive construction.[21] In the fourteenth century, however, there were certain calamities like the territorial wars of the Scottish Bruce invasions of 1315–17 and the Black Death of 1348–50 that temporarily halted the construction boom. But when prosperity returned in the fifteenth century, construction began anew, this time in the school of Irish Gothic, in which "Irish masons produced their own style which was an amalgam of the past and present."[22] This Gaelic resurgence in the arts in medieval Ireland stretched back to a longstanding repertoire of native motifs. The Ballinderry Castle Sheela in County Galway, with her knot-work patterns, triskeles, and marigolds, is one of the finest products of the renewed interest in native Celtic arts (see figures 4.4 and 4.5).

Figure 4.4. Ballinderry Sheela on keystone over the entrance of Ballinderry Castle, County Galway, Ireland, 16th century.

During the turbulent twelfth to sixteenth centuries the Irish Sheela was still set on churches, but more often this religious motif is found on the secular architecture of fortified tower houses. Built for defense on the lands of affluent lords, these castles also served as centers of the surrounding communities.[23] With her growing popularity, the Sheela became a figure of great importance, often the only figure on the building. Reflecting an increase in the power of the image, it's as if some of the structures were built just to frame the Sheela na gig, showing her enduring and perhaps changing meaning for the populace. The Sheela also began to appear on round towers, holy wells, town walls, menhirs (standing stones), and yes, even the funerary monument of a bishop (see figure 4.6). This figure of aggressive sexual display adorned architecture throughout much of the country.

The Sheela na gig certainly excited the imaginations of those Irish artists who used the symbol of the female exhibitionist but had the bold

Figure 4.5. Gundestrup cauldron, Gundestrup, Denmark, 2nd or 1st century BCE (La Tène III). This Iron Age work of silver was found in a peat bog in 1891; the female is sometimes identified as the Celtic goddess Medb. She was created more than a thousand years earlier than the Ballinderry Sheela, but the two figures both have rosettes as well as braids. *(Courtesy of the Collection of Classical and Near Eastern Antiquities, National Museum of Denmark)*

inspiration of deep-rooted pagan themes to create the formidable Sheela na gig. In the spirit of the times, they "forged ahead with renewed enthusiasm and gusto, producing more and better Sheela-na-Gigs than anyone else."[24] In her, the masons saw the duality of their goddesses who had powers of both creation and destruction as conceptualized by the display of her immense vulva—an image of regeneration and death. The vulva, while a portal for new life, is also an image of return, witnessed by the burial practices of interring the dead in the womb of Mother Earth to, in some way, be born again. That awareness that death is near is mirrored in her haglike appearance of dried-up old age, with withered breasts, emaciated ribs, and skull-like face. The Irish Sheelas became bigger, more wild, and more glorious in their display of themselves than their earlier continental sisters found in France and Spain.

At what point does the exhibitionist figure earn the magical name of Sheela na gig? Some call the result of the blending of the Norman and Celtic cultures the "true" Sheela na gig, which takes place in Ireland. But what about the Sheelas of England, Scotland, and Wales? Unlike the Irish Sheelas, all the British Sheelas remain on churches, and generally speaking enthusiasm for the motif doesn't last into the seventeenth century as it did in Ireland. Except for a few figures, like the Llandrindod Sheela in Celtic Wales (figure 9.12), the British Sheelas are usually not as menacing as the Irish ones. But in time, they too become free of the restraints of the Romanesque corbel table, and the figures become larger and more prominent in their placement on church walls, as in Oaksey, Fiddington (see figure 4.7), Church Stretton, Buckland, Crofton-on-Tees, Easthorpe, and Pennington.[25]

Eamonn Kelly, of the National Museum of Ireland, proposes that the English Sheelas might have influenced the Irish ones. He suggests that

Figure 4.6. Bishop's Tomb Sheela, Kildare Cathedral, County Kildare, 16th century. Tucked under the corner slab of the monument, this Sheela grasps both feet to affect her display as the bishop makes his last journey. Outside in the graveyard are the remains of the famous fire temple of Brigid, whose flames were guarded by Celtic priestesses and later by nuns. (*Courtesy of Labyrinthos Photo Library, www.labyrinthos .net; photograph by Jeff Saward*)

Figure 4.7. Fiddington Sheela, St. Martin's Church, Somerset, England. On a quoin stone of the south wall, she squats low while raising her left hand high in an exuberant gesture. She is carved on red sandstone with incised round eyes and a curious column of four holes on her torso.

exhibitionist figures may have been reintroduced into Ireland by the Anglo-Normans in a second wave of invasions in 1171. These invaders came from Wales and the contiguous border areas of England, including the Bristol Channel—the very areas where there is a concentration of Sheela na gigs on churches.[26] As Joanne McMahon and Jack Roberts put it, referring to the above history, "This may account for an even more bewildering mix of carvings."[27]

We must remember that Celtic culture had also established itself throughout Britain beginning as early as 600 BCE, so the hag tradition is there too, as is the aggressive reputation of Celtic women.[28] The Celtic warrior queen Boudicca led a revolt in 60 CE against the might of the Roman Empire and almost won. Britain as well had a Neolithic goddess background. All of these factors influenced the British Sheela. But there's something about the Irish Sheela in her enduring popularity (her numbers are nearly three times that of Britain) and in her ferocious presence that sets her apart.

Guardian of Entrances

The quintessence of the Sheela is her naked displayed vulva. From that exposed entrance, all meanings radiate. Just as she is liberated from the narrow spaces that confine the Romanesque exhibitionist, so the true Sheela na gig is liberated in her purpose. When she is freed from a Christian, misogynist disgust of the female body, a relish in her powers is reborn. Whatever negative function the exhibitionist motif may have had, it is not the function of the Sheela.[29] If the earlier figure was used as protection against sin, the later Sheela is also used for her powers of protection, an icon to guard over the boundaries of a territory, the boundaries of a building, and, more subtly, the boundaries between states of being.

How is she put to use? Through a harmony of associations. By their placement, Sheela na gigs became guardians over doors, watching whomever might come through them. But regardless of her placement, any Sheela can be considered a "liminal entity" who represents "the divine, or at least a gateway to the divine,"[30] for the vulva is itself a door, a site of entrances and exits. Certainly, the mysteries of sex, of life, death, and rebirth, have accrued around the image of the vulva. It is an open invitation to sex, a birth canal, and, paradoxically, a symbolic return to Mother Earth following death.

We are all familiar with the practical, daily uses of doors, which are necessary for our comings and goings. Yet the door exists in another imaginative realm: the lure of what's past an open door beckons us to enter into a change of consciousness. Be it a small pair of English Sheelas at Tugford, in Shropshire, one indolent, one aggressive, just inside the church's south doorway (figure 9.14), or a massive solitary Sheela at the Killinaboy Church in County Clare, Ireland (figure 8.1), she draws in those who must pass under her legs spread above the entrance, to transition from a secular to a sacred space. Over eight hundred years ago, clerics and the congregation walked through her field of power to cross into the inner sanctum, or womb, of the church, a temenos of spiritual communion.

The talismanic powers of the Sheela na gig were employed by masons by setting her next to windows on churches and tower houses. These castles were built between the fourteenth and sixteenth centuries as residences for native Irish lords and Gaelicized Anglo-Norman aristocrats. Through her placement and sexual display, the Sheela creates a double drama of openness. Perched near a window, she watches from her wall over the boundary between the metaphorical inside and out, between the physical indoors and outdoors. Her appearance can be ferocious, often with a menacing face and massive shoulders, and sporting fearsome tattoos.

While a majority of Sheelas are no longer in their original locations, making it impossible to know precisely how many once existed, many Sheelas still exist in situ. From so many centuries ago they have survived the storms of time, alongside changing religious attitudes. To name just a few of the Sheela na gigs still found in their original settings on church or castle walls, by doors or windows: in Ireland, there is Blackhall, Ballinderry, Ballyvourney, Killinaboy, Kilsarkin, Shanrahan, Taghmon, and Moate; and on churches in Britain, there is Iona, Oaksey, Holdgate, Tugford, Buckland, Church Stretton, Romsey Abbey, Whittlesford, and Taynuilt (see figures 4.8, 4.9, and 4.10).

An early affirmation of the apotropaic power of the Sheela na gig was recorded in the 1850s by topographer John Windele when describing a possible Sheela at Barnahealy, in County Cork. He calls her an old fetish figure,

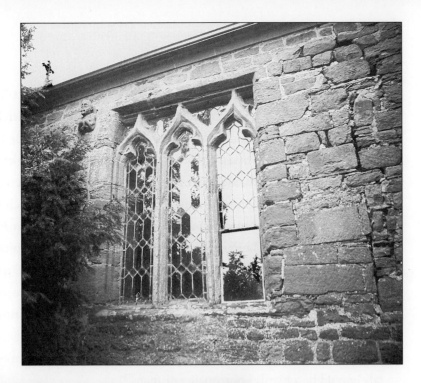

Figure 4.8. Holdgate Sheela (upper left of window), Holy Trinity Church, Shropshire, England, 13th century.

Figure 4.9. Taghmon Sheela over window, St. Munna's Church, County Westmeath, Ireland, 15th century.

Figure 4.10. Oaksey Sheela (right of window), All Saints Church, Wiltshire, England, 13th century.

a Hag of the Castle who, when placed above a door, possesses "a tutelary or protective power so that an enemy passing by would be disarmed of evil intent against the building on seeing it."[31] In his essay "The Worship of the Generative Powers," written in 1866, collector Thomas Wright claims it was "well understood that [the Sheelas] were intended as protecting charms against the fascination of the evil eye."[32] Contemporary Celtic scholar Anne Ross attributes the potency of the Sheelas to the continuum of energies held by earlier goddesses. Sheelas protect the ground that was once protected by the hag. The Sheela, as a repellent hag, echoes the appearance of "the territorial or war-goddess in her hag-like aspect" and canalizes "the evil-averting powers" that the local goddesses were once thought to possess.[33] Ross considers Sheela na gigs to be portraits of ancient goddesses, remembered in the "traditions and festivals of the people," and notes that their prominent genitals "would be a highly apotropaic talisman."[34]

Just as she guards over the open, penetrable parts of a wall by her nearness to doors and windows, the Sheela as a Hag of the Castle shields her turf from intruders when placed high on castle and church walls. From this strategic vantage she commands a grand surveillance of her *túath,* or territory. Frequently a hag is set on the external angle of a wall, the quoin, or cornerstone, because wherever she is placed on a building she adds strength.[35] Two well-known hags on late fifteenth-century castles in County Laois, in Ireland, defended the boundaries of the troubled Fitzpatrick lands. Each figure faced out to the borders, one on the north at Ballaghmore Castle, and the other on the south wall at Cullahill Castle (figure 1.4). That no Sheelas are found on any other of the Fitzpatrick castles indicates "a clear apotropaic function as territorial guardians."[36] The figures may have also acted as powerful status symbols of "clan totems" in these areas of affluent lands, which had the greatest need for defense and thus the greatest concentration of Sheelas.[37] Chieftain families traditonally had their own "specifically named divine hag."[38]

The Hag of the Castle as a territorial guardian links back to the local sovereignty goddess of the area. Irish kings and chieftains placed Sheela na gigs "on their castles as an assertion of their ancient sovereign right to the land of Ireland."[39] As part of their cultural assimilation, Anglo-Norman lords did likewise. Figuratively speaking, the rulers were considered the spouses of their territories. Eamonn Kelly cites many instances of Sheelas being placed on tower houses of Irish high kings as well as Anglo-Norman rulers. To name two such examples: the Sheela na gig found by a window in Bunratty Castle, County Clare (see figure 4.11), on the fifteenth-century home of the O'Briens, the titular Earl of Thomond; and the Sheela discovered among the ruins of Carne Castle, County Westmeath, a sixteenth-century tower house belonging to the O'Melaghlin family, descended from the kings of Meath and high kings of Ireland.[40]

Some examples from the Anglo-Normans are the Sheela set to the right of the door at Blackhall Castle, County Kildare, home of the Eustace family; and the figure's placement on fortified town walls at Fethard (figure 8.10) and at Thurles, in County Tipperary.[41] Scholar Maureen Concannon notes that many Sheelas are also found at the "Seats of the Provincial" kings: "two

Figure 4.11. Bunratty Sheela, Bunratty Castle, County Clare, Ireland. Originally placed in a window reveal high on a tower house, she has been reset in a wall of the hall of the great keep of the castle, which is now part of a popular tourist folk park. (Experience village life in the Middle Ages!) The Sheela has an unmistakable air of death about her, with her monstrous skull head in contrast to her widely splayed legs revealing the source of life. *(Courtesy of Shannon Heritage; photograph by Starr Goode)*

Sheelas near Cruachan in Roscommon—seat of the O'Conor kings of the province of Connacht, and in Leinster there is the Sheela on Adamnán's stone at Tara" (see figure 4.12).[42]

But the enigma of the Sheelas, as castle hags is not solved yet, for what meaning can be ascertained from the fact that not only are they positioned up high beyond any easy visual recognition, they are also often set sideways? The stone slabs on which the Sheelas crouch in their usual posture are inserted horizontally on the quoin so that now they appear to be reclining. What kind of protection can they offer when their presence is so obscured? One notion is that it is part of the Sheelas' magic not to be seen by enemies until they are too close to escape—the better to ensnare them and repel them.[43] This deception adds to their power: the figures don't need to be in plain view; they just have to be there. Clearly, these Sheelas are not there for ornamentation, to make the castle look prettier. This kind of setting was a conscious choice on the part of the masons, who "must have followed a convention which had meaning for them," and was founded on a belief in "some form of magic behind the employment of sheelas."[44]

One of the most splendid castle hags is the Tullavin Sheela from County Limerick, found on the south wall of a fifteenth-century peel, or watchtower (see figure 4.13). She is a very sculptural Sheela, created to stand out from the surface in high relief, with a sensually rounded body. Particularly noticeable are her strong legs, feet splayed out in the classic squat of the prehistoric frog goddess who ruled over death and regeneration. She possesses the powerful raised shoulders of many castle hags, but with odd curly hair or a headdress. Her left hand is raised to her ear in the same prophetic gesture as the Kiltinan Sheela (figure 1.3), a hag also inserted sideways, but on a church. The Tullavin Sheela's right arm reaches long under the thigh to tenderly touch herself.

Just how is a displayed vulva apotropaic? What makes it so? Historically, cross-cultural traditions attest to the well-known belief that exposing human genitals acts as a powerful apotropaic gesture. Carvings of female displays as depicted on everything from wooden doors on granary huts in Africa to gravestones in Ecuador to gables over the entrances of ceremonial houses in Micronesia all employ the protective powers of the vulva (more on this in

Figure 4.12. Tara Sheela, County Meath, Ireland. Carved on a standing stone, or menhir, this rare Sheela is located in a church graveyard on the famed Hill of Tara, an archaeological complex where the Irish high kings were crowned. Around this weather-worn figure whirls much controversy; earlier scholars call her a perverted representation of a Celtic deity, while others believe she was once affixed to the church doorway. She is half-standing, half-dancing, with one arm straight, while the other makes the typical Sheela gesture toward her sex.

Figure 4.13. Tullavin Sheela, County Limerick, Ireland, 15th century. In her original setting, this fine carving is placed high up and sideways on the quoin, or cornerstone, of the south wall.

chapter 11). The belief in the vulva's apotropaic force reaches back to Roman and Greek times, as explicated by historian Frederick Elworthy in *The Evil Eye: The Classic Account of an Ancient Superstition.* This is not just superstition relegated to a less enlightened past; today we use horseshoes as tokens of good luck and nail them over doors for protection against malefic forces, and—no surprise here—the horseshoe is also a symbolic representation of the mare's vagina (in earlier times, the actual generative organ of the mare was used).[45]

Further testimony as to the strong belief during the Middle Ages of the apotropaic powers of the vulva can be found in the bawdy badges that pilgrims from northern Europe and England wore as they journeyed to holy sites. Affordably made from a lead and tin alloy, "the badges were indeed quotidian and common objects."[46] While their iconography included representations of human genitals as well as the figure of a displayed Sheela na gig, a particular favorite was the Pudendum Pilgrim (see figure 4.14), a walking vulva with a pilgrim's cap and boots, in which the figure holds in either hand a rosary and a staff, the image resembling the vulva-as-body of the classical

Figure 4.14. Bawdy Badge. As an evil-averting vulva, she safely walks the pilgrim's way.

figure of the Priene Baubo (figure 5.2). The purpose of these badges was to provide their "medieval owners magical protection from the threat of the evil eye and the Black Death."[47]

To live in such times was to suffer a catastrophe almost beyond imagining—the bubonic plague, outbreaks of which reoccurred for centuries. A common thought was that the disease could be transmitted through eye contact with a victim, and that "even a glance from the sick man's distorted eyes was sufficient to give the infection to those on whom it fell."[48] As Shakespeare writes in *Love's Labor Lost,* "They have the plague, and caught it of your eyes."[49] Folklore held that the startling appearance of an ambulant vulva with its ludic qualities could neutralize the malefic gaze; evil energy is attracted to the bawdy badge and thus it diverted harm away from its wearer.[50] (This process may also illuminate part of the dynamics behind the Hags of the Castle.) Calling on enduring traditions, medieval pilgrims wore the bawdy badges to dispel the evil eye by invoking the shielding spirit of the vulva.

Certainly the Sheela's not-so-secret source of power lies in her sacred display. With her great allure, her power of attraction, she watches over the threshold, a goddess of passages. In essence, her mysteries—her fearsome, paradoxical powers—are beyond our knowledge; her sexual "invitation in" is juxtaposed to the repelling menace of her countenance and her haglike body. These attributes strengthen her apotropaic powers to repel evil. An enduring belief in the Sheela's healing abilities to bring good luck is seen in many figures, such as the Kilsarkin and Castlemagner Sheelas, who are within human reach. They bear the evidence of being rubbed for centuries, of receiving worshipping caresses because the stone dust from the vulva is also thought to have "curative powers" (see figure 4.15).[51]

A secondary source of the Sheela's apotropaic power comes from our full-frontal view of her. We experience the impact of a direct view of her supernatural body with a vulva such as no mortal woman ever possessed. Scholar Jørgen Andersen describes the Sheela's frontality as an element that all primitive art relies on "for dramatic effect in an intended confrontation between a carved or a painted image and the enemies mortal or spiritual, against whom one directs that image."[52] The Sheelas could be considered

Figure 4.15. The author touching Kilsarkin Sheela, Kilsarkin parish church, County Kerry, Ireland. All good-luck blessings to those on the Sheela pilgrimage! *(Photograph by Mark Rhodes)*

primitive art—crude, unsophisticated, powerful. Yes, there is a raw energy in most Sheelas. The fineness of the Ballylarkin (figure 13.21) and Tullavin (figure 4.13) Sheelas is an exception. But *primitive* also means "primal," or "first," or "original," and few could doubt the shocking originality of the Sheela image.

Fertility Figures?

As is so often the case due to patriarchal bias, a female figure is viewed as a symbol of fertility, a bias that narrows her power, reducing her to the role of either bride or mother. In this role she becomes just an attachment to a male god, no longer an original power in her own right. Certainly some scholars in the long study of Sheelas have labeled them as fertility figures, even after just a superficial glance. Her capacious vulva begs the question: Are the Sheelas fertility figures? Yes and no. No, not fertility, in that one of her essential functions has to do with entrances. Her apotropaic power of protection resides in the sine qua non of her display. Certainly the vulva is an organ of fertility, but here its creative powers are used metaphorically, not literally, offering protection from evil influence, attracting good fortune, and providing safe passage into the sanctity of a church or the secure interior of a castle keep.

If our answer is yes to fertility, then how so? It is possible to see the Sheelas as having a fertility function from a feminist point of view. One of the first female scholars of the Sheelas, anthropologist and Egyptologist Margaret Murray, calls them fertility figures belonging to a goddess archetype she calls the "Personified Yoni." In a refreshing analysis, she sees the erotic quality of the naked vulva as stimulating not only to men but to women, too. She also cites the folk custom of brides on the way to their wedding looking at the Oxford Sheela to ensure a fruitful marriage.[53]

Some Sheelas look pregnant. The Moate Sheela from County Westmeath, Ireland (figure 8.3), has, beneath her monstrous face, a swollen, pregnant-looking belly that hangs out above her display. Two other Sheelas depicted with bulging or sagging bellies are the Sheela on the Dowth Old Church, County Meath, Ireland, and the weathered Sheela on the Nun's Church on the Isle of Iona (see figure 4.16), in Scotland. Both show a "sagging, rounded belly combined with spread out small legs, a posture strongly reminiscent of pregnancy in its last heavy stage before birth."[54] One Scottish Sheela on St. Clement's Church in Rodil, Isle of Harris, appears to have just given birth and may be cradling her newborn baby (see figure 4.17).[55]

Scholar Edith Guest states flat-out in a 1937 issue of the journal *Folklore*

Figure 4.16. Iona Sheela, Inner Hebrides, western Scotland, 15th century. Nuns saw this Sheela daily sitting on a lintel above the window.

Medieval Mindset on Pagan Soil

that the Sheela na gigs are fertility figures, and she reports that the Castle Widenham Sheela has been "frequently touched for help in childbirth within very recent years."[56] Reliance on the figures to provide this kind of support continues to the present, as witnessed by James O'Connor in his 1991 monograph on the Sheelas, *Sheela na gig*. The eccentric, long-time owner of Kiltinan Castle, County Tipperary, known locally as Lady La, told O'Connor while he was in his teens that the two Sheelas in Kiltinan "represented an ancient fertility goddess and that barren women used to scrape the stone in the churchyard for its healing dust."[57] O'Connor felt gratified to have his father, a local farmer, confirm this explanation.

Another contemporary account of the belief in the generative power of the Sheelas was recorded in 2012 by researcher Sonya Ines Ocampo-Gooding. She collected extracts from the writings of as well as an oral history from author P. J. Curtis, who grew up near the Sheela na gig on Killinaboy Church, County Clare. His ancestors have been buried in the churchyard since the seventeenth century, just to the right of the doorway that displays the Sheela. He recounts some local practices:

> Infertile women came to pray to Her usually in the dead of night to escape the notice of the people and especially the priests. . . . For as many years as anybody could remember, childless women who craved a son or a daughter came to this place and prayed to the Sheela directly for help. They would first kneel in front of the Sheela. Then they must walk around the church seven times and fall on their knees to beseech her to answer their prayers. . . . Some left little offerings, as they would at the holy wells—coins, medals, keepsakes, that sort of thing. . . . But I also know of many women who after bearing ten or more children came to pray and plead with her that she might grant the opposite and make them barren![58]

In her recent book *Sheela-nag-gigs: Unravelling an Enigma,* scholar Barbara Freitag contends that the central function of the Sheelas was their use as "folk deities in charge of birth."[59] Beyond their aid with parturition, Freitag writes that the Sheelas ensured "fertility in humans, animals, and crops."[60] The life-giving powers of the vulva guaranteed that nature would continue to be fruitful. Freitag also chronicles the high mortality rates for mothers and babies during the gruesome Middle Ages and hypothesizes that this created an urgent need for magical interventions in order to survive. To intensify her claim about this necessity for supernatural agency, Freitag emphasizes the lack of medical training of medieval midwives. Yet it seems inconceivable that through uncountable ages of women giving birth, midwives had accumulated little useful knowledge about the process of labor or of helpful medicinal herbs.

In Freitag's view these medieval mothers-to-be, in their time of need, turned to a belief in the magical energies of the Sheelas. Through the ritual act of touching the stone vulvas, women could secure divine support to help them through the painful task of childbirth. Folkloric customs testify to this, as in Edith Guest's above-mentioned example of the Castle Widenham Sheela's use as a birthing aid. Thus as folk deities the Sheelas have two separate functions that have been named here: ensuring fertility and ensuring a safe birth. Freitag is not exactly clear on how touching a Sheela's vulva translates into the process of giving birth. Most Sheelas are not portable but built into structures; many others are located high up on castle walls, making physical contact with them impossible. Before their confinement, did expectant mothers touch those stone vulvas that were within reach? It is easy to imagine some Sheelas being used for this purpose, but was it their original purpose? Or did it come out of the multiple powers of female sacred display and develop in time as women saw something ancient and familiar in the figure of the Sheela? Freitag suggests an odd chronology in which the stones were carved first for use in parturition and kept in a special location or by "certain old women," then later set on walls, intentionally placed beyond human touch by the church to suppress such practices.[61]

Freitag also examines the look of the image of the Sheelas, pointing out their squatting stance, a time-honored bearing-down position for giving birth. Obviously, the essential feature of the Sheelas is their genital display. The appearance of their swollen vulvas (the portal of birth) certainly could indicate the physiological process of parturition. Freitag further believes that many figures, like the Oaksey (see figure 4.18), Ballinderry, Ballyportry, Bunratty, and Killinaboy Sheelas, may have the amniotic sac protruding out from between their legs.[62]

One cannot address the fertility of a Sheela and ignore the rest of her body. One cannot speak only of her full lower lips and not of their opposite, the upper half most often depicting barren old age—emaciated ribs, a menacing countenance, and shriveled paps (no milky breasts here). The whole image of the Sheela embodies a conjunction of beginnings and endings. In the liminal state of birth, death is always a possibility. In the rural agricultural areas, country folk growing crops and tending to animals lived in nature's great round; they were intimate with the cycles of birth, death, and renewal.

Figure 4.18. Oaksey Sheela, Wiltshire, England, 13th century. Is that the amniotic sac between her legs, or is her merry smile due to a large clitoris, almost the same size as her breasts?

While Freitag stops short of calling the Sheelas goddesses, referring to them only as folk deities or idols used for fertility, she recognizes the veneration of a divine feminine for millennia on European soil (although still employing the pejorative word *cult* to characterize such worship).[63]

Any observer of the Sheela might easily connect the unity of life and death in the features of the figure. She can represent fertility but also so much more. As the Dark Goddess of death and regeneration (more on this in chapter 6), the Sheela's supernatural vulva symbolizes a place of entrance (sex), exit (birth), and return (burial of the dead as children in the womb of Mother Earth for rebirth in another season). The Sheela's link with the realm of the ancestors is forged from her powers to create new life. Clearly, she is a multivalent image with many possible functions, no final word can be said on the scope of her powers.

The Power of Display and Folklore Customs

Whatever the original purposes of the Sheela na gigs, over the years many folk customs have become associated with the figures. In popular belief, Sheelas were employed as healers, bringers of good luck, and aids to parturition, as seen previously. These later country traditions may have expanded on the Sheela's primary purpose: as a guardian rooted in the apotropaic display of her naked sex. Such rural customs are not just local but reflect the numinous energy in the image of the vulva.

When Irish antiquarians first began cataloging the Sheela na gigs in the nineteenth century, some, like John O'Donovan in his Ordnance Survey Letters, connected the figures not with Christianity but rather to a "Pagan origin."[64] Even as late as 1931, H. C. Lawlor, in the journal *Man,* thought that the sexuality of these "grotesque" carvings "must by no means be taken as indicating a Christian connection."[65] The name Sheela na gig was well known and commonly used by country people for the stone figures, whom they believed to possess tutelary powers. An 1840s report to the Royal Irish Academy describes them as "*fetishes* or charms to keep off the evil eye."[66] Depending on the folklore of the area, the Sheela was known by other names, such as "The Idol" at Lusk, County Dublin (later buried by the minister), or seen as the effigy of a legendary local female like Cathleen Owen, in Moykarkey Castle, County Tipperary.[67] In fact, "The Idol" is one of the earliest recorded names for a Sheela on Binstead Church, mentioned in 1781 in the *History of the Isle of Wight*.[68]

Edith Guest, in her thorough taxonomy "Irish Sheela-Na-Gigs in 1935," records rural traditions surrounding the supernatural powers of several Sheelas. At Carrick Castle, County Kildare, the figure was characterized by local people as an "Evil Eye Stone" to guard against unwanted influences; a Sheela at Cloghan Castle, County Offaly, was known by the peasantry as "The Witch" even into the late nineteenth century.[69] In her 1937 *Folklore* article, Guest chronicles the stories and customs around many Sheelas, often involving a holy well and a magical shrub or tree.[70] These remnants of a powerful belief in the image may be the last records of deeply rooted customs no longer available for our understanding.

Guest ends her 1935 catalog of the Sheelas with the observation: "But that pagan ideas and practices were associated with these figures in comparatively recent times and are so even today can hardly be doubted."[71] The word *pagan* has the familiar definition of non-Christian people (derogatorily called *heathens*), but its etymology from the Latin *paganus*, "of the country, rustic," carries a second meaning, one connected to the Sheela na gigs. After all, the Sheelas are not an urban creation but exist mostly in the countryside. It follows that rural people living more intimately with their natural instincts would form unique ties to these earthy figures so well known to them over the centuries.

In popular belief and practice, the Irish did not lose their awe at the sight of displayed female genitals. In 1843, Johann Georg Kohl, a German writer, published the results of his two months of travel in Ireland seeking out the Sheelas. Fascinated by the carvings that the superstitious Irish thought could avert ill luck, he discovered that the Sheelas existed not only as stone monuments on walls but also as living women! For those caught in the spell of the evil eye, their affliction could be lifted and good luck restored by these wise women. Just how? By lifting their skirts to display their female nakedness: "These women were called and are still called 'Shila na Gigh.'"[72] Kohl perceptively notes that with the deeply rooted Irish customs, "if anything ever existed in Ireland, so can one almost always believe that it is the same now."[73]

An even earlier reference to the existence of human Sheelas comes from the seventeenth century, in the diocese of Kilmore, County Cavan. A synod or council of the church refused to offer sacraments to a category of women known as *gieradors,* whom modern scholars Anthony Weir and James Jerman believe might have been called "living sheela-na-gigs."[74] They contend that this reference gives evidence that in some rural areas Sheela-na-gig was a name for "women of loose morals or simply old hags."[75] To the church, was it a crime for a woman to lift her skirts or to be an old woman? Could the powerful women who so interested Kohl two hundred years later be the descendants of the earlier *gieradors* banned from the church? Closer to our own time, in the twentieth century the traditional belief in the power of the naked female display still persisted in the Irish countryside. In a letter to the *Irish Times* dated September 23, 1977, an old man, Walter Mahon-Smith, recalled an incident of his youth:

> In a townland near where I lived [Caherfinsker, Athenry, County Galway], a deadly feud had continued for generations between the families of two small farmers. One day, before the First World War, when the men of one of the families, armed with pitchforks and heavy blackthorn sticks, attacked the home of the enemy, the woman of the house (*bean-a'-tighe*) came to the door of her cottage, and in full sight of all (including my father and myself, who happened to be passing by) lifted her skirt and underclothes high above her head, displaying her naked genitals. The enemies of her family fled in terror.[76]

Another such story comes from Edith Guest in 1935. Guest indirectly affirms the ancient custom of females displaying themselves to dispel evil, and that such females were called Sheela na gigs. From her travels in the Irish countryside to conduct research, Guest recalls a time when she used the term Sheela na gig when talking to a woman from a long line of farmers in the Macroom district. The woman "derived some puzzled amusement from it, wondering why I should desire to seek out old women of the type which I may describe for brevity as 'hag.'"[77] From her early childhood she had known the word as a common one used by people with this "connotation" of the human Sheela na gigs.[78] It seems that the professional Sheelas were elderly women. Jørgen Andersen speculates that the name Sheela na gig was originally a folk term concerned with the ritual of display performed by these women and "not with the witches on the church walls."[79] Does this mean the stone figures took their name from the living Sheelas and *not* the other way around?

In a second oral history taken in 2012 by scholar Sonya Ines Ocampo-Gooding, the Martin family of County Sligo shared their knowledge of folk traditions connected to the Behy Sheela na gig (known as the Red Sheela due to her color). She is now housed in a shed on their farm next to the ruins of Behy Castle, which was apparently built by the high kings of Connaught. It is widely believed locally that once "there were four Sheelas erected on each wall of the castle."[80] For generations, the family witnessed an abiding belief in the many powers of the figure: "We always felt protected by the Sheela, and we would never sell or move her from her resting place. . . . As the Sheela still holds a lot of secrets, many people come to pray to her to relieve them of their illness. They also pray for fertility and well being and bring gifts such as candles or money. It is completely personal to each individual why they come and see her."[81]

A thread runs through all these examples. Once again, the Sheela, whether made of stone or flesh, evokes the image of the old witch, a link to the powers of the Dark Goddess who is capable of destruction in the service of regeneration. Such powers were forced underground by the patriarchy, or as Jørgen Andersen puts it, this is the "last survival of an ancient practice, that of displaying the genitalia as a means of opposing evil, slighting enemies, etc. Trust the Irish to have treasured such a relique and to have kept it very much in the dark."[82]

Whether there are still-living Sheela na gigs today practicing their art in the Irish countryside one cannot say, but the display of the stone Sheelas persists, as does the faith in the power of this arresting image. Certain folk customs still live even now for "the restoration of health and protection against illness."[83] To obtain their good-luck stone dust, contemporary rubbings on the vulvas of the Kilsarkin, Castlemagner, and Clenagh Sheelas demonstrate an enduring belief in their powers.

Nineteenth-century antiquarians documented the remnants of local legends and old names by which rural people called their Sheelas. Some of these figures have been missing for over 150 years, yet traditional practices around some Sheelas continue to thrive into our own time. Pilgrimages to the sites of the holy well at Castlemagner (see figure 4.19) and to St. Gobnait's Abbey (figure 3.10), both with Sheelas replete with pagan associations, remain popular. Often there exists no recorded folklore connected to any particular Sheela and never any text to explain their function. We only have the appearance of the figure itself, but that is enough.

One singular Sheela, alas, no longer in situ but in the confines of the

Figure 4.19. Castlemagner well house, County Cork, Ireland, 17th century. A late, more "polite" Sheela with little genital display. She stands in a classic goddess posture with arms raised to welcome seekers to her holy well, dedicated to Saint Brigid.

HISTORY

National Museum of Ireland, deserves special attention: the Seir Keiran Sheela na gig (see figure 4.20). Originally from a church just south of Birr, in County Offaly, the Seir Keiran Sheela was described in an 1834 issue of *Dublin Penny Review* as a "grotesque figure," with an illustration of the figure set on the eastern gable wall of the church.[84] Later she was found against

Figure 4.20. Seir Keiran, County Offaly, Ireland—a singular Sheela by any measure.

the bank of an earthen wall of the enclosure that encompassed twenty-five acres of monastery ruins, a graveyard, and a holy well about which "stories of miraculous happenings" are still told.[85] An area rich in ancient traditions, once part of the old kingdom of Ossory, the area around Birr may have been a pagan sanctuary according to the *Shell Guide of Ireland*.[86] Currently the figure is one of the few Sheelas on permanent display at the National Museum; one can readily understand the curator's choice.

This is a formidable piece of sculpture. The strength of the massive shoulders and weight of the barrel chest of this Sheela give a rounded dimension to the figure. But as a visual image the eye is first drawn to what makes this Sheela unique: the eleven cup marks sculpted into her torso. Eight round and square holes encircle her vulva in an irregular grouping that punctuates her wide display. Of the remaining marks, one pierces the base of her throat and the other two rest on the crown of her head. There can be no architectural purpose for them, only a ritualistic one, and certainly not for any recognizable Christian rite.

One can imagine the Seir Keiran Sheela decorated with the horns of the moon, with branches, flowers, or other such offerings. Perhaps the largest of the holes, just below her vulva, contained water with which worshippers could bless themselves. A cup mark is like a small holy well that gathers the life-giving moisture of the Goddess, her waters of life.[87] No other Sheela possesses a face so animated, a mouth so pursed in an *O* of awe or ecstasy. Whatever rites were performed around the figure, clearly she herself was also having an experience.

Calling Seir Keiran the most pagan of all the Sheelas, Jørgen Andersen believes that "certainly, at some stage, there must have been people who believed in the power emanating from that image, some ritual must have centered on it."[88] His encounter with the figure seems to have left him mesmerized, engendering a rapture of possibilities about her purpose. For him, the image "obviously involves significant beliefs of a past age . . . [and is] the only absolutely convincing fertility image among the Irish carvings . . . [It has] that air of potency, that aura of myth."[89]

In Ireland, "that aura of myth" is created by a longstanding belief in the primal power of genital display. We have seen this traditional thinking in modern examples and in the earlier Sheela na gigs, but it goes back even further to the Old Irish legends written down in medieval times. In one tale of the great warrior Cú Chulainn, he flies into an uncontrollable frenzy and threatens to turn against his own people. To temper such seemingly invincible energies, his uncle, King Conchobor, calls on a force greater than the mighty blood rage of the youth, perhaps the only force that could overpower him:

> to send a company of women out toward the boy, that is, three times fifty women, that is, ten women and seven times twenty, utterly naked, all at the same time, and the leader of the women before them, Scandlach, to expose their nakedness and their boldness to him. The whole company of women came out, and they all exposed their nakedness and their boldness to him. The boy lowered his gaze away from them and laid his face against the chariot, so that he might not see the nakedness nor the boldness of the women.[90]

Even the strongest of heroes must admit defeat before the concentrated energy of such an array of female sexual power!

The Sheela na gig's authority comes, of course, from her revelation of a primal, if not *the* primal, symbol of creativity. In his wide-ranging study on the image of female display, "The Heraldic Woman," Douglas Fraser, a professor of art history and archaeology, concludes his work with these insights (and tellingly Jørgen Andersen ends his monumental study of the Sheelas with the same words by Fraser): "The displayed female, whether in reality or in image, belongs to a small class of images that are unusually compelling. Like the frontal face, it has the power to ensnare the viewer's glance and hence capture his [*sic*] subjectivity or selfhood. Effective with supernatural powers and human beings alike, it bends all outside forces to the will of those behind the image and thus is equally useful to attract good or repel evil."[91]

The Passing of the Sheelas

The mystery of the medieval Sheela na gig is not that she existed, but that she was created at the very time when the last vestiges of the Old Religion were being stamped out.[92] The energy behind her image cannot be destroyed, for not only did the Sheela burst forth in the midst of the misogyny of Roman Catholic Europe, she did so in a startling, bold form. As far removed from the submissive, heavenly ideal of the Virgin Mary as can be imagined, the Sheela is aggressive and sexual, much like the Celtic goddesses and heroines of legend. She does not ask for permission to exist.

The Sheela na gig is an old figure: precise dating is often impossible, and the arguments over her origins are many, complicated, and elusive. The female exhibitionist motif as part of the Romanesque sculpture of the twelfth century fits in well stylistically with her companions on the corbel tables of northern Europe. What was in the minds of those who carved the figures? Did she rise up, unbidden, from a dark, unconscious memory of an earlier world, a poor mason's imaginative nightmare, or perhaps as a dream of relief from a repressive church condemning the instincts of his body? Or, more likely, the Irish mason drew from Celtic traditions of myth and stone sculpture as well as thousands of years of Goddess worship so deep-rooted in his native soil to create the Sheela na gig.

For over five centuries, the Sheelas appeared on churches and tower houses as prominent figures, especially in Ireland, becoming increasingly powerful in whatever setting they appeared until the seventeenth century. Alas, the disintegration of the Celtic way of life was initiated by another invasion of Ireland, this time by English troops under Elizabeth I in the late sixteenth century, and by the continuation of repressive penal laws against Catholics under the Stuart monarchs. Then came the brutal war on the Irish led by Oliver Cromwell in 1649, which effectively marked the end of Gaelic Ireland. Another factor in this demise was the seventeenth-century importing of Scottish and English Protestants into northern Ireland by the British Crown, which became known as the Plantation of Ulster. This usurped not only the native Irish population but its ancient culture as well. Celtic scholar Maureen Concannon believes this is why there are so few Sheelas in northern Ireland. They may have been destroyed in a puritanical zeal to annihilate Celtic culture, the Irish nobility, and the Sheelas who functioned as a symbol of the sovereignty of the native land.[93] Finally, due to the rising tide of Puritanism and the resulting Counter-Reformation of the Catholic Church, the image of the Sheela lost the power of its official sanction, and this too marked the end of her era.

With the onset of the Reformation, the Old Irish ways were attacked from the pulpit by the clergy, and more drastically a campaign was launched to remove the Sheela na gigs from sight—in fact, to bury or destroy them.[94] Post-Reformation, the church felt powerful enough to finally do away with an image it had tolerated over the centuries. Barbara Freitag makes a compelling point that the church had allowed for the presence of these heathenish, certainly not Christian figures as a way to subdue and control the country folk. The Sheelas were part of a folk religion "too important and too intimately bound up with the welfare of peasant communities to be disregarded by the Christian Church."[95] It had put up with the traditional customs of the country people as a way to bring them into the church until the changing social conditions that led to the Counter-Reformation allowed the church to finally move against the figures. As well, it can hardly be an accident that midwives who carried the wisdom of the old pagan ways and were often connected to the Sheelas were also usurped in the seventeenth century by the rising male medical establishment. Male doctors seized the chance to control birthing practices "to stamp out midwives," their major economic competitors; in parts of Europe, "a good number of these midwives" were prosecuted for witchcraft.*[96]

The destruction of the Sheelas began in earnest during the seventeenth century. Unfortunately, the earliest known reference to the Sheelas is a church statute in Tuam, County Galway, written in 1631, which ordered "parish priests to hide away, and to note where they are hidden away, what are described in the veiled obscurity of Latin as *imagines obesae et aspectui ingratae,* in the vernacular 'sheela-na-gigs'"[97] In 1676, a regulation in the Irish diocese of Ossory ordered the burning of Sheela-na-gigs; also in that year, Bishop Brehan of Waterford, Ireland, ordered the exact same burning.[98] One is reminded of the eighteenth-century fanatics who went

---

*Freitag points out that in the sixteenth century the church issued licenses to some midwives only on the condition that they would not use any herbs or "witchcraft" to relieve the suffering of women in labor.

through an elaborate process of heating and cooling to crack and destroy the megaliths in the great stone circle of ancient Avebury, or in more recent times, the destruction of the ancient giant Buddhas carved into the cliffs of Bamiyan by the reactionary Taliban. Some Sheelas still survive in their original locations but bear marks of mutilation, their lower halves hacked away, such as those found at Ballyvourney (figure 3.11), Bilton (figure 9.9), Killinaboy (figure 8.1), and Taghmon (figure 3.1). The Llandrindod Sheela (figure 9.12), found in 1894, was saved, concealed by being built into the north wall of the church facedown.[99] Many others, like a tattooed Clonbulloge Sheela, in County Offaly, Ireland, have been retrieved from the rivers in which they were thrown.[100]

The destruction of the Sheelas continued for centuries, even into our own time. In November 2004, in Sussex, the Buncton Sheela na gig, located by the chancel arch in the All Saints Chapel, was destroyed by vandals who defaced the carving with a chisel and then stomped the shards to dust—an immeasurable loss. Nevertheless, there still survives a pagan tradition that newlyweds should climb a small stepladder to rub the Buncton Sheela's vulva for fertility; she was well used, worn from centuries of such rites of touching.[101]

We can still see in the longstanding traditions of the countryside a lingering belief in the power of the Sheela, despite centuries of church suppression. This belief probably ensured the survival of many Sheelas. In 1781, when the Binstead Sheela, on the Holy Cross Church, Isle of Wight, was taken down from her guardian position over the keystone of the north door, this so displeased the local people that they demanded her restoration, thus showing that the Sheela held a place in the popular imagination and that removing her would be "a breach of custom."[102]

Perhaps some figures were concealed by those who wished not to bury them but to save them from destruction. New figures continue to be recovered from where they have lain for centuries. A more recent discovery occurred in the early 1980s during an archaeological dig at Glanworth Castle, County Cork. Beneath a floor sealed with collapsed rubble, through a trap door and down into a vaulted ground chamber, lay a heavy-shouldered Sheela, hidden there in the seventeenth century during the troubled times of persecution.[103]

Although over 120 Sheelas still survive in Ireland, many safe by virtue of being high up on castle walls, it is impossible to know how many once adorned sacred architecture before these stone witch-hunts occurred. Church regulations that demanded their destruction also reveal evidence that "once upon a time there may have been a great many more than we can see today."[104] How many more Sheelas have yet to be unearthed from their hiding places?

We can be grateful for what remains: some Sheelas still exist in this world to enthrall us with their strange beauty, showing us what our distant ancestors once thought sacred. Like any other living image, her particular form was shaped by the needs and aesthetics of her time, but times change, forms change, and the age of the Sheela passes. And yet the energy animating the image endures. The Sheela is a visual antinomy of the forces of destruction and creation, a hag who offers up her ever-regenerative vulva, a manifestation of the Dark Goddess with the power to renew. Many such goddesses have preceded her; others will follow.

5

The Sheela's Classical Forebears

The Sheela na gig cannot be understood by just looking at the cultural setting of the late Middle Ages in northern Europe. She cannot fully be explained as a Romanesque motif or a Celtic figure or a blending of both. To trace the Sheela's historical forebears illuminates her purpose. Two strong figures of female display are found in the classical world of Greece and Rome: Baubo and the Gorgon Medusa. The characteristics of these predecessors—exhibitionism, apotropaic magic, and the display of the powers of creation and destruction—hold a mirror to the quintessence of the Sheela na gig.

Baubo

The name Baubo, meaning "belly" or "womb," has been given to a set of figures found around the Mediterranean that are bound together by their sexual display. This name may not be what the figures were called in their time, as the first recorded use of the name did not occur until the second century CE, by Clement of Alexandria.[1] Indeed, the Baubos from the ancient Greek city of Priene, in the eastern Mediterranean, in what is modern-day Turkey, were not given this designation until the early twentieth century by classical scholar Hermann Alexander Diels; later, "generations of scholars followed his lead."[2] Nevertheless, Baubo, the umbrella term for these figures, which are also called Iambe, Isis, and Bau, seems to have stuck, uniting these figures through recurring symbols of the energy rooted in the vulva.

Baubo, although appearing in many forms throughout classical times, is best known for playing a brief but transformative role in the story of Demeter and Persephone. This mythic cycle of separation and then reunion of a mother and daughter was enacted in a secret ritual of the Eleusinian Mysteries for close to two thousand years. No initiate ever revealed its inner truths, powerfully sacred no doubt, but also a capital crime (punishable by death) if one were to break one's oath of secrecy. The myth tells of the grief of the grain goddess Demeter after losing her daughter, Persephone, and the subsequent barrenness of the world. It is Baubo, the old servant, who brings Demeter (and thus the neglected, dying earth) back to life by making the goddess laugh. How does she accomplish what all the gods of Olympus failed to do? By lifting her skirts in an act of *anasyrma,* a ceremonial gesture of naked vulvic display.[3] Here, the act of display conveys not a terrifying power but rather an invocation to joy.

Lest one think the pagan rites of classical Greece are a far cry from the activities of medieval masons who carved the Sheela na gigs on Christian churches, a connecting link exists in the writings of the early church fathers. Clement of Alexandria, born ca. 150 CE, was immensely knowledgeable about Greek myths; it was he who recorded the legend of Baubo. The story survived down through the generations of ecclesiastical writers and monks, such that "the tale of Baubo in Christian writings, and the figurines themselves, played a possible part in the creation of the female exhibitionist carvings" known as Sheela na gigs.[4] Not to say, of course, that the early church fathers approved of these explicitly pagan figures. Pope Clement railed against ancient Greek temples, calling them "godless sanctuaries," and the story of Baubo "that shameful tale."[5] He writes with incredulous disgust that Baubo "uncovers her secret parts and exhibits them to the Goddess," and that such a sight actually gives pleasure to Demeter.[6] To revere a myth about a woman who displays her naked sexual organs was proof enough for him to condemn the Greeks as licentious pagans. Thus, Clement helped set the stage for the repressive Christian view of sex. Indeed, Constantine Psellos, an influential eleventh-century Byzantine monk, considered Baubo a demon.

In the story, the boundless grief of the mother of Persephone meets the irrepressible mirth of Baubo. After the loss of her daughter to the underworld, Demeter wanders the earth as an old hag, tearing her clothes and refusing to renew the growing power of the earth. Nothing can pluck her from the depths of her sorrow, until one night, resting by a well in Eleusis, she meets Baubo, who brings Demeter, now disguised as an old woman, to her home and mixes a special drink for her, the beverage known as *kykeon,* made of mint and ground barley. When this does not restore the spirits of the grieving mother, Baubo dances, tells obscene jokes, and, merry with joy, reveals the source of all human life by raising her skirts to expose her genitals in the act of anasyrma. This gesture pierces the thick carapace of the mother's grief. In a world of values far from the Christian church fathers, what Demeter sees restores her to life, making her laugh with delight. Then the goddess reveals her true self in all her golden glory.[7] This story is the basis for the reverence for Baubo in the classical world, as she represents the ever-renewing power of life as symbolized by her sacred display. Death happens, but life *must* come again. With Demeter's heart softened, the immortals forge a compromise, and Persephone returns to the upper world in time to inaugurate the planting season. Demeter teaches the people of Eleusis her sacred rites and mysteries, then she orders that her temple be built there, and so starts the longest-running ritual drama in the world.

The Eleusinian Mysteries began in late September, which is planting season in Greece, the time when the rains come following the hot, dry summer. After the Greater Mysteries concluded, weeks later in October, a second great festival was widely celebrated in cities throughout ancient Greece—the Demeter Thesmophoria ("bringer of treasures," "bringer of laws"). Here, no men were allowed; only women could organize and participate in the rites that dramatized the autumn sowing of new crops and honored the grain goddess for her gift of agriculture to the human race. Beginning the Thesmophoria was the Stenia festival, which enacted the restorative influence of Baubo, who transforms the desolate, barren crone into the laughing fertile mother (figure 5.1). With the lighthearted gaiety of bawdy humor and sensual dance, female participants evoked the magic of Baubo's invigorating energy.[8]

What a relief from the stratified world of patriarchal Greece these

Figure 5.1. Baubo riding a pregnant sow, terra-cotta, 1st century BCE, 11.8 x 8.5 x 3.5 cm. Baubo in a posture of display is as open as any Sheela na gig. She rides the animal most associated with Demeter, the abundantly fertile sow. Is she about to give birth? She might be holding a soul ladder or a sistrum, which connects her to her alter ego, Isis. *(Image © The Metropolitan Museum of Art; courtesy of Art Resource, NY)*

festivals must have been for the common people. The central rites of the Eleusinian Mysteries welcomed everyone, citizen or slave, women as well as men. None were forbidden except those who didn't speak Greek or those who had committed the crime of murder. Such rites were one of the last refuges of the earlier matristic culture of Old Europe; they "provided a way to feel religious in the old ways."[9] What a relief and what awe an authentic experience of the Mysteries must have inspired in the female and male initiates. In the Homeric Hymns, such Mysteries are described in the closing verses of "To Demeter": "No one may in any way transgress or pry into or utter, for deep awe of the gods checks the voice."[10]

One aspect of the Eleusinian Mysteries had to do with the human fear of death, and at the center of such ceremonies stood the goddess of death and regeneration, Demeter, as played out in the seasonal flux of nature. Scholar and artist Jennifer Reif, in her authoritative work *The Mysteries of Demeter*, speculates that on the last day of the Eleusinian Mysteries prayers and rites were conducted for the dead and for the fertility of the land in the coming planting season. In their essence, the Greater Mysteries provided some kind of ecstatic revelation about life after death. Although there is no last word on the substance of the Mysteries, we do know that "the initiates returned from their pilgrimage to Eleusis full of joy and happiness, with the fear of death diminished."[11] With fervor, Sophocles exulted, "Thrice happy are those mortals, who having seen those rites, depart for Hades; for to them alone is it granted to have true life there," while Plato reminisced, "Let me linger over the memory."[12]

For nearly two millennia, the Greek world celebrated the Eleusinian Mysteries. Excavations have found evidence of a shrine at Eleusis from as early as the fifteenth century BCE, and by the fifth century BCE the Eleusinian sanctuary had entered a golden age. The site had become "an impressive complex of sacred buildings and handsomely decorated open spaces," and ceremonies held there dedicated to Demeter and Kore were "at the center of the pan-Hellenic religious life."[13] Almost a thousand years later, in 380 CE, the Byzantine emperor Theodosius issued an edict forbidding the practice of pagan religions, effectively making Christianity the official state religion of the Roman Empire. The end came soon after, when the invading Goths completely destroyed the Eleusinian temple complex. Over the next century its marble was hauled away for use in the construction of other buildings, including Christian churches. Greek archaeologist and art historian George E. Mylonas, in his erudite study of Eleusis, raises a poignant question about those Christians who had participated in the Mysteries but maintained their vow of silence: "Can we assume that the recruits to the new faith, even after their conversion to Christianity, kept her secret because they still held the Goddess in awe?"[14]

Beyond the Eleusinian Mysteries and the festival of Thesmophoria, Baubo's image appeared throughout the Mediterranean world in various forms: lifting her skirt, touching her genitals, squatting down Sheela-like, spreading her legs while atop a sow, or, most amusingly, as a walking vulva. Such images span centuries in the ancient world: from the archaic to the classical to the Hellenistic Greek world and, lastly, to the Roman Empire, Baubo appears in poetry, rituals, and sculptural art. Her form may change, but the essence remains: delight in the powers of her displayed vulva.

Surely in such a figure one can expect a range of manifestations, all well documented in the masterwork of artist and writer Winifred Milius Lubell, *The Metamorphosis of Baubo: Myths of Woman's Sexual Energy*. Even so, the Priene Baubos take us by surprise (see figure 5.2). On the Ionian coast in the ancient city of Priene, seven small statuettes from the fifth century BCE were unearthed at a temple to Demeter. Once again, Baubo is associated with Demeter; however, these figures are quite unlike any other classical figures. Each is imaginatively rendered as a walking vulva with a human face cradled between her short legs, while the cleft of her chin doubles as the cleft of her vulva. All have thick ropes of hair tied back with ribbons. One wonders how they were used, and for what ceremonies. Not so far from these terra-cotta statuettes other images of Baubo were discovered, this time carved on gold plaques in the tomb of a priestess of Demeter from around the fourth century BCE in Scythia, north of the Black Sea. Just what does the soul of the priestess need to take with her into the afterlife? Three golden Baubos dancing as they raise their skirts!

Baubo lifts her garment yet again in the classic gesture of anasyrma, but this time farther west, in Egypt, where she had many cultural connections. In the Hellenistic period and under Roman rule, the ancient goddess Isis merges sometimes with Demeter and sometimes with imagery of Baubo. Numerous Isis/Baubo/Demeter figures were created (some even mass-produced), as she was an exceptionally well-liked goddess. She became the central deity of "some of the popular new religious cults" that had as their basis a blend of archaic religious rituals and local cults, along with the old traditions of Attic religion (like the female festivals of the Thesmophoria).[15]

Some noteworthy figures connect Baubo more deeply to the Sheelas, as

Figure 5.2. Priene Baubo, clay, from a *bothros* (altar), Sanctuary of Demeter and Kore, Priene, Turkey, 5th century BCE. Women were probably the primary worshippers at the sanctuary. Unique in Greek art, these personifications of the vulva evoke a modern sensibility in their feeling of wit. *(Image © The Metropolitan Museum of Art; courtesy of Art Resource, NY)*

they both have apotropaic elements in their display. One small Baubo sits atop a large eye as she widely splays her legs; the other squats in the classic Sheela frog posture to display her naked sex, while atop her head rests an elaborate, three-tiered crown whose centerpiece is an eye. In a double whammy of protection, the powers of the vulva combine with an unblinking gaze to ward off the evil eye.

Two accounts by Greek historians written four hundred years apart illustrate traditions in Egypt of a Bauboesque anasyrma. In 445 BCE, Herodotus describes with verve the exuberant festival of Bubastis. Sailing down the Nile on barges, women caught up in the spirit of the festival dance and sing, yell mocking jests, and lift their skirts at other women standing on the shore of every town they pass by. When the women reached the temple at Bubastis, the historian reports, the crowds could reach seven hundred thousand![16] Centuries later, in 60 BCE, this time in Memphis at the temple of Apis, the Egyptian bull god Diodorus witnessed the custom of women performing the ritual gesture of sexual display before a living bull, considered to be an incarnation of the god.[17] They stood before the animal and exposed their naked genitals in a primal exchange of energy to stimulate the procreative powers.

Another look at Egypt, but in the Roman period, is described in a startlingly original article published over eighty years ago, "Female Fertility Figures," written by pioneering scholar and folklorist Margaret Murray. In it, she examines figures of Baubo found in the women's quarters as well as in women's graves, thus showing the use of the regenerative vulva to the dead as well as to the living (see figure 5.3). For Murray, Baubo is "an ancient goddess in a new form" whose meaning is reflected in the much later Sheela na gig.[18] Thus Murray sees the medieval Sheela as a descendant of the classical Baubo. Both figures exist as manifestations of the archetype of the Personified Yoni, whose whole emphasis is sexual display. She recounts a local tradition with the Sheela at St. Michael's Church in Oxford, England: "All brides were made to look at the figure on their way to church for the wedding" to excite them and ensure a fruitful marriage.[19] Murray connects this medieval custom to the fact that since the Baubo figures were found in the inner rooms of women, "the use of such figures may have been to rouse and stimulate the sex desires of women."[20]

As a woman, Murray suggests an interpretation of the Sheela that is quite

Figure 5.3. Baubo touching herself, Asia Minor–Egypt. A woman made for women, Baubo reaches down between her parted legs in that characteristic Sheela gesture. *(Collection of Classical and Near Eastern Antiquities, National Museum of Denmark)*

the opposite of the view of many male scholars: an attraction to, rather than a repulsion from, their sexual display. Murray puts forth her ideas "as a basis for discussion, for so much of the published work on female psychology is founded on the masculine ideas of what a woman should feel or be."[21] She concludes her essay with the observation that Baubo was a goddess for women only, a Bona Dea belonging to a category of goddesses whose rituals were solely for women. With certitude, she claims that the long survival of such figures is because their connection with pleasure and laughter appeals to women's essential nature.

From the Ionian coast to Egypt, from pagan sage (as she is called in the Homeric Hymns) to medieval Sheela na gigs, the spirit of Baubo endures.

In fact, she emanates strong female energies that defy annihilation, even through the onslaught by patriarchal religions and even through the murderous medieval Inquisition.[22] Lubell warns us that it would be "a sad mistake for us to lose sight of Baubo and her icon, the vulva, to relinquish her playful joking, to let her slide out of Western consciousness into scholarly obscurity or into the netherworld of demons or pornography."[23] We remember that with an unfailing joy she continues to display the power of her sex.

The Gorgon Medusa

The second figure in the classical world we look to as a forebear to the Sheela, with similar apotropaic abilities that make her a guardian, is the Gorgon Medusa. Power resides in those lethal eyes that turn men to stone, her grinning lips with protruding tusks and pendant tongue, all framed by a head of writhing snakes, a visage often compared to a vulva (see figure 5.4). This is how we know her best. Yet she is a more complex figure than that, representing a convergence of opposites. We experience paradoxes in looking at her image, in knowing that more than one thing can be true at the same time. Much like the Sheela na gig, Medusa has powers of creativity as well as destruction. As a gorgoneion her ferocious face produces a terror that can ward off evil influences, and yet she can also be regenerative in her capacity as a sun goddess. When she assumes the shape of her full body she often becomes a protective mother. As a plumed serpent, her wings give her the ability to fly into the sky, and her hair of snakes gives her access to the underworld. She can be desirably beautiful or repellently hideous. Her blood can heal; her blood can kill. She is the Gorgon Medusa, the "ruling one."

Such a female is not born overnight; she originates in Old Europe with the Neolithic bird and snake goddesses of death and regeneration. According to Marija Gimbutas, "The masks of the Goddess of death (mid-5th millennium B.C.) with large mouth and fangs and sometimes hanging tongue may have generated the gorgoneion."[24] Gimbutas adds that this Gorgon was a potent goddess ruling over life and death, not the later version, an Indo-European monster to be murdered by such heroes as Perseus. From her earliest literary reference in Homer (ca. 750 BCE) to Ovid, with Hesiod, Euripides, Pindar, and Apollodorus in between, the writings of her myth took nearly a thousand

Figure 5.4. Medusa Antefix, Artemis Temple, Corfu, 620–600 BCE. The figure is one of the upright roof tiles running along the eaves so that she may protect the temple by warding off evil. *(Courtesy of the Kerkyra Archaeological Museum; photograph by Gregory L. Dexter)*

years, and for those thousand years the Gorgon Medusa was "extremely popular in art from the beginning" and was found in "monuments by many thousands."[25] She appeared throughout the classical world as the gorgoneion on the aegis to a full-bodied Medusa on classical temples and, in both forms, on tombs, roofs, coins, dishes, clothing, ovens, and mosaic floors. Her image may have shifted over the years, but despite the patriarchal usurpation of the earlier goddess culture, Medusa maintained a connection to her ancient roots. Otherwise, why would she have been such a threat and, at the same time, so popular?

The Dark Goddess resides in the face of the gorgoneion. Her essence conveys terror through the threat of death when she is placed on the shield of a goddess or a warrior. In Greek art, numerous warriors are depicted carrying shields bearing the apotropaic Gorgon head; the ominous powers of her deadly eyes and devouring mouth offered protection against enemies. In the *Odyssey,* she guards the entrance to the underworld, watching over the threshold between life and death. To attain transformation we must pass through her "gaping mouth of death [that] is the vulva, the cave through which we reach the Underworld, which may be compared to the womb of the birth-mother."[26] Out of destruction comes renewal.

Similar to the Sheelas, the image of the gorgoneion conveys death and life. In one of her many manifestations she exists not as a visage of terror but as an emblem of the sun goddess. Here, her powers originate not from fear but from solar energy, a productive and fertilizing energy through the action of light and heat on the earth. Over a century ago, art historian and archaeologist Arthur L. Frothingham dared to offer his interpretation of Medusa, which he was sure would be "so distasteful to orthodox votaries of the Olympian cult."[27] Presciently, he identified Medusa as pre-Olympian, with prehistoric roots as the Mother Goddess and a vegetation deity, one who watched over the life continuum and, in time, evolved into the solar disk. Later, throughout the classical world, the creative and sometimes destructive power of the sun was represented on numerous tombs decorated as the gorgoneion surrounded by garlands, an image of the end and the beginning, the vegetation indicating her power to renew life beyond the grave (see figure 5.5).[28]

In our own time, groundbreaking scholar Patricia Monaghan closes her book *O Mother Sun!* with a meditation on Medusa. Monaghan identifies the gorgoneion, with her snake hair, as a sun goddess, since her face, "a circle surrounded by rays—is eminently solar," and one cannot safely look at the face of the sun or the face of Medusa (see figure 5.6).[29] Once again, we see in this figure a combination of both life and death symbols; she is a goddess of both the dark and the light.

But she does not exist in the plastic arts or in myth merely as a head; the Gorgon Medusa can also assume the shape of a full-bodied female. And

Figure 5.5. Gorgon with garlands on a sarcophagus, front panel, Phrygian Marble, Roman, Dokimeion, Phrygia, Asia Minor, 140–170 CE, 91.5 x 226 cm. Cupids hold up garlands of oak leaves while standing on hybrid sea monsters. A Medusa head and two tragic masks fill the spaces above the garlands. *(Digital image courtesy of Getty Museum's Open Content Program)*

what a female! The architectural Gorgon comes into full flower in the next century when, like the medieval Sheela na gig, images of her are placed on sacred buildings to serve as guardians of the gates. Because of the great apotropaic power of the Gorgon's face (as in the Sheela's display), she watches over temple entrances, providing protection by repelling harm.

Surely, the most magnificent visual realization of a full-bodied Medusa exists on the highest point of the western pediment at the Artemis Temple on the island of Corfu (see figure 5.7). Considered to be the apogee of the architectural Gorgon, at nine feet tall she looms over the scene; too energetic to be contained, her head breaks out of the pediment borders. A

Figure 5.6. Gorgon antefix fragment, terra-cotta with polychromy, Capua, Italy, 550–500 BCE, 26.2 x 39.1 cm. Stylized red snakes frame her face. *(Digital image courtesy of Getty Museum's Open Content Program)*

great potency to the figure is created when symbols double and triple. She
has wings on her feet and great wings spread out from her back. She bears
a crown of eight snakes on her head, and pairs of snakes jet out in opposing directions from her neck and waist, while intertwined snakes face each
other as they girdle the center of her body. She is a goddess of snakes and
of birds, and since her two children are at her side, she also represents the
Mother Goddess. In the earlier myth of her brutal murder as written starting with Hesiod (ca. 700 BCE), Perseus decapitates the mortal Medusa. As
she is dying, this mother gives birth to two children, who leap forth from
her severed neck: Pegasus, the winged horse, and Chrysaor of the golden
sword. Thus her face acts as a vulva with an upper womb.[30] But here,
gracing this archaic temple, on the oldest stone pediment in Greece, she
appears not as a dead mortal slain by an ambitious hero, but as an immortal
goddess alive with her children, thereby refuting the myth.

Another Gorgon who dates back to 600 BCE is the winged Gorgon
from an Athena temple in Syracuse, Italy (an area known then as Magna
Graecia). Under her right arm she carries her child Pegasus, and under her
left, though missing now, would be her other child, Chrysaor (see figure 5.8).
The face presents a frontal display of a mouth with tusks and a large pendant
tongue. But her legs are in profile, running in the pinwheel pose. A small
skirt parts in a suggestive manner, showing a naked thigh and barely covering
her private parts.

Figure 5.8. Gorgon tablet, terra-cotta, Syracuse, old Temple of Athena, 610–590 BCE. Most likely this Gorgon was once part of an altar or served as a sacred image for the temple. *(Image © DeAgostini/SuperStock)*

■ ■ ■

The magical power in the act of genital display began in prehistoric religions and never died. It is an elementary idea whose apotheosis in the classical world was animated in the figures of Baubo and Medusa; it continued in time down through the boldness of the Sheela na gig. Baubo and the Gorgon Medusa can be seen as chronological mothers of the Sheela, for all their powers over death and regeneration emanate from the transforming energy of their sexuality. Through iconic images of their femaleness, Baubo stimulates pleasure and the return of life, while Medusa's fierceness can destroy threatening forces to protect those who need her. To observe the different responses of men and women to this feminine power makes one ponder cultural identities and natural instinct. The spirit of delight visits Demeter in the form of an outburst of pleasurable laughter when Baubo displays her naked genitals. Yet this same exposed vulva terrorizes male warriors across the centuries, from the Greek Bellerophon to the Irish Cú Chulainn, causing them to back down in battle.[31]

Margaret Murray insists on an enduring tradition of women's delight in Baubo and in the much later Sheela because "it appears certain that the figures made and still make an appeal to women's [sexual] nature. This then is the reason for their original use and long survival."[32] Proof of the Gorgon Medusa's enduring popularity in the Mediterranean world can be found on thousands of sacred monuments and in more quotidian forms like dishes, clothing, and ovens.*

French scholar Jean Claire links Medusa and Baubo as "twin embodiments of female sexual power"; Medusa's face is a vulva, while Baubo's vulva is made into a face, and they, as "creatures of the vulva, tend toward those things which are strange."[33] To say the least! Their disruptive displays can divert grief or danger. They are sisters of the Sheelas in their possession of contradictory powers centered in their sex, and all are transformative figures permeated with the ancient death and regenerative symbolism of vulvas, birds, snakes, and eyes. Just as the Sheela na gig has unbroken roots going back to the Celtic goddesses of sovereignty who protected the land, so do these roots extend back to the apotropaic Gorgon watching from temple walls and golden Baubos dancing with the dead. The energies of the archetype of display pass down through time, despite patriarchal domination that demonizes that which it fears: the force of female sexuality. Her eternal energies are always alive, always being called on to take yet another shape in life's continual play of forms.

---

*The Medusa lives! In California she can be seen in courthouses, at the entrances of state buildings, on documents to which the governor's signature is required, and even on the badges of law enforcement agencies. How is this so? Because the Great Seal of the State of California displays a seated Athena with her hand resting on her shield, which is emblazoned with the face of Medusa, the gorgoneion.

6

The Dark Goddess
of the Neolithic

Archaeological breakthroughs in the twentieth century have revolutionized what we know about our past. The deeper roots of European religion have been unearthed, revealing the Great Goddess of nature and cosmos who, in her myriad forms, ruled over all cycles of life. Knowledge of this pre-patriarchal, Neolithic civilization of Old Europe links the iconography of the Sheela na gig back to the earliest patterns of Western worship, all the way back to the images of vulvas created in Upper Paleolithic caves nearly forty thousand years ago. With her hunched-over shoulders and hunkered-down posture, the Sheela na gig physically resembles a frog goddess, often a hybrid figure whose squatting frog body reveals a prominently marked human vulva. This female deity also evokes the Sheelas by dint of her dual functions as a dark wielder of destruction and a restorer of life. The ubiquity of her image, also alive in ancient Egypt and Anatolia, bears witness to the reverence with which she has been held in human consciousness.

The Frog Goddess
of Death and Regeneration

The frog goddess endured as a subject of devotion through millennia in prehistory and history (see figure 6.1). As a sacred image, she appears on amulets, figurines, pottery, and shrines. Throughout Neolithic Europe, figures of the frog goddess were carved from amber, alabaster, ivory, marble, green

Figure 6.1. Vinča frog, terracotta, classical Vinča, first half of the 5th millennium BCE, approx. 6 cm. Standing in a human posture with arms raised in a ritual gesture of the Goddess, she is over six thousand years old. *(Courtesy of the Marija Gimbutas Archives at Opus Archives)*

or blue stone, and clay, and her image adorned temple walls. Toad sculptures created in materials from terra-cotta to bronze were also discovered in much later Bronze Age sanctuaries and graves in Greece and Rome.[1]

One of the earliest artistic renderings of the frog goddess dates back to the beginning of the sedentary agricultural period that transformed the nomadic ways of our Upper Paleolithic ancestors. This "Neolithic masterpiece" was a frog-woman pendant (with perforations for suspension) that some unknown artist lovingly carved out of gleaming, jet black stone nearly nine thousand years ago (see figure 6.2).[2] She was unearthed at the site of the once-flourishing Neolithic culture of Achilleion, Thessaly, in northeastern Greece. Excavations by Marija Gimbutas at this site in the 1970s uncovered seven archetypes of divinities, including the frog goddess. This motif of a frog body with a human vulva reaches all the way back to the Paleolithic caves of southern France. A series of frog-woman images engraved on bones were discovered in the Cave of the Trois Frères, and another is engraved on a bone found at Fontales, a rock shelter in Tarn-et-Garonne in southern France.[3] The longevity of this goddess in the Old European spiritual canon speaks to the human concern for the continuity of life.

Prominent deities like the frog goddess embody seemingly opposing powers. As a goddess of death and regeneration she could simultaneously bring death and restore life, mirroring the ever-repeating rhythms of nature. Through the potency of her inexhaustible womb she is both the creatrix of all matter and its destroyer when she calls all things back to her, and she also possesses another supreme power, that of renewal. It was thought that to bury the dead in a fetal position in the womb of Mother Earth meant that from this dark womb the person could be born again. This belief lasted into Elizabethan England and the plays of Shakespeare:

> *The earth, that's nature's mother, is her tomb.*
> *What is her burying, grave that is her womb.*
> *And from her womb children of divers kind.*[4]

The vulva is a portal for new life and an image of return, as witnessed by this ancient burial practice—a custom we still practice today.

In the worldview of the Neolithic culture of Old Europe, these natural forces are not in conflict but interdependent qualities. At the end of *The Language of the Goddess,* Marija Gimbutas comments on *The Great Mother* by Jungian psychologist Erich Neumann. She observes that Neumann's division of the Great Mother into a good and a terrible mother never occurred:

Figure 6.2. Achilleion frog, early Sesklo, Achilleion lb, Thessaly, ca. 6300 BCE, 3.2 cm. The frog goddess is a major archetype of Old Europe. *(Courtesy of the Marija Gimbutas Archives at Opus Archives)*

the archaeological record shows that the life-giver and death-wielder are one. Revivifying life starts at the moment of death and begins within the body of the Goddess. In this sense, Gimbutas says, "the Great Goddess is the magician-mother."[5] Thus, the antinomies present in the image of the Sheela's body are part of a long tradition of a conjunction of seeming opposites creating a unity. Like the Sheela na gigs, the frog goddess is a conundrum of the continuum of life and death, part of the moment when a mystery turns inward and creation comes forth again.

In temples used for the performance of death and regeneration rituals, worship often centered on the Goddess in the form of a frog or toad.[6] One such site is the great urban temple complex of Çatal Hüyük, which dates back to the seventh millennium BCE. Located on the Konya Plain of Anatolia (present-day south-central Turkey), this site testifies to the geographical range of veneration for the pre-patriarchal Great Goddess. A splendor of shrines, artwork, and houses have been found that offer insight into the spiritual practices and daily life of its builders. In 2014, Professor Ian Hodder, director of excavations at the site, announced his latest findings: women and men lived under the principle of gender equality. Hodder added that modern scientific techniques have shown that "the same social stature was given to both men and women. . . . There was no leader, government or administrative building; men and women were equal."[7]

In his *Çatal Hüyük: A Neolithic Town in Anatolia,* James Mellaart, the site's original excavator from 1961 to 1963, found twelve successive building levels; almost a third of the rooms are shrines.[8] Designed for ceremonial use, many of them are dedicated to the theme of death, as shown in paintings of flying vultures pursuing headless bodies and the energies of rebirth shown in plaster reliefs of female figures in postures of sacred display. Hodder believes "that artworks were made to get in touch with the dead or to protect them."[9]

While Mellaart certainly recognizes the figures mounted repeatedly on numerous shrine walls as goddesses, he never identifies them as frog goddesses, unlike in the decades-later work of Marija Gimbutas, who emphatically sees these figures as frog goddesses in postures of magical significance, with upraised arms and parted legs. She points out that frog-woman hybrids as symbols of regeneration are "quite common" in Anatolia, as seen in a ceramic frog goddess with a human head and vulva found at the Neolithic site of Hacilar some 220 kilometers west of Çatal Hüyük (see figure 6.3).[10] Both archaeologists agree that the Goddess appears in an anthropomorphized form, and as Mellaart puts it, she is concerned with "the mysteries connected with life and death, birth and resurrection."[11] Both also agree that as indicated by the shrines themselves and by their reliefs and paintings, many rites must have been performed in these Neolithic temples.[12]

In one striking shrine, an anthropomorphized frog or bear or hybrid human-animal figure is shown in relief on a wall, legs spread wide, her belly marked in concentric red circles, symbols of the whirling life force

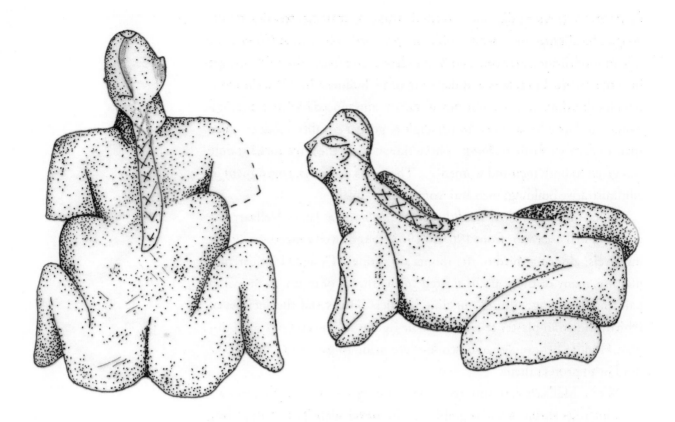

Figure 6.3. Frog woman, illustration of a ceramic found at Hacilar (Level VI, House Q.VI.5), Central Anatolian Neolithic, end of 6th century BCE. Great Goddess in the shape of a frog. *(Courtesy of the Marija Gimbutas Archives at Opus Archives)*

(see figure 6.4). Placed below the Goddess's body are bulls' heads or bucrania, as if to stimulate and strengthen her powers of regeneration. In addition to the association of the massive bull with masculine strength, the bulls' heads and horns also have a feminine connection—their shape is thought to resemble the life-giving uterus and fallopian tubes.[13] This point is undeniably made in another shrine's depiction of seven stylized female torsos with the image of the bucranium placed right atop the area of their reproductive organs (see figure 6.5).[14] Mellaart, as a man in the grip of a mystery, describes with awe the "simple serenity of this shrine dedicated to the goddess."[15]

In one final, crucial feature of the shrine, below the floor lay the dead. Again, through the magical portal of her vulva, not only does the Goddess give birth, she also takes back the dead and creates new life. Thus the Goddess fulfills the promise, a yearning deep within the human heart, that life *will* come again.

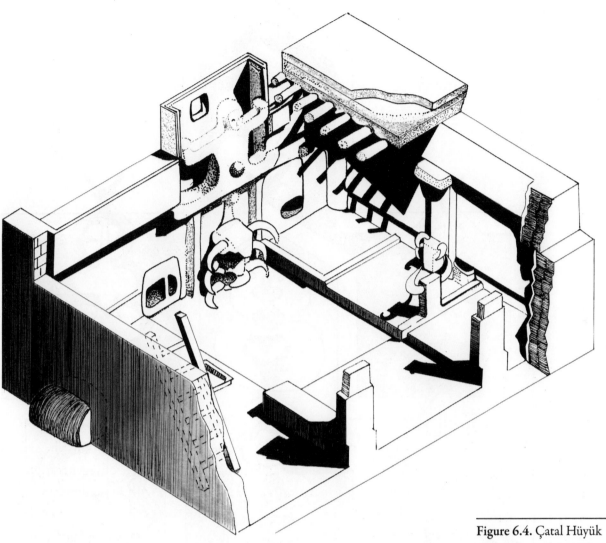

Another utterly unique site dedicated to rites of death and regeneration deserves to be mentioned: Lepenski Vir. Here we are back in Old Europe, on the banks of the Danube between what is now Serbia and Romania, at one of Europe's greatest gorges, the Iron Gates. This is a dramatic landscape with the bare cliffs of the Koršo hills and dangerous whirlpools (*virs*) in the river; modern visitors report a feeling of haunting mystery at this site to this day.[16] Such primal energies must have drawn prehistoric people to this site as well. In a period of over a thousand years, between 7000 and 5500 BCE, some fifty shrines were built one by one to the residing deity,

Figure 6.5. Bucranium
Mural, Çatal Hüyük (Temple
A.III/11), 6000 BCE.
*(Illustration by Ruth Ann
Anderson after figure 27 in* The
Living Goddesses, *by Marija
Gimbutas)*

this time to the fish goddess. Appropriately, all the structures face the river.
Even though the primary devotion at Lepenski Vir was to the fish, not the
frog, both equate in Neolithic iconography with the sacred vulva and the
womb of the Goddess.

Fifty-four stone sculptures were also discovered here, as original in
their own way as the walking vulvas of the Priene Baubos or the Sheela na
gigs. These anthropomorphized fish goddesses stood about 50 to 60 cm

high and were carved from egg-shaped river boulders, fashioned to have strange fish eyes and gaping mouths, but with human noses. Several stones were designed with human breasts and bird-of-prey feet as hands—once again, like the Sheela na gigs, a perfect hybrid of the properties of life and death. And in a staggering continuity of imagery, some sculptures appear to be Stone Age precursors to the Sheelas, as they employ her classic gesture of reaching down to pull apart a triangular-shaped vulva (see figure 6.6).

Figure 6.6. Lepenski Vir fish goddess, Lepenski Vir II, Iron Gates region, Serbia, 6000–5800 BCE, 51 cm. Once again, an image of a female deity displays her supreme power—regeneration. *(Courtesy of the Marija Gimbutas Archives at Opus Archive and the Lepenski Vir Museum; photograph by Gregory L. Dexter)*

The Dark Goddess of the Neolithic

To enter the shrine of her body-temple, one had to pass between two rows of stones in the shape of the Goddess's open legs leading to her womb-altar, on which stood a stone offering of the fish goddess. These red sandstone sculptures were often painted with red ocher; the shrine had reddish lime-plaster triangular floors; the altar was surrounded by V-shaped stones set vertically, forming a pattern of triangles. Graves of the dead had a similar triangular structure with red floors.[17] To reinforce a symbolic point, triangular shapes abound. They invoke the regenerative powers of the Goddess's pubic triangle, and the use of red, the energy of her life blood. All of this is necessary because the dead need her help. Clearly, such a site is meant not for secular daily living, but for the practice of sacred ceremonies serving the mystery of how the Goddess restores life out of death. Ancient people constructed shrines and graves and conducted sacred rites, whether at Achilleion or Çatal Hüyük or Lepenski Vir, to call on the Goddess's sovereignty over renewal, whether she took the form of a fish or a frog.

The Frog Goddess in Egypt

Revered throughout the ancient world, the frog goddess has deep roots in Egypt, where she was known as Heket (or Haquit, Heqet, Hekat), the "primordial mother of all existence."[18] Portrayed as a frog or a frog-headed woman, her hieroglyphic sign was a frog. An early Egyptian deity from the Old Kingdom, she is first mentioned in the Pyramid Texts (one of the oldest known religious texts in the world, ca. 2400–2300 BCE). Like in Old Europe, her abilities are complex and multivalent; Heket had "life-giving power" and "was associated with the afterlife."[19] Heket aids the departed on their journey into the Beyond; magical "amulets of frogs were found in tombs from all periods in Egypt" (see figure 6.7).[20]

As a goddess connected with the waters of life, Heket's powers were imaginatively conceived out of what the Egyptians experienced in nature: Every summer when the rains flooded the Nile, "millions of exuberantly singing frogs would appear as if spontaneously generating in the salty mire emblematic of the unformed matter before creation and the interval between death and rebirth."[21] From this primordial material, Heket helped to shape

the embryonic child in the uterine waters. In Old European imagery, the frog was frequently equated with the uterus. Such meanings accrue around the frog, who in its own life cycle undergoes a remarkable metamorphosis, from water dweller with gills into land creature.

Egyptian myth has it that the frog goddess breathed life into the unborn. Later she presided over the labor of birth, protecting both the mother and her newborn (much like Barbara Freitag's view of the Sheelas as birthing stones protecting the life of the mother). To ensure this divine support, pregnant women offered up their devotion to Heket through their prayers and invoked her energies through talismans of frog amulets and rings (much like the prayers and gifts offered to the Behy Sheela, discussed in chapter 4). Her priestesses trained as midwives and became known as "servants of Heket."[22] Hence once again we see that the frog goddess's realm encompasses death and the ever-rejuvenating waters of the womb of nature.[23]

Figure 6.7. Eight frog amulets, late period, New Kingdom, Egypt, ca. 1200 BCE. The ubiquitous frog in Egypt. *(Image © The Metropolitan Museum of Art; courtesy of Art Resource, NY)*

The Dark Goddess of the Neolithic

The Frog, Baubo, Heket, and Hekate

Taking another look at our old friend Baubo, she has many associations with Egypt and the frog goddess, from her physical stance to her very name. As noted earlier, many statuettes of the wildly popular Baubo were mass-produced during the Roman era in Egypt. Often the figure is squatting, with knees raised and feet turned outward, all the better to exhibit her yonic display—a sacred and universal gesture whose power can only be perceived when viewed from the front. Margaret Murray called this the "Baubo-Phryne," or frog attitude, and it is of course also seen in the posture of the Sheela na gig. Phryne was the most famous courtesan of classical Greece, and by Murray's etymology her name means "frog." She states that many classical scholars equate "Baubo-Phryne (Frog-Baubo) with the frog-goddess of birth Heket," for it is "hardly possible that these figures should appear suddenly and in such numbers without any precursors."[24]

A direct response to Murray's ideas appears in the 1935 journal *Man*, written by art historian K. de B. Codrington. He describes a "Baubo-toad goddess" terra-cotta figurine from Mathura, capital of the Kushan dynasty in northern India, perhaps dating from the early second century CE (see figure 6.8).[25] From the front, one sees a naked squatting female in classic frog-goddess posture replete with a large vulva, and on the reverse side is the back of a frog. To see this artifact is to be convinced of the direct link between the frog and female sexual display. While Codrington understandably associates the sexual exhibition of the Mathura frog woman with Baubo, the Mathura figure is actually a Lajjā Gaurī figure found in India (more on these goddesses in chapter 10).

The connections continue. Marija Gimbutas points out that Baubo has associations with the frog goddess Heket, whose name is similar to Hekate, who in "ancient Greece has an epithet, 'Baubo,' i.e., Toad."[26] In some European languages, "the root *bau* or *bo* is used in association with names for toads or witches."[27] *Witch* is considered derogatory by some; it is a name often given to denigrate the Sheelas. The medieval Inquisition and witch hunts, which lasted into the seventeenth century, certainly targeted the very existence of women healers;[28] now they were called "witches," considered no longer servants of the Great Goddess, but agents of Satan. Hekate, whose totem was a frog or toad, was targeted as a demon in the *Malleus Maleficarum,* a manual for the torture and extermination of the lineage of traditional healing women that gave Hekate the name "Queen of the Witches" and damned as the most dangerous "those whom Hekate patronized: the midwives."[29] Because of this era of officially sanctioned terror, probably the lowest point of Christianity, it bears repeating and can never be said enough that the traditions of these "witches" goes back to a happier time, when the priestess "servants of Heket" were revered midwives, practicing under the sacred aegis of the frog goddess.

Figure 6.8. Molded terracotta figure of frog and woman, Mathura District, Uttar Pradesh, India. *(Courtesy of Wiley Publishers; from Codrington's "Iconongraphy: Classical and Indian")*

The Frog in Folklore

Yet she survives. The Dark Goddess of death and regeneration, in her many manifestations, never leaves us; from frog goddess to Sheela na gig, her energy cannot be eradicated. As one of the most enduring images in the archaeological record, the frog goddess's powers continue to fascinate us long after the disintegration of Old Europe. She still exists in folklore, ritual, language, and dreams. As Marija Gimbutas affirms, despite "the horrible war against women and their lore and the demonization of the goddess," memories of prehistoric motifs condemned by Christianity live on.[30] The sovereignty of the frog goddess over death and the waters of life can be seen in the folktale of the German goddess Holla, the old hag of winter, considered the mother of the dead. As a frog, she jumps down into the waters of a well to bring back to earth the red apple, symbol of life, dormant there since it fell at harvest.[31]

Modern beliefs echo old beliefs. The frog, a prominent symbol from Neolithic times, simultaneously holds the meaning of being lethal and restorative. Alongside its squat, Sheela-like display, frogs are identified with the transformative uterus of the Great Goddess. This association of frog to the womb of the Goddess persists into modern times, when women suffering from barrenness or difficult pregnancies appeal to the Virgin Mary for help through votive offerings of toads made of wax, iron, silver, and wood; these can "be found to this day" in churches in Austria, Bavaria, Hungary, Moravia, and the Balkans.[32]

An astonishing example of this enduring belief in the powers of the frog and the association of the frog woman with the Goddess's vulva is an ex-voto tablet dated 1811, from a church in Bavaria. It bears the image of a heavenly Madonna with child next to a human-headed frog with a vulva carved on her back (see figure 6.9).[33] A similar image carved from hematite was found in Cyprus; it depicts a frog with a vulva on her back. And in a demonstration of the longevity of this motif, the Cyprus figure dates back to the second millennium BCE.

An even longer span of time separates a final example: two renderings of toads, both with heads in the shape of a flower bud, representing new life (see figures 6.10 and 6.11). One is a wooden tombstone from nineteenth-century

Lithuania, and the other a terra-cotta figurine from Sesklo (what would now be northern Greece) from 6000 BCE.[34] Thus the symbolic tradition connecting the frog with regeneration has endured at least eight thousand years.

It can hardly be surprising that in folk traditions the frog or toad also has apotropaic powers, as shown in the practice of hanging up dried toads "to protect the house against all evil."[35] Much like the Sheela na gig and the Gorgon, the toad's magic was invoked to guard entrances; toads were nailed on doors and stalls to protect humans and animals from sickness and death. In another link to the Goddess, Marija Gimbutas asserts that in Bavaria it was believed that such healing power was only effective if the toads were sacrificed on the Virgin Mary's holy days, August 15 and September 8.[36]

Figure 6.9. Illustration of a Bavarian votive tablet. From the earth to the skies: the frog, the vulva, the Mother. *(Courtesy of the Marija Gimbutas Archives at Opus Archives)*

The Dark Goddess of the Neolithic

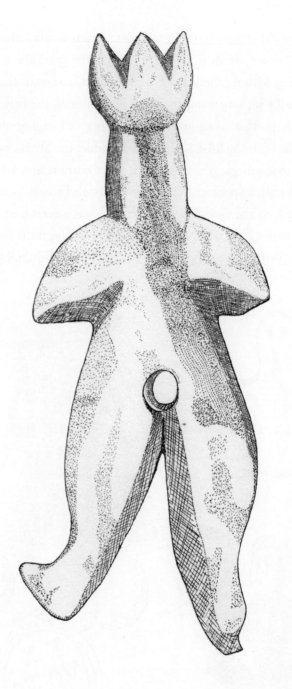

Figure 6.10. Illustration of Neolithic toad, terra-cotta, Sesklo, ca. 6000 BCE, approx. 1.6 cm. *(Courtesy of the Marija Gimbutas Archives at Opus Archives)*

The deep association of the frog with the waters of life is well described by Anna Ilieva and Anna Shturbanova, senior research fellows at the Institute of Folklore Studies, Bulgarian Academy of Sciences. These reseachers have documented old village people who still remember this disappearing way

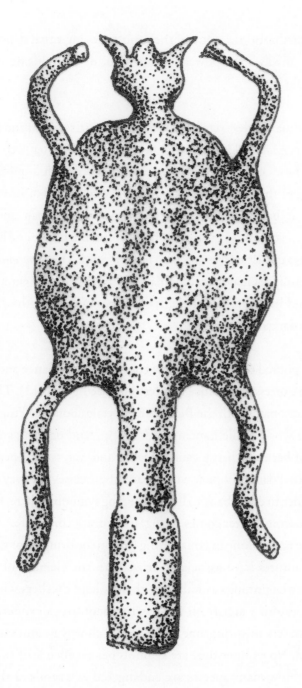

Figure 6.11. Illustration of toad, wooden tombstone, 19th century, Nida, Kuršių, nerija, western Lithuania, 4.5 cm. *(Courtesy of the Marija Gimbutas Archives at Opus Archives)*

of life. They have also studied women's ritual dance, which survives to this day, "in order to discover the message handed down to us from antiquity, despite layers of cultural transformation," a "living experience of the dance" passed down through generations (Bulgaria having once been a center of Old

European civilization).[37] One of their most moving ritual dances, called the Peperouda, involves the power of frogs to bring the rains necessary for the return of life:

> In the ritual's oldest version, the *Peperouda* girl is naked and barefoot. The *Peperouda* held green twigs in her hands, and frogs were fastened to her head and girdle (belt). . . . She danced with a quivering and shaking of the body, running forward and backward or in a circle . . . aimed at balancing the relationship between human and cosmic realms . . . [releasing] the forces of new life within nature and humanity. . . . This same ritual was repeated in every yard. The *Peperoudarki* (the ritual groups of maidens accompanying the Peperouda) entered with a song and lined up in a circle. As they began to sing, the *Peperouda* started dancing.[38]

Water was poured over them as they continued their dance and roared with laughter to express abundance and fertility (see figure 6.12). This prayer for the waters resonates with the Bulgarian fairytale about the Frog Queen, who created the world while dancing and dancing and dancing and then, with the wave of her right hand, caused forests and waters to appear.[39] Humans, through ritual dance, hope to vivify natural processes as a way of aiding the Earth Mother to come back to life. In the frog symbolism here, from drought comes rain, from winter comes spring, from death comes life.

Europe is not alone in considering frogs to be bringers of rainfall. Many different cultures have associated frogs with the element of water. With their watery beginnings as tadpoles, then as land dwellers with permeable skins that absorb water from the environment, frogs exuberantly emerge from the waters in springtime, croaking in chorus to announce an awakened world. No wonder they are symbols par excellence of transformation and (sadly, now many species are endangered as a result of the toxicity of our polluted waters). These creatures of the waters were used as rainmakers in ancient China; Native American tribes linked frogs to the purifying energy of water as a cleansing power; in the *Rig Veda* frogs are invoked as deities, their croaking seen as a prayer for rain.[40] In Old Europe and in

Egypt, a figurative use of the frog associated it with the waters of the womb of the Goddess, the shaping of uterine life, and renewal (see figure 6.13).

Such meanings persist down through the centuries, as shown in Marie-Louise von Franz's *The Feminine in Fairy Tales,* which notes that the frog in folklore is a maternal animal who helps women become pregnant and aids in childbirth—again, much like the folk traditions associated with the Sheela na gig. Franz adds that in many countries, "the croaking of frogs in the springtime is said to resemble the cries of unborn children, and therefore represents the soul of the not yet incarnate child."[41] From a psychological point of view, just as the frog comes out of the waters of spring, it arrives in dreams out of the waters of the unconscious to reveal "the ending of a stage of psychological sterility; it indicates a spirit of nature,

Figure 6.12. Frog girl in Peperouda ceremony, Bulgaria, 1950s. *(Courtesy of Wikimedia Commons)*

Figure 6.13. Woman and frog vessel, faience, eastern Greece, Archaic, late 7th–early 6th century BCE, 11.4 cm. Double-spouted vessel of a kneeling woman holding a jar; she mirrors the frog with her green skin, warts, and amphibian legs, and as a carrier of life-giving water. *(Image © The Metropolitan Museum of Art; courtesy of Art Resource, NY)*

or a vital impulse."[42] Here is yet another arena for the play of the frog's revitalizing powers.

If in folklore the frog or toad has protective, life-giving properties as an incarnation of the Dark Goddess, so it must also possess destructive properties. It was believed, even as late as the early twentieth century in Europe, that the toad can be a messenger of death; it can kill a sleeping person by crawling onto the chest and stealing the breath from a body.[43] In time, the original associations between the toad and the Goddess were applied to the toad and the witch. As noted earlier, in many European languages the names given to the toad also mean "witch." It is not by chance that in folklore one of the principal animals of the witch is a toad or a frog, just as the witch is a form of the prehistoric Goddess. Hence, this transformative Great Goddess "was not erased from the mythical world but lives on throughout Europe as the Baltic Ragana, the Polish Jedza, the Basque Mari, the Irish Morrígan, and the Russian Baba Yaga."[44] Such witch-goddesses like Baba Yaga can turn into a toad or, like Ragana, have a toad for her totem.

The Body of the Dark Goddess

The dark side of the Goddess can seem destructive from our human viewpoint, but her functions serve all of life. She keeps the necessary balance, implacably sweeping away the old or what has gone too far: "She stops growth, waxing, blossoming, productivity, and fertility lest life powers flourish forever."[45] Her reanimating powers come out after this need for finality, for limitation. Or to put it another way: without death, there would be no need for sex, for fertility. In folklore, the witch-goddess and her animals inherit these powers, watching over any needless waste of energy, influencing the rhythms of nature: death and rebirth, the cycles of the moon, the energies of the sun, and human sexuality.[46]

And this, more than anything, is at the root of patriarchal fear: female sexuality. A potent factor behind the medieval Inquisition, lasting into the seventeenth-century witch burnings, was a fear of the feminine. The female body, with its mysterious powers beyond male control, terrified the clergy, especially since "witches" carried the formidable powers of millennia of the

Great Goddess's reign. This hysteria, this terrible need to destroy the connection to our physical instincts, aroused the "enormous energies spent by missionaries and the inquisitors to fight this powerful goddess."[47] She was considered a demon from the point of view of the church, but from that of the country people she was a healer, a wise woman, a midwife in service to mothers.

Let us never forget that the medieval Sheelas also came to be considered of the devil by the clergy, who ordered them burned as witches even though they were made of stone, not flesh. It is impossible to know the number of Sheelas who suffered such barbarity; in later centuries and to this day, many are being recovered from where they were sometimes tossed into rivers or buried deep beneath castles. Other carvings had their vulvas hacked away, but, no doubt, many were hidden by the people to preserve their beloved Sheelas.

The degradation of the Goddess in all her aspects began with aggressive invasions of Old Europe in the fourth and third millennia BCE by Indo-Europeans, a hierarchal warrior society from the steppes of southern Russia with a male-dominated pantheon. The destruction of the Goddess as a symbol of the unity of all life continued through the historical period, intensified "by the entire array of Hebraic-Christian traditions."[48] This lethal dominance culminated in Christianity's holocaust against the female sex—the burning of women at the stake. Whether tens of thousands or hundreds of thousands or millions of women were tortured to death, no one knows for sure. The powers of the Dark Goddess of Old Europe have been demonized as an evil projected onto women to justify the longest war on the planet: the war against women, which continues to this very day.[49] Yet without the Goddess, there is no life.

The startling figure of a female displaying her powers manifests as an archetype throughout the world. In fact, the earliest known figure displaying her vulva was recently discovered in southeast Anatolia, at Göbekli Tepe (Navel Mountain), a site that dates from between 9600 and 8000 BCE (see figure 6.14).[50] Excavations begun in 1994, which still continue, have uncovered a vast temple complex located on top of a hill between the Tigris and Euphrates rivers. As of today, it is the oldest dated human-made structure, built over eleven thousand years ago. Radical speculation as to Göbekli Tepe's function occurred in a *National Geographic* article published in June 2011, which stated, "We used to think agriculture gave rise to cities and later to writing, art, and religion. Now the world's oldest temple suggests the urge to worship sparked civilization."[51] Not a scarcity of food but the need to gather together at a sacred place gave rise to this culture that had no evidence of social hierarchy.[52]

In one of the ten enclosures excavated so far was found the only unambiguous human figure. It is the image of a female guarding (yet again!) the entrance to the lion shrine, protecting her worshippers. (This association

Figure 6.14. Illustration of Göbekli Tepe female figure, early Neolithic. Is this the source of civilization?

of females with felines will also be seen in the Paleolithic caves.) Carved on a stone slab, she was found between two pillars with lions sculpted in relief, seemingly for ritual purposes.[53] With pendant breasts, exaggerated labia clearly depicting her sexuality, and her knees bent in a frog posture, it seems as if she were the dancing mother of all Sheelas to come (figure 6.14).

The Dark Goddess in all her forms represents life and death, the mysterious source of the ever-renewing life force, the unfolding cycles of manifestation in all of nature, and, to be sure, in the entire cosmos. In his sweeping study of female display figures in prehistoric times and across world cultures, Douglas Fraser concludes that not only in early examples like the frog goddess of the Neolithic period, but in all of the displayed figures he researched, he finds a convergence of opposites like birth and death. This continues right up through the Sheela na gigs, "who symbolize a goddess of creation and destruction of the sort in which Celtic mythology abounds."[54]

In our current age of a conscious return to the Goddess, older meanings are revived. Certainly the Dark Goddess has never left us, although she exists in the realms of the deep: sex, death, awe of the feminine procreative energies. As one of the later manifestations of the Dark Goddess, the Sheela na gig brings back to consciousness the radical meaning of the earliest display figures. She disrupts the lethal narrative of patriarchy when she asserts in the boldest manner the sanctity of the vulva—a sanctity that reaches back to the origins of culture.

7

The Cave Art of the Paleolithic

In the European art of the Upper Paleolithic Stone Age nearly forty thousand years ago, the image of the vulva took hold in the human imagination. The image was incised onto stone or bones or painted on walls found in rock shelters and caves throughout Europe, from Spain to France to Russia. While this era was certainly not the beginning of artistic creations, there was an undeniable intensification of art making and aesthetic refinement and symbolic representation. This Ice Age explosion of creativity most likely was grounded in a rich tradition going back hundreds of thousands of years.[1]

The Imaged Vulva in Deep History

Europe's Ice Age art is not the beginning of the story. In 1981, a female figurine with a groove suggestive of a vulva was discovered at Berekhat Ram, Israel. Dating back some 230,000 to 800,000 years, she was hailed in newspaper headlines as the world's oldest figurative work of art. The Blombos Cave, on the Southern Cape coastline of South Africa, was first excavated in 1991 and is known for its nearly eighty-thousand-year-old pieces of ocher engraved with lozenge and triangle designs, both enduring female symbols (see figure 7.1).[2] Such creations suggest that the cave-art tradition may have originated in Africa and migrated north to Europe. But there can be no doubt as to the flowering of artistic expression in the Upper Paleolithic era. Paleolithic archaeologist Alexander Marshack, in

Figure 7.1. Symbols eighty thousand years old, from the Blombos Cave, South Africa.

his *Roots of Civilization,* makes a formidable inquiry into the beginnings of art and symbol making. He believes that the art from all periods of the Upper Paleolithic, roughly thirty-five thousand to ten thousand years old, raises "profound questions about the nature of evolved human cognition and intelligence and human culture"—questions he considers as world-changing as those raised in the mid-nineteenth century by Darwin.[3]

Nowhere is the importance of Stone Age images of the vulva better demonstrated than in those monuments of magnificence, the Paleolithic caves. What better place to create such art, as the caves themselves very likely were seen as symbols or embodiments of the life force rising from the Goddess's womb.[4] The vulva as entrance to the womb, cave as womb, the womb of the Goddess—that entrance to her mysteries is the center of all images of female display, the source of power for the frog goddess, the Gorgon, Baubo, the Sheela na gig. This is the *point finale*—one cannot take it back any further; this is the first resting place of the imagination. While in the Upper Paleolithic era there are many of the so-called Venus figures (Willendorf, Laussell, Lespugue, Hohle Fels, and Dolní Věstonice, to name a few out of at least a hundred), our focus here is on sexual display and the bedrock foundation of its power, the image of the vulva. As an Upper Paleolithic symbol of a world-creating energy, its essence remains, a synecdoche, a part to represent the whole of the cosmic Creatrix.

In *Juniper Fuse,* his erudite meditation on the Upper Paleolithic imagination, poet and writer Clayton Eshleman writes that the "imaged vulva is possibly the oldest and most enduring force in creative imagination."[5] Henri Delporte, an authority on prehistoric art, observes that "although Paleolithic artists were able to depict animal forms with astonishing skill and verisimilitude, they choose to depict the vulva abstractly," revealing an astonishing power of conceptual thought.[6] Because it functioned as a symbol of renewal, birth, and return, the abstracted vulva became a widespread image with a story or myth so well known that it was "understood by every adult in the culture that it was a traditional image with a traditional story."[7] Thus, the reason why an Upper Paleolithic gravestone is incised with a single vulva is clear. Here we find the origins of the later Neolithic goddess of death and regeneration.

Male Interpretive Bias

Unfortunately, not all scholars are as informed as Eshleman, Delporte, and Marshack. As we have seen, the sway of entrenched patriarchal bias can result in misinterpretations of the obvious. As cultural historian Riane Eisler contends in "A New View of Ice Age Art," images of vulvas found in prehistoric caves have been dismissed by many archaeologists as incomprehensible. But, she points out, "the meaning of these images is comprehensible—indeed unmistakable—once we free ourselves from the still-popular notion that Paleolithic cave art was made by men for men to use in some kind of 'hunting magic.'"[8] Marshack elucidates the obvious about the carvings long interpreted as barbed weapons with "thrusting lines"; upon closer inspection they turn out to be line drawings of plants. The association of the life-giving vulva with sprouting seeds and plants found in paired vulvas and branches from Upper Paleolithic caves continued well into the Neolithic era (see figures 7.2 and 7.3).[9]

The October 1988 issue of *National Geographic* devoted to Ice Age discoveries displays an all-too-familiar bias: a male artist painting in the Lascaux cave, described as "a Paleolithic Leonardo da Vinci." A woman sits by his feet, passively holding up an animal-fat lamp (see figure 7.4). In fact, some cultural historians claim that it is quite probable that this sacred art

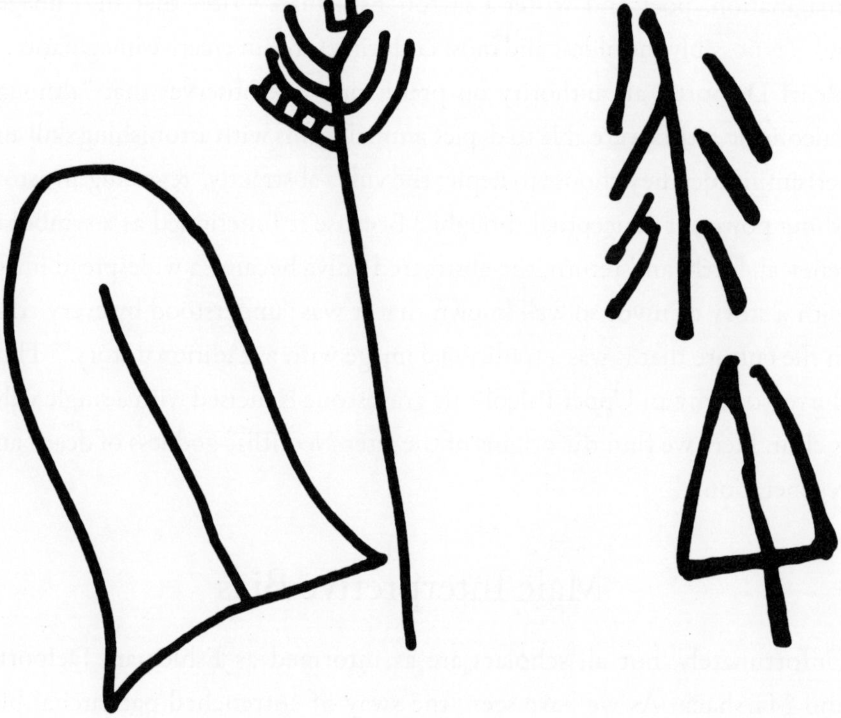

Figure 7.2. Vulvas and plants in Paleolithic caves, El Castillo, northern Spain, and La Mouthe, southern France. *(Courtesy of the Marija Gimbutas Archives at Opus Archives)*

was created by women for other women and men in their community.[10] A quarter of a century later, *National Geographic* questioned its earlier position on the creative origins of cave art in an article published on October 8, 2013, "Were the First Artists Mostly Women?" When archaeologist Dean Snow of Pennsylvania State University analyzed the relative lengths of ring and index fingers in hand stencils found in eight cave sites in France and Spain, his research determined something astounding: three-quarters of the handprints in ancient cave art were left by women. This discovery upends what Snow calls a longlasting "male bias . . . of unwarranted assumptions."[11]

Finally, let us dispense with the puerile notion that these images are Paleo porn, as some commentators seem to think it the height of wit to call this early art. Marija Gimbutas says rather that this art expresses "persistent awe of female sexual and procreative energies."[12] Surely an image that has endured throughout history and is so prominent in the archaeological

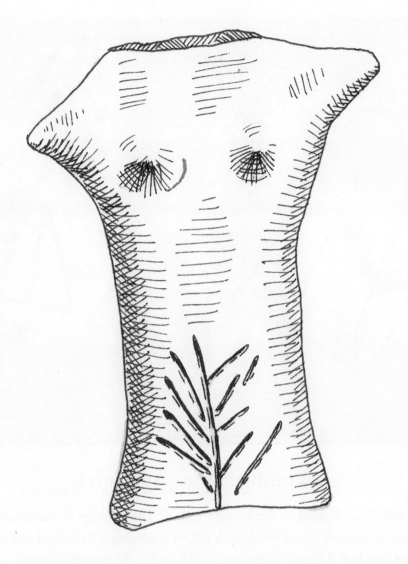

Figure 7.3. Association of the vulva with plants continues, as seen on a Neolithic figurine, early Vinča terra-cotta, Jela, Serbia, ca. 5200 BCE. *(Courtesy of the Marija Gimbutas Archives at Opus Archives)*

record of prehistory speaks to a meaning essential in human perception and understanding of the world. As conceptual art, the Paleoithic vulva is often depicted in disembodied form, abstract and schematic—a solitary image or in clusters, carved in relief, sometimes painted in black or red ocher. Some are etched on rock shelters; some are found by entrances, others in the deepest recesses of caves. Created in various designs, the vulva can appear to be triangular, bell-shaped with plants, or an oval, representing the waters of life from the cosmic womb of the Goddess, the regenerative sprouting of new life and the process of birth.[13]

Figure 7.4. Yet another male view of the supposed origin of Paleolithic cave art, as imagined by 20th-century artist Charles R. Knight in *Cave Painting at Font De Gaume*: men painting mastodons. *(Courtesy of Wikimedia Commons)*

A Wealth of Stone Age Vulvas

A wonder to behold in the Spanish cave of Tito Bustillo is a celebratory panel of swollen vulvas awash with red, in a subterranean cavity known as the Chamber of Vulvas. In the cave of El Castillo, three vulvas assume a red-painted bell shape and are paired with sprouting seeds, while a young plant is painted in black (figure 7.2). Sometimes, however, more of the female body is shown, as seen in two French caves from the Upper Paleolithic, which, like the Spanish caves, date from 16,000 to 12,000 BCE. At the La Madeleine Cave, two sculptures carved in relief, enhanced by the natural rock face, portray a pair of languorous females who recline at their ease—all the better to display their vulvas as they watch over the entrance (the guardian once again) from either side of the cave walls.[14] At the cave in Angles-sur-L'Anglin, many thousands of years ago an artist shaped three female figures in a continuous

flow of forms, evoking an intense feeling of grace and aliveness. A triple goddess of vulvas emerges from the cave wall, a tableaux of swelling abdomens gently rising from the rock surface, yet each anchored to the stone's surface by boldly etched sexual triangles.

The Dordogne region of southwest France possesses an embarrassment of riches in prehistoric rock shelters and caves. Not far from La Madeleine Cave is the rock shelter of La Ferrassie, where stones were engraved with clusters of vulvas that seem to dance on the hard surface (see figure 7.5). The La Ferrassie carvings date back some thirty thousand years to the Aurignacian period; earlier it was a site for Neanderthal burials. Also in the Dordogne there exists a complex of six rock shelters (shallow cavelike openings at the

Figure 7.5. Images of vulvas at La Ferrassie, Savignac-de-Miremont, Dordogne, France, Aurignacian. The carvings of vulvas and cupules are found on a block in the rock shelter. *(Photograph courtesy of Don Hitchcock, www.donsmaps.com)*

The Cave Art of the Paleolithic

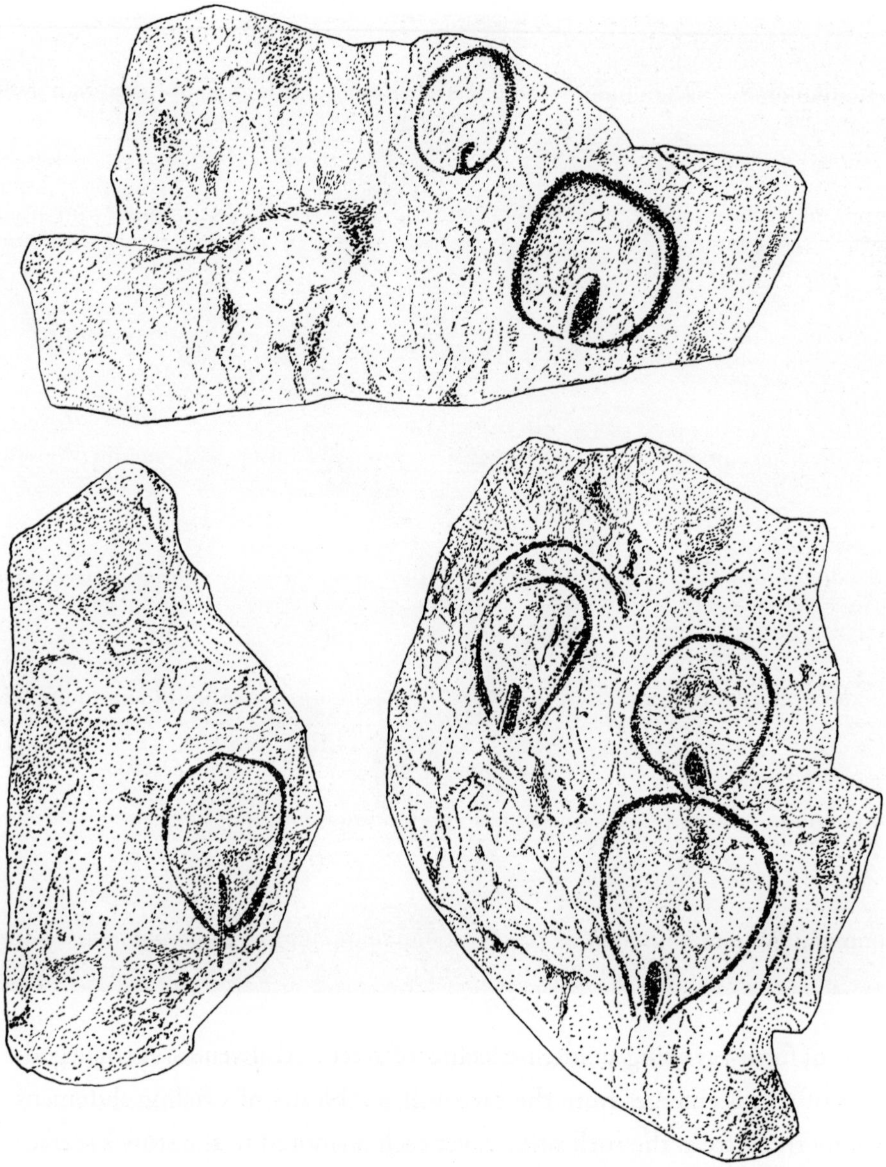

Figure 7.6. Abri Blanchard vulvas, Castel-Merle, Dordogne, France, Aurignacian. The thirty-thousand-year-old symbols of the sacred feminine are engraved in rock. *(Courtesy of the Marija Gimbutas Archives at Opus Archives)*

base of a cliff) collectively known as Castel-Merle, located in the Vallon des Roches, or Valley of Rocks, which could be renamed Valley of Vulvas! At Abri (Shelter) Blanchard (see figure 7.6), and further up the cliff face of Abri Castanet, and even further, on Abri Cellier, archaeologists have uncovered a number of limestone blocks marked with vulvas, and several have multiple images of the symbol, which can be seen as "early representations of the divine feminine in art" (see figure 7.7).[15]

The 1994 discovery of the Chauvet Cave in the cliffs of the Ardèche Gorge, a few hundred kilometers southeast of these rock shelters, became a "bombshell," overturning longstanding conceptions about cave art by pushing back the timeline of parietal art. Sealed off by a massive rock slide some twenty thousand years ago, the art remains remarkably vivid. Now considered the oldest cave paintings known to science, the Chauvet images date back at least thirty-two thousand years or more, and even though they are almost twice as old as those in Lascaux, they display an equivalent sophistication. This revelation indicates that Paleolithic artists transmitted their techniques from generation to generation. After her visit to the Chauvet Cave, *New Yorker* staff writer Judith Thurman mused that "for the conventions of

Figure 7.7. Abri Cellier vulvas, Le Moustier, Dordogne, France, Aurignacian. Rounded, almost sculptural vulvas are carved on limestone blocks. *(Photograph courtesy of Don Hitchcock, www. donsmaps.com)*

cave painting to have endured four times as long as recorded history, the culture it served [must have been] deeply satisfying."[16]

In the powerfully affecting documentary by Werner Herzog, *Cave of Forgotten Dreams,* we see the Chauvet Cave's stone engravings and paintings of over four hundred animal figures, with separate panels of horses, lions, and reindeer, and the hall of the bears. In his writings on the cave, one of its three discoverers, speleologist Jean-Marie Chauvet, expresses his belief that, based on the evidence of footprints and handprints, some of the paintings were created by women as well as men.[17] Visitors to the cave, whether journalists, historians, or archaeologists, report experiencing a strong sense of the presence of the original artists—as if they had just been in the cave and are alive still in the vibrant expressions of the animals and the dynamism of their portraits. No human conflict is recorded in this cave art.

And what is at the heart of all this magnificence? This Upper Paleolithic site reveals yet another ancient manifestation of the sacred triangle of the Goddess (see figure 7.8). At the end of the 1,300-foot cave, she resides in the Salle du Fond, the last and deepest of the chambers, amid a frieze of lions and rhinos following one another. There, she occupies a privileged place, the central topographic setting on a cone of limestone descending from the ceiling of the vaulted space, which includes over a third of the art found in the cave.[18] On the outcrop of rock, the vulva is not etched but painted in black charcoal—large, dark, imposing, and at eye level. Drawn later (by the account of most experts) are images on either side of her: a bison and a lion (a feline association we saw in Göbekli Tepe).[19] The Goddess is the unifying source of the life depicted in the cave, the mother of the animals drawn next to her and on all the walls throughout the caverns. In a striking continuity of the powers of display, she protects the space; she watches over a corridor opening just behind her and is considered one of the oldest images in the entire cave.

The *International Newsletter of Rock Art* reports that four other drawings of vulvas exist inside Chauvet, "indicating each time the entrance to the adjacent cavities" in the Galeries des Megeceros and the Salle du Fond.[20] What clarity of purpose! This apotropaic quality of the vulva is a primal virtue, there from the very beginning, an entrance guarding an entrance. Later this

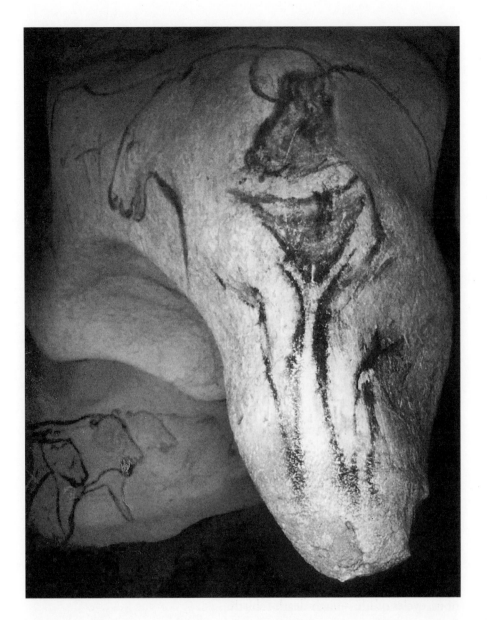

Figure 7.8. Chauvet Cave vulva, Salle du Fond, Ardèche, France. This image of the fount of life has an apotropaic quality even at the dawn of human culture. It was discovered only through the use of a remote-control camera on a telescopic pole. Note the lions in the background. *(Photograph courtesy of Yanik le Guillou, Mission Recherche du Ministère de la Culture)*

manifests in the Gorgon Medusa and later still in the Sheelas, both daughters of the vulva. Here in the deepest recesses of the most ancient cave paintings yet to be discovered we find again the astonishing power of this image.

Just as we rest in the knowledge of the great antiquity of the Chauvet Cave, the creative spirit of discovery has more surprises in store for us as new works of art surely will be found and, in fact, have already been found. In 2007, at Abri Castanet, in Dorgogne, France, a team of scientists overturned

The Cave Art of the Paleolithic

a section of a one-and-a-half-ton block of limestone that had fallen from the roof of the shelter ages ago. And they found—what else?—an engraving of a vulva that dates back thirty-seven thousand years. It has a rounded shape similar to those found at Abri Blanchard. Anthropologist Randall White, who led the excavations at Abri Castanet, reported that "while there are animal figures, the dominant motif is considered to represent abstract female vulvas."[21] Archaeologist Harold Dribble acknowledges that "the repeated use of this image [of the vulva] at other sites" in the rock shelters along the Vallon des Roches suggests that these ancient people shared a common iconography.[22] Indeed, devotion to making images of the sacred body of the Goddess continued for tens of thousands of years, well into the historical era, and it is resurfacing in our own time.

Randall White points out that whereas the paintings at Chauvet are located deep within the uninhabited chambers of the cave, "the depictions at Abri Castanet were on the rock shelter ceiling right above the spaces where prehistoric humans slept and ate, making them a kind of everyday and public art."[23] Prehistoric artists would have reached up, chisels and ocher pigment in hand, to embellish their home.[24]

French archaeologist and paleo-anthropologist André Leroi-Gourhan, in his monumental tome *Treasures of Prehistoric Art,* observes that there are "two categories of cave compositions—those executed in daylight, either in rock shelters or at cave entrances, and those executed deep inside the caves, where daylight doesn't penetrate."[25] Might this not imply that Chauvet and other Paleolithic caves were sanctuaries to be used for rituals to lift people out of the realm of the ordinary and into the sacred? Or to put it another way, they were a place to align with the sacredness of the ordinary, yet mysterious, cycles of life—birth-death-rebirth.

Archaeologist Alexander Marshack, from his great overview of Paleolithic art, maintains that the symbol of the Goddess could be used as part of a continuing myth: "Obviously the meaning of the female image in life and death could not be explained except in terms of an encompassing story."[26] Myth, story—here we are in a realm that calls for ceremony. Even the very making of art on the cave walls must have felt like some sort of rite. Far from the outer world of light, the cool refuge of a cave exists as an inner realm of the deep, back to the Source, the primordial womb of the Mother. Shifting to the objective language of that eminent specialist of prehistory André Leroi-Gourhan: "The cave as a whole does seem to have had a female symbolic character, which would explain the care with which narrow passages, oval-shaped areas, clefts, and smaller cavities are marked in red, even sometimes painted entirely in red."[27]

The processes of life are the same for us as they were for our prehistoric ancestors. As Julien Monney, one of the Chauvet archaeologists, in *Cave of Forgotten Dreams,* overcome by his experiences in the cave, by the presence of those long-ago artists, states simply: "They were human, I am human." Marshack too realizes that the Paleolithic images of the Goddess serve to explain external as well as internal processes that are human, whether they be "female processes of birth and pregnancy or more general processes of disease, death, dreams or trance, or even the origins of man himself [*sic*]."[28]

Creation-destruction, destruction-creation: there is no end to the thread of the ever-whirling life force that must also contain death as a necessity for renewal. From the Sheela's bold display back to the etched symbol of a vulva made by an obscure ancestor artist some unimaginable thirty-seven thousand years ago, this emblem represents the source, the origin of the world, and, after death, a sanctuary of return. In the prehistoric caves, the artists' use of figuration gave them a way to make deeper sense of their own world, and a way to communicate to us in the future.

This is our cultural inheritance from our Paleolithic forebears, who perceived with awe the natural processes of life. They created images such as the abstracted vulva, which by the very nature of symbols holds more than our conscious minds can, to touch on an understanding of the mysterious womb of the Goddess. From our Neolithic ancestors of Old Europe, with their exuberant celebration of life and acceptance of death; down through the Gorgon Medusa, who also carried creation and destruction in her blood, which could harm or heal, and her lethal face that guarded the temple gates but could also give birth to children; down to the belly laugh of Baubo, merry in the display of herself, also a force of regeneration when, as a dancer fashioned in gold, she is placed in the tomb of a priestess; down further to the Celtic goddesses who protected the land and gave prophecies of warning, and the hag of Irish legends who decided who should live and who should die; and, finally, down to the Sheela na gigs, monstrously beautiful in the terrifying power of their sacred display, who watched over the entrances, could repel enemies, and could be a portal for life and help women in childbirth. And still, life flows on. Who knows what form this Dark Goddess of destruction and creation will take next? What form will bloom again, wither back to the root, only to start again?

PART II

Journeys

8

On the Trail
of the Sheelas

Ireland

Killinaboy Sheela

I waited many years to come to Ireland. Since my youth I had wanted to stand in front of Yeats's grave and read his epitaph: "Cast a cold Eye/On Life, on Death." At last, one hot Sunday afternoon in May, my journey began when I arrived at Shannon, a small, negotiable airport in County Clare. As I drove to my bed-and-breakfast, I had a jet-lagged sense of unreality, then disappointment. Here I was, finally in Ireland, but the countryside seemed washed out, a dull yellow. Where were the famous forty shades of green and the atmosphere of magical mysticism described in the ancient lore? Old men sat on stone walls and looked out over the monotonous flat land.

The next day I drove inland from the coast to see the Burren, or Boireann, a lunar landscape of limestone rock where Neolithic dolmens no taller than a human body have stood for thousands of years. On the way to the Burren I stopped at a small spot known as Killinaboy to see the remains of an eleventh-to thirteenth-century church on which was the sole figure of a Sheela na gig. I carried with me a catalog of Sheelas based primarily on a taxonomy compiled in 1935 and amended with references to various archaeological journals. Each entry described in a few vague sentences the locations of some seventy existing figures. Now, I was about to see my first Sheela "face to face."

I parked the car on the side of the road where several men were building a dry stone wall. One laborer, eyes alive, smiled and jerked his thumb up to the direction of the church and asked, "Have you seen our Sheela na gig? The Christians put her up to bring in the pagans."

"I'm going right now," I replied, and walked up the hill to the roofless ruins of the church. Once this was a holy community, a monastic site, and even earlier, a pagan sanctuary, but today one finds a broken stub of a round tower built to provide refuge from Viking raids, the double-armed cross of Lorraine on the east wall of the church, and a graveyard, old but still in use. The burials marked by granite slabs and red plastic flowers have crept into the interior ruins of the church.

I scanned the stones looking for the Sheela. When I turned a corner, on the south wall, there she was, nestled in green ivy, placed over a round-headed doorway, the only entrance to the church. She is carved in high relief with a monstrous bald head, a thick-lipped grimace of suffering, and tattoos streaking down from neck to breast; one could count the ribs on her emaciated body (see figure 8.1). Her legs splay out and she squats, all the better to frame the fierce pull of her crude hands on her exaggerated labia. She is female, but she is not human. A figure of duality, of menace and openness, she offers an invitation into her body, into the church, to an altered state of mind. No one could pass through this portal without seeing this Sheela na gig—all must enter beneath her. Imagine this scene centuries ago, monks and nuns and country folk passing under this sexual display, entering to participate in the rite of the Christian Mass. What could their consciousness have been?

How does this symbol, this conceptual figure, fit in with that particular time during the Middle Ages? What two worlds does this Sheela connect? The laborer putting stones in a pile knew her name and saw her as a pagan deity. Oh yes, he tells me, they *had* to put her up there to get the people into the church; otherwise they wouldn't come. Implicit in his comment is that the image of the Sheela, a rude supernatural woman exhibiting herself, was a pre-Christian image that would have been recognized by the unedu-cated populace of centuries ago. In Ireland, the church tolerated "worship

Figure 8.1. Killinaboy Sheela, County Clare, Ireland, 11th to 13th centuries. She watches over the south-wall entrance.

of local deities to continue in cases where it was possible to bless them and cause them to serve Christianity instead of paganism."[1] Locally, this Sheela is known as Bhaoith, after St. Inghean Bhaoith, the founder and first abbess of the church.[2]

From her place, the Sheela na gig commands a grand view of the countryside. She has reigned there for over eight hundred years. In the Irish tradition, she *is* the land she protects. Her purpose is to guard the entrance of this sacred site. As I stood before the gray stone antiquities surrounded by green farmlands, I felt overcome by the wonder at being alive. Now I saw before me what I had previously only read about. Now I was present with the birds above in the sky and, at my feet, the churchyard graves decorated with small statues of Jesus and Mary, images of divinity. But I preferred the Goddess on the wall, with the parted lips of her vulva, that dark space, beckoning us into the unknown. Amid the ruins, at last I'd found the magic I'd been looking for.

Kilsarkin Sheela

I drove five miles east of Farrnafore to find the ruins of the medieval church of Kilsarkin, County Kerry. It is not listed on any map but lies north of the Lakes of Killarney, between the Dingle Peninsula and the Ring of Kerry, like the base between two parted fingers. All I could do was approximate as I drew closer, asking shopkeepers, strangers in pubs, farmers. "Kilsarkin," I inquired of an old woman standing in front of her store, "can you tell me how to get to Kilsarkin?" She seemed puzzled, almost angry at the question. "Kilsarkin? You might as well go to Timbuktu."

This is how it is when on the trail of the Sheelas. For the past three hours I had been reading a twenty-year-old map drawn from a sixty-year-old map, trying to find her—circling round like a reverse spiral trying to find its point of origin. Ten kilometers away and no one had heard of that Sheela na gig on that ruined church. Drawing closer, one bit of information led to another, and finally to some local who knew which dirt road to follow.

The men at a construction site next to the old parish church of Kilsarkin seemed surprised at the sight of a tourist coming to such a remote place, then returned to their work cutting back roadside weeds. On the edge of anticipation, after all the research, all the labor to get here to this very spot, I strode around the outer walls of the sixteenth-century church to look once again for her. A thrill passed through me to find her, legs straddled over the spandrel of a narrow south window (see figure 8.2). Carved in one solid block of stone, the Sheela and the arch of the window seemed as if they were one continuous entity, each completing the other.

She is a small figure, less than a foot high but nearly two feet wide. Even for a Sheela she has an unusual body (or, one could say, lack of body)—a head, then a neck sprouting two long legs that stretch out above the window to reveal her wide display. In a cartouchelike effect she appears set into the stone, centered within a scalloped border. A thick coil of braid tops her head and cowlike ears stick straight out. Her face is animated by startled

Figure 8.2. Kilsarkin Sheela, County Kerry, Ireland, 15th to 16th century.

round eyes composed of uneven circles chiseled deep in the stone. Below a thick nose, the lips of her mouth part. Surprisingly, she has no arms.

I stand on my tiptoes to touch her genitals with my fingertips, then I rub her for good luck, as generations of pilgrims have done, as evidenced by the worn stone of the old shrine. Folk wisdom holds that the stone dust from her display has magical properties: it can bring good luck and promote fertility.[3] The ritual touching of her vulva continues to this day. There are few facts, but the truth of lingering customs remains. As Michael Quirke, a woodcarver from Sligo, once said to me, "Here in Ireland, local rumors last a thousand years."

A column of vertical white crosses is spray-painted on the stones flanking the window. A contemporary remedy to a perceived ancient evil? Originally she was an integral part of the creation of the church. Clearly, the Sheela is still venerated as a beneficial image, but do some people now view her presence as a desecration of the holy site? Nevertheless, she continues her watch over the opening. Leafless vines break through gaps in the wall. The cold winds of centuries blow over the tufts of grass and crooked gravestones. The Sheela na gig endures. I make my way over and reach up to her again. I aspire never to forget the Great Mother in the stillness between the gusts of wind.

Moate Sheela

She resides above a green door. To find her, I drove east from Kilbeggan on the Dublin road. But, like many Sheelas, she was not so easy to find, and the steady rain and fog was beginning to feel oppressive. A locked front entrance and a house surrounded with barking dogs did nothing to lift my mood. All one could do was ask for help. At the Bon Bon shop on the edge of town, the women clerks pointed the way to Seamus, who worked at the florist shop and also as a gardener on the estate. He, in turn, pointed the way to a little alley: "Just climb over the fence when you get to the beech trees. Walk through the field, aye, but the field's very wet." In my time here, to be sure, I had been through wet fields full of cow dung, crawling bugs, flies, mosquitoes, and the rain, all to see the Sheelas, and today, to see one of the strangest figures ever carved.

Behind the Moate Castle (really just a large country house in County Westmeath), a wall was rebuilt in 1649.[4] Centrally placed above an arched door that leads to a yard, the oval-shaped Sheela was sunk into the keystone (see figure 8.3). She is a remarkably well-preserved figure. Scholars disagree as to whether she was initially carved for this location as a "late grotesque treatment of the subject," or if she is of an indeterminate date and not in her original position, wherever that might have been.[5] If she was carved in 1649, she is a late figure indeed, created near the end of the era of the Sheelas.

Less than a foot high and singularly monstrous in expression, she has the muzzle of a predator combined with large teeth and protruding tongue. With a misshapen body and tattooing across her forehead, the Moate Sheela is an altogether menacing Irish Sheela na gig. Her disturbing appearance

Figure 8.3. Moate Sheela, County Westmeath, Ireland, 17th century.

empowers her apotropaic function as a guardian over the gateway door. This figure also has a pregnant-looking belly that spills over her display. Coupled with a face that is anything but maternal, this Sheela is young enough to be fertile. In the mysterious antinomies of the Sheela na gig, she appears to be a pregnant hag.

Her breasts, however, are barely noticeable. A beltlike shape passes beneath them. Freitag calls this a birthing girdle, those long strips of parchments or any material with inscribed prayers to aid in parturition, which could be tied around the abdomen and then loosened at the beginning of confinement to quicken birth.[6] Fingertips touch the white slit of the vulva. For once, her sexual exhibition is not prominent but instead seems small in proportion to the head. This Sheela's entire body is a plane of conflicting shapes and patterns. Her face emanates force with its bulbous cheeks, swollen mouth, and the asymmetrical eyes of a stroke victim. She is not at ease but exudes a coiled-up danger, as if she could spring from the wall to attack. At such an arresting sight, so full of character, and despite all the rain, how could I not cheer up?

Ballinderry Sheela

From Tuam, you take the Athenry road. Ballinderry Castle, in County Galway, sits a few hundred yards from the road. It was completed around 1540 by an Anglo-Norman family. Later, during the brutal invasion of Ireland in the 1650s, Cromwell's army took the castle. The last military use of Ballinderry was as a British outpost during the troubles of the Irish War for Independence in the early twentieth century. A picture appearing in a 1936 journal of antiquities shows the building with no door, and inside, a pile of rubbish.[7] In recent times, the tower house has been renovated and is currently a private dwelling. Through all this, the Sheela na gig has survived.

Set above the entrance to the castle, the Sheela was created during a relatively stable period in the sixteenth century. At that time there was a flourishing of interest in native Celtic arts fostered by the patronage of the Anglo-Norman lords, colonists who, in time, assimilated into Irish culture so completely that some no longer spoke English. More than any other Sheela na gig, the design of the Ballinderry carving illustrates the artistic traditions of the Celtic past.

To get to the Sheela, I park my car on the Tuam–Athenry road and walk up through the high grass of a huge field, past grazing sheep, to the castle. When I round a corner of the building and stand before the entrance I read a warning on the door painted in big red letters: EXTREME DANGER BEWARE. I turn to see a bull standing twenty feet away, watching me. But he remains motionless, and I have a Sheela to see. Whether in arrogance or feeling blessed in my quest, I go about my business and am allowed my visit to contemplate her and take pictures.

Like so many others, this figure confirms a custom enacted "throughout the Middle Ages even down to the Renaissance," which was to set Sheelas by doors and windows.[8] The placement of the Ballinderry Sheela as the voussoir keystone over the arch of the door, the only entrance to the castle, emphasizes her ability to lend strength to the structure (see figure 8.4). Her location

Figure 8.4. Ballinderry Castle Sheela, County Galway, Ireland, 16th century. A most Celtic-themed Sheela na gig.

at this strategic point demonstrates yet again the power of her apotropaic presence. The design of the wedge-shaped stone clearly shows that the carving is in its original position, just where it has been for over 450 years.

Unlike the case with other Sheelas, the eye goes immediately not to her sexual display but to the elaborate ornamentation surrounding her. This is not to say her vulva is dull! Something is going on between her legs, but precisely what? Rounded, tubelike arms meet at her groin, where a stream of liquid pours out of her. The weathered stone makes it hard to tell if it is urine, menstrual blood, or the amniotic waters signaling birth. Some observers offer other interpretations: it's just a stool she sits on, or, in a more extreme view, she has a penis. I see the waters of life flowing from her wellspring of creation. Whatever process her body is undergoing, her blank eyes are closed in concentrated effort to complete a primal task. One cannot help but think of a wooden carving from southern India, of a squatting female with her menstrual blood in a triangular flux out of her vulva, most likely representing a Yoni Pūjā (see figure 8.5).[9] And like the Irish figure, the Indian figure is also decorated with flower images.

If in the Ballinderry Sheela that flow can be hard to discern, the geometric designs surrounding her body easily capture our attention. The background of Celtic motifs gives her a pagan aura. Three different circles have patterns of 3, 6, and 8—respectively, the triskele, the rosette, and the marigold. Such numbers express a myriad of meanings and basic systems of nature experienced by humans. Lunar cycles can be seen as the three phases of the moon and solar cycles in the eight divisions of the year of the ancient calendar.[10] The rosette circle with its six divisions into twelve can represent the zodiac, or the first six months of the unfolding year in winter/spring, and the next six completing it in summer/autumn.[11]

The number 3 dominates in the ornamentation of the design. In addition to the triskele (three interlocked spirals), a triquetra (three interlaced arcs) is carved below the marigold circle (six spokes, or 3 + 3). This pattern is as ancient in Ireland as the triple spiral carved on the back altar of the prehistoric temple at Newgrange (figure 4.1)—as ancient as the downward-pointing triangle of a Neolithic goddess, a symbol par excellence of the vulva, and the three sides of the yoni creative triangle found so often in Paleolithic

Figure 8.5. Kālī in the yoni tantra, wood carving, South India, 18th century.

caves. Three is "the formula of all creation," the birth waters of the feminine pouring down.[12]

More goddess connections can be mined from the images encircling this complex Sheela. The rosette has associations with the Celtic goddess Epona, protectress of horses, as well as with many other ancient female figures, such as the goddess Inanna/Ishtar.[13] Perched on the rosette is a bird, similiar to a Celtic sovereignty goddess, Medb, often depicted with a bird on her shoulder.[14]

Finally, there is the ornamental border at the top of the stone, Celtic knot work woven as hair plaits flying out from the sides of her head. Each braid has a different pattern of weaving, and she bears Irish tattoos across her forehead. The sculptor who carved the Ballinderry Sheela drew from the art of the Celtic past. The Gundestrup cauldron (figure 4.5), a creation of the La Tène culture between the fourth and third centuries BCE, has a female figure whose hair is arranged in braids and is flanked by rosettes, two motifs echoed in the Ballinderry Sheela.

So much to see, so little time. When I am done, the bull starts moving toward me. I rush back down the field and do not look back even when I reach the stile bordering the property and the road. Probably I was in no real danger, and, in any case, when on the trail of the Sheelas, I am under her protection.

Four Sheelas, County Roscommon

It was the first day of autumn, the sky clear after a morning rain. The earth seemed to have its own inner light that came up from just below the surface as if the summer sun had been baked in the soil and was now reemerging. I stood amid the ruins of the Rahara Church as my guide, Albert Siggins, the curator of the Roscommon County Museum, pointed out the graveyard (see figure 8.6): "People want to be with their own. There's peace here. The burials go back for over a thousand years. The gravestones only mark one percent of the people here." He informed me that even before the Normans there were diosecan boundaries, and that in 1308 Rahara was listed as being in the parish of the nearby village of Elphin. As we walked around the grounds,

Figure 8.6. The Rahara Church, County Roscommon, Ireland, dates back to the 14th century.

and for all the rest of the day, Siggins pointed and I looked, ecstatic over the beauty of the countryside, the atmosphere of these ancient places, and the pleasure of the curator's company.

Back in 1990, during a cleanup campaign of the old graveyard, an organizing team found several treasures. On the corner of the long east wall a stone head carved on a quoin, or cornerstone, was found about ten feet above the ground.[15] Close by was a wedge-shaped stone sunk in the earth. When a member of the group turned it over, he discovered the female figure of the Sheela na gig.[16] For just how long the true nature of the underside of the stone was hidden, no one can answer. Most likely, she once functioned as a keystone over the main arched doorway. I like to imagine the church at the height of its splendor, the stone head decorating the corner wall, the whole scene dominated by the large Sheela (twice as big as the Ballinderry Sheela) centered above the main entrance, watching over all those who pass beneath her.

It seems likely that general decay through the passage of time (and not, in this instance, through the repressive malice of the Reformation or Counter-Reformation) dealt the Sheela na gig her fate as an element of the crumbling medieval church sank into the boglike land. (Although a local legend exists that claims the church was "knocked down by Cromwell's guns.")[17] Ironically, that the Rahara Sheela sank down into the earth preserved the details of the carving (see figure 8.7).

The most striking of these details are the Sheela's thick braids, plaited into the pattern of Celtic knot work and flowing down to her bent elbows.

Figure 8.7. Rahara Sheela, County Roscommon, Ireland—a Sheela discovered in 1990! *(Photograph courtesy of the County Roscommon Historical and Archaeological Society)*

An imposing, wedge-shaped head and nose echo the lines of the voussoir, or arch stone, on which she is carved. Another singular facial feature is the quite odd-looking nostril channels between her nose and mouth, deeply etched like a ritualistic scarring. As with the Ballinderry Sheela, her pendulous breasts fold under her arms and hang down toward a prominent navel. Her flexed arms reach under the symmetrical display of her wide-open thighs. Fingers reach to touch a vulva formed like a falling tear. The three middle fingers pull open her lips from each side, with thumbs up and delicate little fingers pointing down. Is that a clitoris inside there? The figure is framed in a cartouche and sits on a cube of stone similar to the square seat of the High Priestess from a tarot pack.

Less than a mile north of the ruins of the Rahara Church is Tobar Largan, an ancient holy well. (Wells are frequently located near Sheela sites like Ballyvourney, Castlemagner, Killinaboy, Dowth, and Seir Kieran.)[18] Resting on the well's stone wall is a basin-shaped stone with a head projecting at one end. Possibly serving as a holy-water font at one time, this stone connects it to the Rahara Church, as the face has the same "almond-shaped eyes" as the head carved on the quoin stone and the Sheela.[19] Rich traditions are still told about Tobar Largan. Country people believed that if the stone was removed, the well would run dry, and so when drawing water from the well they would throw a few drops of water onto the stone with their prayers. Finally, local tradition has it that Saint Brigid visited Tobar Largan.[20]

The Rahara Sheela is now housed at Roscommon County Museum, where I first met Siggins that morning. I had had an anticipatory thrill to see this newly found Sheela, but when I did, she looked washed out, propped up against a shelf. Even a goddess needs flattering light, and here she was, all cleaned up and sitting in dull shadows. She seemed not alive at all, in stark contrast to the vivid photograph of her I'd seen in a book, taken when the stone had just been overturned from the muck, when the dirt of centuries outlined her contours. The day's pleasures picked up, however, when the curator kindly gave me that original picture, and together we left the museum to begin our tour of the countryside to see the four Sheelas in the area.

After we first visited the Rahara Church and Tobar Largan, the afternoon progressed as Siggins and I made the short drive three miles to the northeast to see the two Sheelas at Scregg Castle. The figures are positioned on the gable of a carriage house, placed there above the entrance when the barn was built in the eighteenth century. It was most likely constructed from stones quarried from Scregg Castle, a tower house now in ruins just up the hill. Also built from the dismantled stones of the old castle is Scregg House, a Georgian country residence dating from 1760.

The two Sheelas were undoubtedly saved from their original setting on the castle and reset by the eaves of the gable wall. They were first documented in 1983 when a local resident brought them to the attention of the National Museum. How they slip through the centuries unnoticed! The Sheela to the left of the entrance may be one of the smallest exhibitionist figures on record, just under four inches high. She evokes the feeling of a merry acrobat with her wide smile and flexible legs flying apart, almost in a horizontal line. She has a round head, round torso, and round vulva, as if swollen with delight. Her larger companion on the right side of the door has a fierce countenance with a pointed chin and the sticking-out cauliflower ears of a boxer who has seen better days. Her upright stance shows the familiar hag features of emaciation—withered breasts and visible ribs. As her angled arms reach for her genitals, she stands deep in her stone, which is pitted with a chisel-punch surface.

What position the figures originally occupied on the castle remains a mystery. The taller Sheela (about a foot high) is carved on a voussoir-shaped stone, so she may have been located over an opening, a window or a door. Her diminutive sister may have been a mysterious talisman high up on the castle wall or set lower down to cheerfully greet guests. Who can say?

At twilight we drove to our last Sheela, down a long road to the Cloghan Castle. She is where she has always been, about twenty feet up on the south wall, set sideways as a Hag of the Castle but with not much castle left to guard: once again, stones have been quarried from this castle, which dates from 1610. But the destruction stopped well short of the Sheela, as if her powers of protection saved herself.[21] She is a formidable figure, only recently documented in 1970.

The Cloghan figure has a cap of hair, and the oval eyes have large pupils, as if in a state of shock. She displays her tongue so boldly that one can discern its center seam. Although the stone is much weathered, no viewer could doubt the gesture to her vulva. Below this is a mysterious, second tonguelike shape enhancing her display.

In the end, we were losing light; the whole afternoon had slipped into evening. I could see no more, certainly not the Sheela high up the dark wall now hidden by the shadows of sheltering trees.

Fethard Sheelas

With twenty identified figures, County Tipperary has the greatest concentration of Sheela na gigs of any county in Ireland, and the environs of Fethard have the greatest density of figures within the county.[22] Located in the center of the country, Tipperary was historically beyond the pale—an area outside of Dublin, beyond the direct control of English law, where the medieval Anglo-Norman lords claimed their territories and constructed buildings enhanced by the presence of many Sheelas.

My first stop of the day was at the Fethard Historical Society. Fethard, which in Gaelic means "high wood" (Fiodh Ard), is well known for its medieval walls that surround the town for defense, built by royal decree granted in 1376.[23] Most of the circuit can still be seen today, some sections towering alongside the river. In the offices of the historical society I heard the tale of Grandmother Fethard, a local woman who used to send her daughters as brides to rub a Sheela for fertility. Then I was off to see the Kiltinan Church, built in the fourteenth century.[24]

The Kiltinan Sheela na gig had been inserted sideways on the corner wall of the church, just below the roof where the gable ascends. Such a dramatic sideways placement was believed to impart physical as well as spiritual strength to the building.[25] The figure is remarkably angular. Her right shoulder is raised to a point, as is the left elbow; her head is the shape of the Goddess's downward triangle. With a thumbs-up gesture, her right hand pulls open the thick, straight slit of her vulva. The left cheek is marked in the same manner as the Bishop's Stone, carved some six hundred years earlier. The stare of her round eyes makes for a fierce countenance (figure 1.3). A strange force emanates from her. The lift of her shoulders feels like a display of power. Her pendulous left breast has two nipples. Feet above the earth, she dances a jig. She lifts her left hand to her ear with fingers spread, all the better to hear, for she seems to be listening for some internal voice from the Beyond, before her open mouth will deliver the prophecy. Surely this is one of the most magical of Sheelas. With her mystical dance and oracular gesture, she resembles the otherworldly crone in the Old Irish story "The Destruction of Da Derga's Hostel" (Togail Bruidne Dá Derga) (see chapter 3).

This particular Sheela na gig is imbued with much history, being the first recorded reference to a Sheela in O'Donovan's Ordnance Survey Letters of 1840. He wrote of his encounter with the Kiltinan Sheela na gig in terms of disgust that she should be placed on a Christian church, repelled by what he considered her lasciviousness.[26] Yet despite his moral reservations, he was compelled to write in a feverish tone about this arresting figure, losing the cool objectivity of his previous entries.[27]

Sadly, all these descriptions of the appearance of this Sheela come from looking at photographs of her, because the Kiltinan Sheela was stolen from the church on January 9, 1990 (see figure 8.8). In Fethard, the people's connection to this Sheela is such that she was missing for only a few hours before her loss was discovered by a local farmer. James O'Connor, a local authority on the Sheelas, tells a boyhood story of being afraid of the dark one night when he had to direct a tractor to his family's wheat field directly across from the Kiltinan Church. His legs, "with a mind of their own," carried him over to the Sheela, and he sat beneath her feeling safe and protected the rest of the night. Since then, he has had a "very benign attitude towards the figure."[28]

Of course, when I visited the Kiltinan Church I knew it was impossible to see the Sheela, as the theft had occurred years ago, but I was not prepared for what happened next. I made a short walk east from the church and down the road to Kiltinan Castle, to visit a second Sheela built into a well house located on the grounds. A pinched-faced guard stopped me in my tracks, refusing to allow me to pass through the property gates. I tried every trick in my arsenal: I was a scholar, a devoted pilgrim, an eager tourist on a once-in-a-lifetime trip . . . He remained obdurate, claiming in an English accent that if he let me see the Sheela, "My job is on the line." I looked out over to a field of horses. The English composer Andrew Lloyd Webber had just bought the

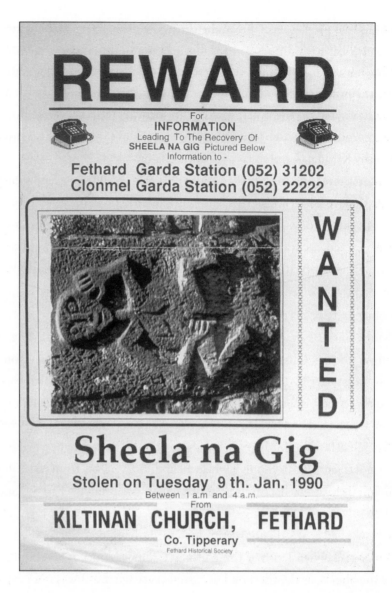

Figure 8.8. Reward poster for the stolen Kiltinan Church Sheela. *(Photograph courtesy of Joe Kenny, www.fethard.com)*

estate of Kiltinan Castle as a stud farm for his equine-loving wife. Far different was the policy of a previous owner of the castle, an eccentric known as Lady La who lived there some fifty years. Earlier in the day, a lad at the Fethard Historical Society had recalled his boyhood on the castle grounds to me: "I know every inch of that place. [Lady La would] have festivals. It was all free. You could come and go. She had fifty ponies and dozens of cats."

The historical record places the construction of Kiltinan Castle back to the twelfth century, making it one of the oldest inhabited castles in Ireland.[29]

Built on a limestone cliff with a sheer drop of a hundred feet, it overlooks the Clashawley River. At the bottom of the cliff is a round well house that supplies fresh water to the castle; it is connected to the courtyard high above by a passage cut into the stone face of the cliff. Since the 1940s the Sheela na gig has been situated on the north wall of this fortified well. While her original position is not known, scholars speculate that she may have once been set on the nearby Kiltinan Church, as a second, smaller Sheela.[30]

In contemplating this Sheela I could only rely on the one existing picture and the descriptions of others. Called "the Guardian of the Well," she protects with the grim, lethal lineaments of her face almost more than she does with the carved vulva at the center of her legs, spread open like her arms (see figure 8.9). In a posture rare for a Sheela, she raises her arms with objects

Figure 8.9. Kiltinan Castle Sheela, County Tipperary, Ireland. What mysteries does she hold in both of her fists? *(Photograph courtesy of Joe Kenny, www.fethard.com)*

The Sheelas: Ireland

in both of her fists, much like a Minoan snake goddess. This leads to the most debated question swirling about this figure: Just what is she gripping so tightly? Some say the figure is too weathered to make any definitive statement, but this doesn't stop the flow of interpretations: in her right hand a cross, a dagger, a comb; in the left, a torque, a birthing girdle, a mirror like some of the mermaids carved on Irish churches hold, since the Sheela is also by water. What exactly she grasps in her right hand is impossible to clearly discern, but a more distinct image is the object in her left hand. It is a horseshoe, as James O'Connor believes. Who better to say, since he has lived near this Sheela all his life and probably has observed her more than anyone else writing about her. It was O'Connor who spotted the evenly spaced nail holes. In this, he is in agreement with an 1840 report to the Royal Irish Academy stating that the Kiltinan figure holds "the lucky horse-shoe."[31] The horseshoe is a well-known symbol for the protective powers of female genitals, in this instance the mare's vagina. Thus the Sheela holds in her hand a symbol in harmony with her display.

Just down from Kiltinan on the Cashel road, a third Sheela watches over the old entry into the town of Fethard from her strategic position on a wall. This is the very road from which Cromwell's forces invaded Fethard in the seventeenth century (he then quartered himself at Kiltinan Castle). The figure is set in a small section of the medieval Old Wall at Watergate Street and looks out over an old bridge on the Clashawley River. She faces south, as I have observed many Sheela na gigs do. An old man on the side of the road kindly felt a need to tell me things such as the fact that fever-bearing winds come from the south, and Clashawley means "beautiful stream."

At last, after this day of not seeing any Sheelas, I now stand before this formidable figure, who under my gaze seems to come alive (see figure 8.10). She is famously known as the "Witch on the Wall," a description bestowed on her by Jørgen Andersen, which became the title of his pioneering book on the Sheelas. Indeed, she blends well into the wall, whose stones have been expertly shaped around her, yet in a moment of concentration the figure pops out into view. I have since learned that a green oval plaque has been inserted under the figure to make her easier to find. How dedicated a seeker

Figure 8.10. Fethard Old Wall Sheela, County Tipperary, Ireland. She continues her watch.

can you be if you need a sign to point the way? Where's the adventure in that?

The Fethard Old Wall Sheela seems startled by her own power. The staring eyes with dilated pupils and her clenched teeth indicate some internal agony, as if to say such power has a cost. Apotropaic in her position on what remains of the fortified wall, what has she seen pass over this bridge through the centuries? Her medieval sovereignty ravished by Cromwell's army?

Her appearance has elements of other Sheelas: molded ribs but no breasts, striations on her neck, and a vulva, yet the totality of her appearance resembles no other figure. Her ham-hock thighs, like an inverted comma, move up and away from her body; both hands pass beneath atrophied calves and down to her display. Her fingers are the only delicate feature about her. Her large, bizarre head is marked on one cheek by a chevron, an ancient symbol of the bird goddess, while a triangle comes to a point below her left eye. This echoes the exact marking of the pagan Janus figure from Boa Island, linking her to the Irish past. On her other cheek is an object that has been called an ear, though it does not resemble any ear I've ever seen; it looks more like an infected carbuncle. Everything about her appearance was deliberately created by the carver to disturb the viewer, and it does. Her agony is the agony she would like to inflict on us if we dared to cross her boundaries without permission.

Then it's back to the east side of Fethard to see the last carving of the day, another Sheela on another wall. One walks through the graveyard of an Augustinian friary to see the carving placed on a low wall next to the parish priest's house (see figure 8.11). The brickwork around the figure indicates that this is not her original setting, which was most likely the ruins of an older (ca. 1300) Augustinian church nearby. During my visit, a priest emerges from the house and states that this is not a Sheela but a Seamus. How he knows this, god only knows, since the figure's genitals are barely discernible. Some think she has been defaced, but others claim that her vulva is merely worn with age. For me, the telling feature is the motion of her left hand reaching down to the abdomen—a quintessential Sheela gesture. In addition, she has the familiar emaciated ribs and tattoos on her face. Her right hand is missing, and she stands on small straight legs. She has a dignified feeling about her, a more meditative Sheela. A quiet end to the day.

Figure 8.11. Fethard Abbey Sheela, County Tipperary, Ireland. With a large pagan head, she stands next to the priest's house.

Castlemagner Sheela

The map stated that I should travel half a mile west of Castlemagner, County Cork, to a field on the north side of the road to Cecilstown. There on the banks of the Catra stream will be the Castlemagner holy well.

After spending the better part of the afternoon trying to follow these vague instructions in Edith Guest's 1935 guide, and warnings from Jørgen Andersen's 1977 template ("by no means an accessible place"), I needed help. After being chased off one farm by a sheep dog and finding another farm deserted, I was lost. Continuing to drive, I found what seemed to be a *shebeen,* a pub on the country road. Once inside I asked at the bar if anyone knew how to get to the holy well. One fellow put down his Guinness and stood up, saying, "Oh, you'll never find it." Soon I was following his red car up the lane, then walking the path through the green fields by the river till I stood before the well house. I can't recall ever being in a more scenic atmosphere—an enchanting stream, lush fields, and the ancient holy well! Every sentimental thought about Ireland being a beautiful fairyland came to mind. And once more, I was standing before a Sheela.

Like her sisters, this carving raises questions, the primary one being: Is she actually a Sheela? She does not display her genitals; in fact, her knees are close together, practically touching (see figure 8.12). Her legs look planted in the earth. Like the Kiltinan Castle Sheela, her arms are raised in the ancient Goddess gesture. But her hands are empty, as if ready to receive or to command the energies about her. Most tellingly, her pubis is marked as a *V* or chevron, a symbol of the generative triangle of the Goddess that began in the Paleolithic era. Nineteenth-century artist and antiquarian George Victor Du Noyer, in his sketches for the Irish Ordnance Survey, dated the Castlemagner figure back to the seventeenth century, near the end of the era of the Sheelas. There is no denying that she is a more "polite" figure than the uninhibited carvings from the Middle Ages. Perhaps she was created as "an adaptation of the sheela-na-gig idea by a more conventional age."[32] But who wants a refined Sheela?

In a familiar function of many Sheelas, she guards the entrance, this time to a holy well. The well house is built from stones formed in a beehive

shape with a ledge above a low opening (figure 4.19); the stream flows in
from the back. Carved on a limestone slab, she stands just over a foot high.
Her incised eyes stare out with a look of anticipation, as if she expects worshippers. She might not be the most daring of Sheelas, but there can be
no doubt that here is a naked female who radiates power. Tradition confirms this, as votaries have scratched crosses on her torso, her forehead, her
palms, her thighs—on every conceivable plane of her stone body, which
gives the look of a severe tattooing. This custom is no relic of a superstitious past. In fact, Andersen's comparison of two photographs of this
Sheela, one from 1935, the other from 1975 (just before the publication of
his book), shows that belief in her powers has only been growing, since she
bears more crosses in the later picture.[33] Is she an object of veneration, or
do the marks indicate a Christian fear of female sexuality, a darkness that
must be contained?

A further clue to this puzzle is her partner guardian. Flanking the other side of the well's opening is the figure of a Roman soldier originally from a nearby manor house. The Castlemagner Historical Society states that the effigy is no mere soldier but an image of the Archangel Michael. Is this the beneficent guardian angel or the fierce spirit known for doing battle with evil? Often depicted in sculpture as a Roman soldier, he slays with his fiery sword the dragon of Satan. No surprise here that the serpent also symbolizes the forbidden powers of the Goddess in a patriarchal world. One is pulled two ways. Is he a companion or adversary to the Sheela? Is the well Christian or pagan, with the water (older than any creed) as the conciliatory third force? Hard to say. The holy well continues to be a popular place to visit due to an enduring faith in its curative powers. The site has a rich history, with a pagan background as a well once dedicated to the Goddess Brigit, and then to the Christianized Saint Brigit.[34] In a book about Castlemagner Parish written in 1911 by Col. James White, he describes the scene a century ago:

> People came to the Holy Well from long distances on St. Bridget's day to drink the water, which is supposed to cure every kind of illness. The water is also rubbed on the part of the body where there is pain. . . . This Holy Well is also called "Sunday's Well," probably from the fact that about eighty years ago over one-hundred cars [horse-drawn carriages] could be seen on a Sunday at the well bringing people to pay rounds.[35]

On the day of my visit, I felt the energies of the place. With the intense green of the trees and fields, the singing sounds of the stream, and, above, the blue sky of May, I relished its natural beauty. Beyond this, I inhaled the soft air of centuries of ceremonies practiced on this sacred land. My generous guide from the pub told me, "The lads and I, we've been coming to this well all our lives."

9
On the Trail of the Sheelas
Great Britain

Buckland Sheela

I'm back in England after a nine-year absence. I never thought I'd say it, but England looks drab to me, washed out and cramped. And Heathrow Airport is under construction—a more hideous scene of destruction under the guise of "progress" I hope never to witness again.

I'm resisting getting back to work, back to the book. I feel overwhelmed by the details and effort ahead of me—research, cameras, maps, organization, record-keeping, writing, describing, condensing, concentrating, observing myself, mining myself for reactions. What writer said writing was traumatic? I want to remain in this cozy bed-and-breakfast, looking out at a garden of roses mingled with yellow and orange nasturtiums; I want to stay in bed and read the new Harry Potter novel that I bought at the first chance in an airport shop. But I've traveled so far to see some more Sheelas . . .

Up early the next day, I drive down the Aylesbury–Tring road to Buckland, in Buckinghamshire, to the thirteenth-century Church of All Saints. There is a yew tree in the churchyard and crenelated battlements atop the church. Despite my anxieties, a familiar excitement pulses through me as I walk around the church, my eyes scouring the stone walls, searching for her. And there she is, in a proper place for a Sheela: watching out from above

173

the priest's door. She is the first Sheela on this trip, but I still feel edgy; the light is not good today for photographs, and she is somewhat obscured by a vertical drainpipe.

I look and look at her heart-shaped lollipop head with a hint of nose and eyes, and I am drawn in and under her spell (see figure 9.1). She has a wide, gay smile, lips stretched open as if invisible fingers pull at its corners, just as her fingers below pull at her vulva. These deep cavities echo each other. She has power in her mouth much like a Gorgon, and a pudendum as large as her entire torso. But despite the etymology of the word *pudenda* ("to be ashamed"), she does not reveal this emotion in the slightest degree.

She is all white and bright, as if carved from plaster, not stone. One finds a crudity in this merry exhibitionist—not in the exposed vulva, but in the execution of the design. Her arms sprout out of somewhere from above her head, disconnected from her body except for their tight grip around her genital lips. She is not menacing, but she is odd. Upon a deeper look, is that a merry smile or an expression of startled openness that could devour the viewer if her invitation in is accepted?

Jørgen Andersen comments on the gap between the reality of this Sheela's appearance and the official version of it. In the 1912 report of the Royal Commission on Ancient and Historic Monuments, the Buckland Sheela is described as "a stone having a rude carving of a half-figure with uplifted arms."[1] Pity the poor antiquarian with no context by which to assess the stone image of such a peculiar nude as a Sheela na gig, whose supposedly uplifted arms are, in actuality, stretched down and clutching her genitals. Andersen also describes a church leaflet that fares no better in terms of accuracy in describing the Sheela—she's "a crudely carved figure with upraised arms traditionally believed to be one of the two robbers executed at Hang Hill some two miles away."[2] Ah, the nature of perception; how can one see something clearly if it is so outside one's system of reality? That pamphlet is no longer available, and the one that I purchased on my visit to the church, *A History of the Parish of Buckland,* highlights important events: the dedication of the church in 1284, an Elizabethan silver chalice, the eighteenth-century restoration of the squat tower, the addition of Victorian "monstrosities" of griffin gargoyles to that tower—but not one mention of the Sheela. Yet on

Figure 9.1. Buckland Sheela, Church of All Saints, Buckinghamshire, England, 13th century, above the priest's door on the outer south wall of the nave.

175

The Sheelas: Great Britain

the day of my visit, a local parishioner came to wind the tower clock, and the Sheela was the *only* object he commented on. He told me his theory of her origins and functions: "For what it's worth, it's graffiti. Perhaps the masons were cheesed off—up to a bit of mischief." Let us hope so. And may her mischief continue to disrupt all views that render her invisible.

Whittlesford Sheela

Broken tombstones, rosebushes, a copper-colored beech tree, crumbling buttresses, and lambs bleating in distant fields. Sitting on a bench staring at the south wall of Whittlesford Church in Cambridgeshire, I am disappointed. I can hardly see this Sheela; the angle of the light makes the carving seem lifeless, so faded into the wall is she. *This is one of the most important . . .* I had told myself this morning in high anticipation as I drove down the walled country lane from Royston to Cambridge. At first I couldn't find her, this most famous carving, this most shocking of Sheelas, so hidden by the dull light of the day, so without detail in the gray stone arched above the round-headed Norman window. A white-haired woman with garden shears points to the tower with the Sheela, never breaking her stride: "It's supposed to be a fertility symbol," she says, moving on into the church to do flower arrangements. She seems nonchalant about the carving, unconcerned.

With apologies to the dead, I stand on a crypt and begin to take pictures, shooting from every conceivable angle, leaving nothing to chance, working with the materials at hand: the quality of my eye, the quality of the light. With all the concentration I'm capable of, I focus to make the image come alive. Unlike any other Sheela I've ever seen, she has a male companion (see figure 9.2). His head almost touching hers, this man-animal rests his pointed, bearded chin on her shoulder, lips pursed in a whisper or a kiss. His long body has been shaped to fit over the rounded top of the window. There's no doubt as to his gender, what with his huge phallus, as exaggerated as her vulva is. She is full-front, he all profile—the best positions to display their respective strengths.

The Sheela is a source of renewal for him; his power comes from her. She has the weight of gravity, the still center that motivates his movement toward

Figure 9.2. Whittlesford Sheela, Church of St. Mary and St. Michael, Cambridgeshire, England. High noon for the Sheela and her companion.

her. She inspires him, to say the least! The capacious opening of her vulva is shaped like a teardrop. In a typical Sheela acrobatic feat, her right arm loops under the thigh to grab and pull at the lips of her vulva. Because of her deep squat, her genitals reach to her feet and her whole body rests on the triangular base of those full lips. Her left hand seems to fondle her own large breast as it rests beneath it.

The two faces are the center of the off-center composition of their bodies. She stares straight ahead, her face impassive. The human part of him is his expressive face; if his lips are ready to kiss or to speak, so too are her lips parted and full. The relationship does not feel obscene but rather one of intimacy, their legs touching.

A ten-pence pamphlet bought in the church contains a bowdlerized drawing of the Sheela and her male companion, describing her as an ancient "heathen" image. Anthony Weir and James Jerman, however, give her a purpose in support of medieval Christianity's moral teachings about the sins of the body; they place a photograph of the couple on the opening page of their book *Images of Lust*. The authors call this sexual tableau "surely one of the most astonishing compositions in Europe" and then go on to denounce the Sheela as "brazen," "indecent even in a bordello," "ugly as sin," and most tellingly, a "whore" whose purpose is to teach morality through her supposed repellence.[3] Any union between the two figures would also be repellent. They are mystified at how "so gross a spectacle" has managed to survive to the modern era.[4] Good question.

While anthropologist Margaret Murray agrees that "the Whittlesford relief is the most remarkable of the series" of Sheelas, she sees the exact same figure as divine and sacred.[5] She bestows on the image an ancient lineage that goes back to the earliest art of our ancestors, thus explaining the appearance of the displayed female on the medieval church. Murray notices that had the male figure "been represented as standing upright, the resemblance to the Dancing God of the *Cavern des Trois Frères* would have been very apparent."[6] One might also think of the archaic definition of *lust:* pleasure, delight, relish—a far cry from the theory of sex as sin, a Christian bias that has led to the repression of natural human instincts and has done so much harm to our culture. In my journeys around these northern isles I have noted that many locals have used words like *heathen, pagan, fertile,* yet not one has ever referred to her as sinful.

I am comforted by the continuity of the image; she is meant to be seen. This Whittlesford Sheela is in her traditional place above a window, guardian of the entrance. Here in this tableau, she seems squeezed between the temporal and the eternal, with the tower clock above and the window below that serves as a dimension of the infinite, an opening to the Beyond. Bells chime every fifteen minutes and blend with a chorus of different birdsongs among the gravestones. Ivy erases the names on the tombs encircled by weeds. Who remembers these people? Perhaps the Sheela, who watches over the dead in silence. She lives on in all her mystery as an emblem of the ever-renewing life force, sovereign here above the mortal remains. Her sacred vulva, ever fertile and moist, is a more powerful note of renewal to me than any cross decorating the church. The old woman reappears. "I've done my bit," she says, and leaves the peaceful atmosphere of the old church. The rains begin, and I too must go.

Oxford Sheela

She lies flat on her back in the oldest building in Oxford, the tower of the Church of St. Michael. She is locked in a glass case on the second floor of the treasury room (she *is* a treasure), on the bottom shelf, next to seventeenth-century wig curlers, a copy of the Book of Common Prayer, and a stone cherub with a countenance of cruelty (see figure 9.3). She is carved in deep relief from a square foot of stone, with much of her face erased by time; what remains is a fierce gaze and a slash of a mouth like the slash of a line between her spread legs (see figure 9.4). This clear incision indicates an opening between her swollen, hanging lips, technically known as the vestibule of the vagina. She has hunched-up shoulders and massive bent arms, but thin, straight legs. Her squat torso, like the squat tower she once adorned, leans to her right, as if ready to break out of the stone frame containing her.

Questions surround the Oxford Sheela. How old is she? Is she part of the original architecture of the eleventh-century Anglo-Saxon tower or a later Norman creation? There is no known record whatever on the figure.[7]

Figure 9.3. Treasure case in the tower of St. Michael's Church, Oxfordshire, England; the Oxford Sheela lies flat in the middle of the bottom shelf.

Figure 9.4. Oxford Sheela, Oxfordshire, England. Countless brides on the way to their weddings looked up to her for a blessing. *(Photograph courtesy of John Harding, www.sheelanagig.org)*

One scholar gives her an improbable date of origin as Roman times; based on what, one wonders? A booklet purchased at the church gives her a more likely date of late eleventh or early twelfth century. She was originally set high up next to a belfry window on the west wall of the tower of St. Michael at the North Gate, the popular main gate into the city. Thus, she guarded two entrances. From her prime position overlooking Cornmarket Street, she oversaw the busy intersection for centuries. Here, she was above the roof of the old Bocardo Prison, which was connected to the west side of the tower, a prison where the Protestant archbishop Thomas Cranmer awaited burning on orders of the Catholic queen Mary.

All Sheela na gig studies pursue the question: What do they mean?

Jørgen Andersen, in his classic *The Witch on the Wall,* takes his time in offering a definitive interpretation. After a thorough survey of the Sheelas set by entrances—above doors, inside doors, over windows, in window lintels—he is finally ready, more than halfway into his book, to make his first argument about their meaning. Based on "a sufficiently large body of material," he makes (to my way of thinking) a self-evident statement: the purpose of the Sheelas is to safeguard the structures on which they have been placed.[8] He asserts that it is "quite logical" that the placement of Sheelas by entrances "in fact had an apotropaic function."[9] Their sacred display defends the open and penetrable parts of walls.

According to a 1929 report by the vicar of the church, the Oxford Sheela was taken down from the tower to prevent further damage caused by the soot-filled atmosphere of the city. When she was removed, a local newspaper reported the local custom of brides looking at the figure to ensure fertility.[10] She was then put in the vestry (and later under lock in the church treasury). So she is safe now—safe in a prison, no longer free to function as herself. Some part of me cannot help but feel would that she could take her chances out there in this polluted world and still be herself, guarding the city from her original high perch, watching over the unfolding generations as they pass beneath her.

Easthorpe Sheela

How crowded England has become; it's a slow road to Colchester, a decayed-looking town that has known better days. My destination is a hilltop castle converted to a museum that houses a Sheela na gig. Colchester Castle is the largest keep ever built by the Normans, constructed in the early twelfth century from the Roman ruins of the Temple of Claudius. In the fifteenth century, heretics were burned at the stake in front of the castle for denying the authority of the pope. And in the seventeenth century women suspected of being witches were also tortured and burned by the notorious "Witch-Finder General," Matthew Hopkins.[11]

But I am looking for an image whose authority rises up out of the earth. At the museum, I rush through the exhibitions, trying to find the Easthorpe Sheela, traversing one floor, then the next. Right now I don't care about

Roman bowls or medieval knights, only this one thing: Where is she? Then I am stopped by something amazing: standing solitary in a clear glass case is the Dagenham Idol (figure 4.2). According to the museum legend, she is 4,500 years old and from the early Bronze Age, one of the oldest human depictions ever discovered in Britain. She was found nearly a century ago in a marsh at Dagenham. To call her an idol is to say she is heathen, a pejorative term for a non-Christian deity. No matter, for she possesses her own sanctity. I regard her as part of a longstanding lineage that made possible the Easthorpe Sheela, whom I will find on the next floor. I can't help but wonder how many people in this museum have identified this Neolithic wooden figure with her medieval stone ancestress located one floor up.

The Dagenham Idol before me stands about a foot and a half high, with a round head and round buttocks. Between the hollow of her eyes begins a long hag nose that ends above a large mouth. She has no breasts; her long nose and the nubs of her arms are both reminiscent of a Cycladic figure. Her legs are marked with horizontal notches (a measure of time?). One feature between curved hipbones signals her prime importance—a capacious womb. She emanates a fearful energy, a feeling of sacrifice that is so hard to bear that one can only offer it up to the universe for transformation.

With the hugeness of her sex, her symbolic connection to the Sheelas is obvious. And there is evidence that not all Sheelas were carved from stone; some were shaped from wood. In 1676, church regulations in the Irish towns of Ossory and Waterford ordered Sheela-na-gigs to be burned like witches.[12] This suggests that "there may have been wooden sheela-na-gigs in existence."[13] To this day, in South Tawton, Devonshire, a wooden Sheela can be found displaying herself as one of the roof bosses in the fifteenth-century church of St. Andrew (figure 3.8).

Up one floor from the Dagenham Idol, I sit down on the floor to stare through the glass at the Sheela (see figure 9.5) displayed between two other artifacts, a female head and a cherublike figure. Other museum visitors pass around me, politely not disturbing my concentration. I am in relative comfort and warmth, with all the time in the world to look at this meditative Sheela. A massive head rests on a straight line of shoulders, as if she doesn't need a neck. Her rim of hair is set off by protruding cauliflower ears. Mysterious

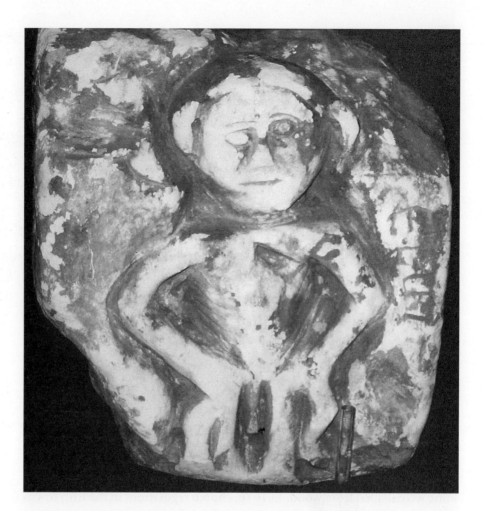

Figure 9.5. Easthorpe Sheela. Not decent enough to be on a church? *(Courtesy of Colchester and Ipswich Museum; photograph by Starr Goode)*

letters are carved vertically along the left side of the stone, ELUI, making her the only Sheela accompanied by a text. No satisfactory explanation has been found as to the meaning. Barbara Freitag connects the word to birth charms, fitting in with her analysis of the Sheelas as folk deities to help women in childbirth.[14] Jack Roberts thinks the letters may postdate the Sheela by some centuries.[15] No one really knows.

Originally, this Sheela belonged to St. Mary's Church, a small parish church at Easthorpe, just southwest of Colchester. From her place above the south door the Sheela fulfilled her function of defending the entrance. Centuries later, in the early twentieth century, she was taken away and donated to the museum by the vicar. His value system judged her as being too "obscene" to keep in a church.[16]

The Colchester Castle Museum booklet gives her a twelfth-century date, an early date for a single figure over an entrance. Debate continues as to whether the Sheela was an original part of the church, because some of the structure was demolished in the thirteenth century.[17] Locally, she was named the "Clunch Stone," as the carving was made from clunch, a kind of gray chalk or clay with a gritty texture used as a building material in eastern England.[18] This explains the strange mottled appearance of the stone.

Standing before the glass case, I look down on her. The left eye rises above the right—are they closed? Squatting, I look up at her. Is that a tentative smile? Though she radiates the stillness of inward attention, the different aspects of her face change with each different view. There is a dynamism to this figure made of stone, as her torso twists to the side. Both arms bend to form triangles of negative space. They flank the downward-pointing triangle of her scrawny hag rib cage, which rests on her sturdy labia. These thick lips are wider than her thighs. A long, skinny clitoris hangs down almost as a root to the ground. Her ability to stand comes not from her useless spindle legs, but from the strength of her vulva meeting the earth.

When I had first entered the Colchester Museum, I asked the young woman selling tickets, "Where is the Sheela na gig?" She had never even heard of this term. I tried to help with a vivid description. "No," she flatly asserted, "we have no nude medieval woman." She called a curator, who set her straight. Then she broke into a laugh, "When I think of how often I've cleaned that case . . ." A surge of yearning as I thought, *You touched her? Oh, how long has it been since I rubbed a Sheela's good-luck vulva* . . . Still, later, as I left the museum, I held in my memory the image of the Easthorpe carving. Altogether an alive Sheela with a wistful look—there is something endearing about her, something about a longing satisfied.

Austerfield Sheela

She floats on the edge of the topmost part of a column along the north arcade of the nave of St. Helena's Church in Austerfield, South Yorkshire (see figures 9.6 and 9.7). Her gravity-defying body traverses the realm of air as if she were the figurehead of some ship, flying from the prow with

Figure 9.6. Austerfield Sheela, Church of St. Helena, South Yorkshire, England, 12th century.

her head thrust forward and body flowing behind, the beauty of her fat, fertile thighs spread open, ready to meet whatever may come their way.

The Sheela blooms at the center of a foliate design that rises from her shoulders like wings, then encircles the top of a heavy stone column. This design is known as "water leaf" (*feuille d'eau*), so perhaps she is not flying above the waves but swimming through the leafy foliage of the sea, the swaying kelp beds floating up from the ocean's floor. Her hair streams down to her thighs. With effortless ease, the fingers of her right hand part the lips of her vulva in a gesture of freedom, the flower of desire.

Like many English or Irish Sheelas, she is not easy to find. Located on a rural road south of Doncaster, just north of what was once the edge of Sherwood Forest, near the River Idle, the Austerfield church was built around 1080, soon after the Norman conquest of England.[19] Thus, one finds

Figure 9.7. Austerfield Sheela side view.

the church in the geographical center of England on "the ancient highway from London to York."[20] The front cover of the church pamphlet (delightful publications one can find in almost any English church with a Sheela) promises visitors that they "will see here one of the best examples of the small Norman church. It is outstanding even in this countryside which abounds in beautiful churches." In the later twelfth century, Yorkshire was considered the most prolific center for Romanesque sculpture in England, deemed the most aesthetically realized.[21]

By the end of the nineteenth century the church was in shambles. An 1898 restoration project stripped away a wall built during earlier repair work done in the fourteenth century. Beneath the plaster, Norman pillars were uncovered, along with the Sheela na gig. Apparently, these discoveries were a shock, as no one "knew of their existence."[22] Despite being enclosed in that wall for five centuries, the Sheela survived miraculously to emerge in another time. Although she bears tool marks that have damaged her face, no facial features were ever carved on the figure—making her the representation of an impersonal archetype. The smoothness of her rounded body radiates self-possession.

To finally arrive at this restored church does not mean one can enter it—it is locked. A crude dragon is carved on the tympanum above the door with zigzag molding. Not far from the weeping ash tree in the church-yard, a telephone number is posted by the south door. I make the call, letting the telephone ring and ring. I'd come so far, I refused to give up. A woman finally answered: "My husband's in the garden; he'll be there in ten minutes."

When Mr. Harrison, the church warden, arrives, he gives me a familiar theory of the function of the Sheela: "a fertility symbol." *That's a comfortable explanation for him,* I thought—to reduce thousands of years of Goddess worship to a single acceptable aspect: motherhood. But it's preferable to the second common theory proposed in the St. Helena's Church pamphlet: "They are a warning against lechery, the third of the seven deadly sins."[23] A pretty poor warning if you ask me. One glance at her graceful design reveals a sheer delight in her own being.

A paradox of weight and weightlessness, her pudgy baby feet are not meant for walking the earth. A rare Sheela to be on a capital, at the topmost part of a pillar, instead of on a wall, she is sculpted in a curved simplicity. The figure harmonizes with her leafy background as one intimate design. And that master observer of the Sheela na gig, Jørgen Andersen, praises her loveliness: "Alone among the English sheelas, the Austerfield temptress is a worthwhile piece of sculpture."[24]

Bilton Sheelas

North of Austerfield, just east of Wetherby on the road to York, is another church dedicated to St. Helena, the mother of Constantine, who was proclaimed the Roman emperor in York in 306 CE. His mother had influenced him to give Christianity official standing as a religion. The church goes back to Saxon times but was in Norman hands by 1150. The remains of three Celtic/Saxon crosses show the earlier influences.

The influences of the northern Celtic Christian church migrated down from the isle of Iona (home of another Sheela) via Ireland, and that of the Church of Rome traveled up via the Continent. The two met in the middle, in the area of Yorkshire. These opposing forces made peace some centuries before the church was built, agreeing on, among other things, the date of Easter. Lest we forget the pagan origins of our current calendar, Easter was fixed to be on the first Sunday after the first full moon following the spring equinox.

But my contemporary concerns about this church lie with the twin Sheelas inside the nave. They sit next to each other on a corbel table that was originally part of an outside wall. In 1869, aisle roofs were built that extended the church and enclosed the corbels. This helped to preserve the Sheelas and the row of their companion Romanesque figures: double-bearded masks, animal and beak heads, and, on the other side of the church, that sister motif of the Sheela, a seductive mermaid.

If the Sheelas are twins, they are not identical. On the east end of the series, the first Sheela has a shape as luxuriant as a Maltese goddess (see figure 9.8). She squats like an ancient frog goddess, while her long arms sprout from the breastbone and hands join at the vulva to form a heart shape resting on her body. The figure's outstanding feature is her ample thighs—massive, world-engendering. No emaciated crone, this Sheela conveys an earthy abundance. No wonder her whole presence conveys serenity.

Her sister, however, radiates menace (see figure 9.9). With heavy shoulders, a grim, downturned mouth, and her very Sheela-ness half hacked away, this figure has suffered. No one knows when this outrage occurred. Her beauteous sister remains intact; Andersen speculates that she was spared maltreatment because of her more modest display, while her sister's bolder exhibition of her vulva caused offense.[25] Did her very power make her a target for mutilation in later, more repressive times? As a pair, it's as if these Sheelas proclaim love and power as dueling forces in the universe, one in pleasure, the other in torment.

For the modern Sheela seeker, the Yorkshire countryside abounds in Norman Romanesque churches adorned with exhibitionist figures on corbels, capitals, and walls. But often one finds them locked up, like in Austerfield and here at the Bilton church. Through the graveyard, I had walked over to

Figure 9.8. Voluptuous Bilton Sheela, Church of St. Helena, North Yorkshire, England, 12th century.

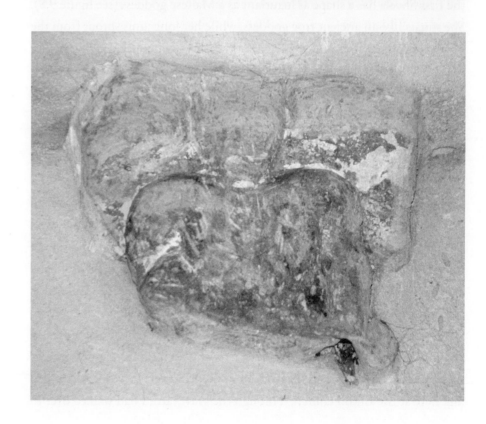

Figure 9.9. Defaced Bilton sister Sheela.

the pub across the street, where the owner watered his geraniums in an outside planter box. I called all the numbers listed in the church pamphlet until a Mr. Schmidt, the church treasurer, generously offered to drive over and let me in. I remember on that day of beautiful Sunday weather how eager I felt to see the Sheelas and pay my respects. I rushed past the horizontal gray tombstones lying as flat as the corpses beneath them to the entrance to the church, to the joy of an open door.

Copgrove Sheela

Another Yorkshire Sheela is described by historians as one of the more remarkable ones in England, but not so to me. The most enjoyable part of the day was the drive to the church on green-edged country roads, and the sky half fleeced with white clouds—a perfect day of high English summer.

Northwest of the city of York lies the Parish Church of St. Michael and All Angels, recorded in the Domesday Book, 1180–86, compiled at the command of William the Conqueror. I find the Sheela on an interior wall in bad light, stuck in a place where she does not belong. Standing before her, I feel distraught; I cannot see her. And, try as I might—flash, no flash, filtered flash—I just cannot get a clear picture of her. Adding to the lack of light is the harsh fact that time has grievously erased her features.

No literature can be found in the church, only notes stapled to a bulletin board. From these I learn that country people called this Sheela the "Devil's Stone" and thought she possessed a great antiquity, with Roman-British origins. So she is, according to local folklore, an image of lust *and* a pre-Christian pagan figure. This strange Sheela is a magnet for many contradictory beliefs. Andersen speculates that she may indeed "represent a remote art which has survived as a kind of folk expression."[26] He doesn't say what that remote art might be, only that its forgotten true meaning "has been substituted by assumptions about its pagan origin."[27] For others, "the primitive nature of the carving" makes her one of the oldest Sheelas in Britain.[28]

Whatever her origins, she is clearly not in her original position on the outer north chancel wall as a cornerstone. Like many Sheelas, she once looked out over the churchyard graves. She has been moved several times:

once during a late Victorian renovation to a northeast corner of a new exterior wall, and finally to inside the church. In her appearance she is an unremarkable, flat carving (see figure 9.10). With her stick legs, stick arms, and stick body, she is far from the sculptural grace of the Austerfield Sheela (figure 9.6). Her round space-alien head looks twice the size of her body, and with large asymmetrical eyes she seems somewhat mad. A long neck melts into her thin torso, from where the long fissure of her vulva hangs down toward the feet. Her left arm forms a jaunty bend for the hand to rest on her lower lips. The left leg is worn away.

Another one of the Copgrove Sheela's curiosities is the capital *T* crudely carved by her head. Does this represent a tau cross or a medieval workman's tool? One charming explanation that has been suggested is that possibly the *T* stands for *terra,* connecting the Sheelas to the earth, as does their squatting-down posture, making them a kind of medieval Mother Earth figure.[29]

But surely the greatest mystery of this Sheela is that her right arm holds some sort of disk away from her body at vulva level at a very awkward angle.

Figure 9.10. Copgrove Sheela, Church of St. Michael and All Angels, North Yorkshire, England. Devil or Goddess? *(Photograph courtesy of C. B. Newham)*

By what physics does her hand grasp the thing and keep it up? This round object excites discussion. Here we encounter the nature of perception (who is doing the seeing?) and enter the realm of symbols (if we ever left it). Thus come vastly different interpretations of the disk from students of the Sheelas, who each make their own biased leaps into meaning. Jack Roberts believes that what makes the Copgrove Sheela remarkable is that she "holds the sacred sun symbol."[30] Anthony Weir and James Jerman, in *Images of Lust,* weigh in with their Christian-based theories: the ring she holds might be the ring of the miser's purse, so this Sheela combines the two greatest medieval transgressions, *luxuria* (lust) and *avaritia* (greed). Surprise surprise, as sin is the core concept in their analysis of the exhibitionist figure.[31] Eamonn Kelly of the National Museum of Ireland sees in her hand the mermaid's mirror, and he connects this with the Irish mermaid, a temptress motif almost as popular as the Sheela and found in areas where Sheelas are common.[32] To Barbara Freitag, the object looks like a birthing girdle to aid parturition.[33] Jørgen Andersen offers no theories except to say the Copgrove Sheela is similar to the Irish Lavey Sheela

Figure 9.11. Lavey Sheela, County Cavan, Ireland, found in 1842 on top of a recently built gate pier at the entrance to the churchyard of Lavey Church, by then in ruins. She has long fingers and toes and a disk tucked under her left arm. *(Courtesy of Cavan County Museum; photograph by Starr Goode)*

(see figure 9.11), since both hold disks, and both were originally on the quoin stones, making them both protectresses of their buildings.[34]

Sun disk, miser's purse, mirror, birth girdle. Now I make my leap. What is the common denominator of all these objects this Sheela supposedly holds? The circle, that ancient image of eternity, completion of all beginnings, transformation of all endings. This resonates with the powers of the vulva: creation, destruction, renewal. Life emerges from this portal; the dead return to the womb of the earth, and life comes round again by the regenerative powers of the earth and the female body. All separations are temporary. Out of the emptiness of circular nothingness comes manifestation. From zero comes something.

Llandrindod Sheela

Another missing Sheela. I spent a day driving west from Yorkshire into Wales, to the old Victorian spa town of Llandrindod Wells, where, historically, people took the waters for their health. But after I arrive I bounce from church to church scouring the walls for the sight of her. How many churches can one small town have? In this case, thirteen, none of which house a Sheela na gig. Oh, to come so far and see nothing. A Sheela I most particularly wanted to find because of her extraordinary un-Englishness—that is, she seems very Irish in her size, in her monstrous menace, and she is considered the most outstanding Sheela in Wales.

I finally find the Old Parish Church, out from the city of Llandrindod Wells, situated on the Golf Links Road with a commanding hilltop view of the surrounding countryside. I am told the door is locked. *This cannot be,* I think, and try for myself. I open the door and walk in. But no Sheela, just a placard by a window saying she used to be here but now she's gone—gone to Radnorshire Museum, which kindly left a placard stating that Sheela na gigs are usually found protecting the thresholds of medieval churches, and rather than representing "the hellish nature of pagan belief" (I never heard *that* analysis before!), contemporary interpretations suggest that it is more likely that their "incorporation in churches possibly indicated continuation of goddess worship, traditionally connected to that site." Sounds accurate to me.

Much about this Sheela is not known, including, most important, her original setting. As she is presently a loose piece of sculpture not attached to any wall, it is impossible to accurately date her. However, it is possible to date precisely when she was discovered: October 24, 1894, during a restoration of the church. The first documents mentioning the church date back to the thirteenth century, but nothing remains of that building. The current Old Parish Church, built by the late Victorians, now stands on the original site. In any case, accounts of her discovery differ. Some say she was buried face-down beneath the threshold of the church; others, that she was built into the north wall, upside down. No one can say how long the Sheela was concealed, but certainly it was for hundreds of years. Was she placed there to protect her from crusading zealots, or was it done by a disgusted puritanical minister to protect his flock from exposure to sin? A happy consequence of this is that the concealment served to preserve the stone carving. After she was retrieved, she was placed by a window; in time, the sunlight did do her harm.

I drive back to the town to find the museum, certain that at last I would be able to view the Llandrindod Sheela. I walk expectantly into the museum after this long day of seeking, only to find, once again, nothing. An attendant informs me that the Llandrindod Sheela is now at the Cardiff National Museum being repaired. The light from the church window has caused her to shed a peculiar crystal grayish dust, I am informed. Disappointed again—to come so far and see so little. I must go home and be content with pictures, never the same as physical contact with the live presence of the carved stone. Such is the lot of a Sheela devotee. I stretch my mind to at least find comfort in the fact that she is being given such care.

When studying her image, the eye goes first not to her vulva, but to her face (see figure 9.12). Strong eyes, nose, mouth, chin—all clearly sculpted. She has rare features in a Sheela: eyes with irises and a mouth with a distinct set of teeth. Above her brows she is tattooed in the Irish manner, and notches of hair rim the scalp. Her face sags with heavy jowls framed by stick-out cow ears.

This Sheela is composed of three shapes: a large head, a large torso, and a large vulva. A square head sits on a diamond of bent arms over a diamond of bent legs. Settled between the spread of these legs hangs a long, capacious

Figure 9.12. Llandrindod Sheela, Llandrindod Wells, Powys, Radnorshire, Wales— one of the most magnificent Sheelas in Great Britain. *(Photograph by Gareth Lloyd Hughes)*

vulva. Her torso bears a navel and incised ribs on which a tool-marked pattern extends past her body to the edge of the stone slab. Most visually striking are the Sheela's high, unnatural breasts, which contrast with her aged hag ribs. Her whole being tilts to the left, looking at the world askew.

According to Jørgen Andersen, carved into one side of the stone slab is a cross-crosslet, a heraldic cross made from four Latin crosses arranged at right angles to one another. Another claim for a cross comes from a website for Welsh cultural history that states that the Sheela has a crucifix marked on her right hand, but that it may have been added later (not part of the carver's original intentions). I am limited to secondhand experience. I can only scour all the images of her available to me, and I can't see either cross. Such is the downside of not being able to stand before her and look with my own eyes, free from any written commentary.

I have seen Sheelas with chalk crosses inscribed on or near them, a Christian countermand to the pagan power of her female body. If these crosses do exist, then poor Sheela, branded with crosses, buried in church walls, so frightening is your sexuality. Still, you have survived, even if it took centuries for your liberation. You are unstoppable.

Church Stretton Sheela

A charming lane of painted cottages borders the churchyard, with the Shropshire green hills in the distance. Passersby turn their heads to watch me, wearing a hat, cameras at my feet as I stare at a wall, then take notes; stare, and take more notes. Senior citizens, all women, come out of a lunch at St. Lawrence Parish Center. Standing in the overgrown grass, I wonder: What do they think of this nude female carving on their church? How much notice have they ever given to their Sheela na gig, this part of their own island heritage and their heritage as women? The *Shropshire Star* recently published an article stating that it was "thankful" that many of the parishioners do not notice the Sheela.[35] Is the sacred display of a female body too lewd a sight for grown women's eyes?

Thirteen miles south of Shrewsbury on the road to Leominster, between Little Stretton and All Stretton, lies the town of Church Stretton and the Church of St. Lawrence. This is one of three Shropshire churches housing Sheelas. St. Lawrence has a familiar history—an earlier Saxon site, then Norman with a later medieval reconstruction, later still a Victorian overhaul, and currently undergoing yet another extensive renovation. Yet the Sheela remains. Today one finds her not by the main entrance but on the humble back wall above an old Norman doorway, which may not be her original setting. The door is no longer in use, but according to a history of the church published in 1971, it "used to be known as the corpse door, as it was apparently used only for bringing in the dead."[36] Then she is described (once more) as a pagan fertility symbol known as a "Sheila-na-Gig." So be it. Let her vulva, passage for the powers of life, balance the door for the dead.

The figure of the Sheela connects with the dead in many ways. Her vulva functions as an image of return to the Beyond. And since many Sheelas are set on the outside walls of churches, they often overlook burial grounds. Of course, the Church Stretton Sheela has an additional association with the dead because she watches from over the corpse door. Barbara Freitag notes that some figures have also been used as gravestones, like the Kilmokea Sheela, County Wexford, Ireland, whose reverse side has a headstone inscription with the date of death.[37] The famous Bishop's Tomb Sheela at Kildare Cathedral, County Kildare, Ireland (figure 4.6), appears on the tomb of Bishop Wellesley, seemingly a fit guide to the afterlife. Some Sheelas, like the Kilmainham Sheela, County Meath, and the Rahara Sheela, County Roscommon, have been found buried in churchyards during cleanup campaigns.[38]

The Church Stretton Sheela stands off-center in a cartouche of weathered red-hued stone (see figure 9.13). Her large, round head has a small crescent-moon mouth and eyes that look downward with the cast of inward attention. Tiny hag breasts hang on a polelike body. Below her is a worn stone and two rosettes carved over the door's keystone, similar to the Ballinderry Sheela in County Galway, Ireland, who actually is the keystone over the door to an Irish castle (figure 4.4).

All Sheelas are the same and different. This Sheela's uniqueness appears in her weight below the waist, in her sturdy legs and heavy horse-hoof feet. The knees look swollen; the right erupts in cracks. Curiously, she is not squatting at all but stands erect on strong legs. Both hands reach to the center in the quintessential Sheela gesture, but her posture makes the motion seem awkward and causes her vulva to seem squeezed between the thighs. I have no information on when this violation took place, but her vagina is plugged with a stone.

Some time later, when I return home to California, far from rural Shropshire, I am mad at myself. Why didn't I take more pictures of some of the corbels on the church tower, of the Saxon stone coffin lying to the right of the doorway? There's nothing I can do about it now on this Sunday night. Perhaps there's a power to that, creating more curiosity about the unfathomable Sheelas.

Figure 9.13. Church Stretton Sheela, Church of St. Lawrence, Shropshire, England.

Tugford Sheelas

Still in Shropshire, south of Shrewsbury, south of Church Stretton, go east at Craven Arms along the Corve Dale on a narrow rural road to Tugford, to the twelfth-century St. Catherine's Church. The church is home to a pair of Sheelas, the smallest I have ever encountered—no larger than a human hand. They live just inside the entryway, on a ledge above the south door, where they can watch from each side all those who cross the threshold (see figure 9.14). These diminutive guardians emanate a strange power. As Shakespeare says of Hermia in *A Midsummer's Night Dream,* "Though she be but little, she is fierce."

It is a wonder how these twin sisters have survived the centuries in their original position, perched on this tutelary spot throughout all the replastering and restoration of the church. They have survived wars, weather, shifting human beliefs. Surely such continuity is a testimony to their powers of protection over the entrance. Any visitor who passes through the church door would have to be a keen observer indeed to even notice them hidden up in the shadows, and would need to climb a ladder to make out their features. For Jørgen Andersen, the image they evoke is that of two furtive gnomes ready to jump from their lintel onto any unwelcome visitors.[39]

Both Sheelas are very sculptural, carved in high relief. The one to the left of the door (as you enter) has distinct facial features: open eyes, bulbous nose, tongue sticking out of her mouth (see figure 9.15). She holds a mysterious breastlike object under her left arm. The prominent head sits low on her chest between scrunched-up shoulders that start above her ears. With a gorilla-like reach, both hands pass under her legs and meet in the middle of her display. Her left knee is missing, as is her left foot. The effects of missionary zeal, or frailty over time? With legs pulled tight to the chest, her whole body squeezes back into a corner, yet she is upright, with an active feeling.

Her sister, the more weathered of the two, reclines with indolence, her big pudendum like a fat cushion she lies upon. One hand touches her open mouth, while the other has a good grip on her genitals. The right leg is caught in the wall through careless plastering. Her thin, weak legs are not made for standing but dangle from her body.

Figure 9.14. Tugford door with two Sheelas, St. Catherine's Church, Shropshire, England, late 12th century. Flanking the entrance, a pair of very small Sheelas on a ledge above the arched doorway.

How do these sisters function together—as two parts of what whole? Active and passive? Grim and languid? Both make gestures involving their mouths. The Tugford Sheelas keep double-double-double watch over the door. First, obviously, because there are two of them; then, because they

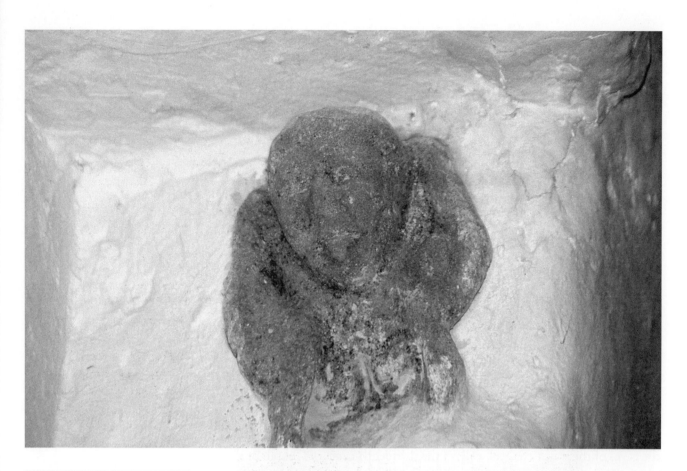

Figure 9.15. One of the Tugford Sheelas on a ledge above the doorway, on the left as you enter the church.

protect with both their vulvas and their mouths. In Anthony Weir and James Jerman's Christian-based classification, these rude facial gestures fall into well-known Romanesque motifs: tongue-sticking and mouth-pulling. By their analysis, medieval churchgoers would recognize these motifs and be familiar with their meaning: playing with the mouth is "blatant sexual exhibitionism."[40] The authors refer to a passage in Isaiah (57:3) that they believe might have inspired the work of the medieval masons: "But draw near hither, ye sons of the sorceresses, the seed of the adulterer and the whore. Against whom do ye make a wide mouth and draw out the tongue?"[41] This is not the first time (or the last) that the Sheela has been called a witch or a whore. Such is the fate of females who step outside the bounds of the patriarchal order, whose power "sinfully" comes from themselves.

Despite their narrow view, which regards the Sheelas as purely medieval phenomena with no links to any heritage from the earlier civilization of the

Goddess, Weir and Jerman do admit that the "classical origin of tongue-sticking could be the Gorgon-mask."[42] Yes, the Gorgon has power in her lolling tongue and her face that acts like a vulva, giving birth to children. And like the Sheelas, she too is a guardian of entrances, a true foremother to two barely discernible medieval Sheelas who, in the quiet Shropshire hills continue to fulfill the purpose they were made for.

Holdgate Sheela

Eternity in her mouth. No Sheela na gig has a mouth like the Holdgate Sheela, a double *O* to form a lemniscate, a horizontal figure eight (see figure 9.16). The number 8 may be written over and over again without lifting pen from paper, in one continuum; thus, the 8 on its side symbolizes infinity. While the central power of the Sheela figures always resides in their vulvas, some Sheelas, through their open mouths, echo and strengthen their display, as can be seen in the Tugford Sheelas, just a few kilometers south of Holdgate, in Shropshire.

But the Holdgate Sheela looks nothing like her Shropshire neighbors. For one thing, she is big. Close to two feet high, she protrudes from under the eaves of the south chancel wall on the thirteenth-century Church of the Holy Trinity. If she opened her eyes she could look out over the Shropshire hills. High on the church wall, she guards the triple-spine mullion window just to her left (see figure 4.8), as well as the fertile green land before her.

Lively hands open wide the lower lips, while fingertips disappear into darkness and prominent thumbs oddly turn up. She appears to be in a magical birthing posture. Her vulva is so dilated it could deliver a human baby; its opening seems to fill her whole inner body. The knees are raised high enough to be mistaken for breasts, but then the legs curve into a knock-kneed, pigeon-toed shape. One could never walk on such puny legs. They serve one purpose only: to part and reveal her sex.

Nothing about her is human, yet she is distinctly female. The chevron marks on either side of her mouth look like cat whiskers (and connect her to her tattooed Irish sisters), and her most peculiarly shaped head resembles a squeezed peanut (like the Clonmacnoise exhibitionist; figure 2.8). This

Figure 9.16. Holdgate Sheela, Holy Trinity Church, Shropshire, England, 13th century.

rounded, sculptural Sheela possesses a distinctive face, with high eyebrow ridges, a narrow nose, and stylized mouth. This mouth is unmistakably echoed on the voussoir of the south Norman doorway, where a mask has the same figure-eight lips. A bit of the personality of the carver shines through, giving the sense of a living artist across the distance of time.

The closed eyes portray a meditation on the condition of her being. Earlier, as I moved through the deteriorating tombstones in the churchyard, my own internal chant of "What's it all about?" vibrated with the moaning of cattle beyond the low stone wall. An imagined cry from those buried in the dark womb of the earth warned me to remember our end. I tramped through the wild ruins of nettle bushes and a jungle of weeds before I could find her, the solitary figure on the church. Ivy once covered and perhaps protected her over the centuries.[43] A church pamphlet reports that she is thought to be a pagan fertility figure. I cannot gainsay this; she is certainly not Christian. Her roots reach deep into the prehistory of Europe. When I look up at her, a Celtic cross sits on the edge of the roof—two contrasting worldviews in one visual frame.

At the end of the day I feel so lucky in all aspects as to feel my enterprise blessed, doors opening to locked churches, good weather, useful directions, and, most of all, more Sheela sightings! On this evening of the last day of June, at 9 p.m., it is still light. I lie in bed studying Sheela materials. Then night overtakes the day and clouds move in. How pleasant to be in this farmhouse in the Shropshire hills, to listen to the music of the rain as the water hits the roof and windows, to look up at arched ceilings of dark wood. And I think again of what I saw today—such a strange Sheela, with her strange head, strange mouth, strange body—and of what I'll see tomorrow at Kilpeck, which will bring me full circle, to the image that initiated my Sheela quest so many years ago, and the end of my journey.

Kilpeck Sheela

This afternoon, I drove east through the English countryside to Herefordshire and to Kilpeck, to see that most famous Sheela whose image inaugurated the romance. Yes, I wanted to see her above all others, but when the rain began, the light disappeared—I swear, the filthiest of curses, and I feel cursed myself, exiled from my pilgrimage. But in the spirit of English pluck I carry on.

On a gentle hill before me sits the three-celled Church of St. David and St. Mary, thought to have been completed around 1140 and often called the most perfect Norman building in the British Isles. Despite the rain, I walk around the corbel table to find her on the outside south wall of the nave, and once again, I ask permission from the departed to climb on top of a crypt and start taking pictures. After that, I wander about the church surveying its wonders: the eighty-five corbel carvings, the west window, and the incomparable south door. Then a miraculous gift arrives in the form of a tour bus. It unloads twenty or so elderly people taking a day tour of local churches. They gather around the gem that is Kilpeck, and a man in a suit begins an erudite lecture about the church carvings, starting with the south door, then making his way around the corbel table. Out of despair and into exhilaration, like a ray of light breaking through the rain, making all pictures possible, I follow the lecture from the edge of the crowd.

Through the on-again, off-again rain, the tour takes over an hour. I ask the guide if I can listen and follow the group; he replies none too nicely, "I can't stop you." As we continue around the church, I take pages of notes while he interprets the rich carvings decorating the church. Then comes the moment I've been waiting for: the group arrives at the Sheela (see figure 9.17). A woman asks, "Is that a frog or something?" The guide laughs, "You couldn't be more wrong." He announces that this is a Sheela na gig, an Irish term for a woman of low morals. Oh yes, it's very bad to be exposing yourself for all the world to see. I, however, think, *Sister, you got it just right. How perceptive of you to notice her relation to the frog goddess!*

I do ask a few questions about the Sheela na gig, and he corrects my pronunciation (according to him) and tells me how to spell it. The crowd and even the tour guide begin to warm to me because of my energetic interest in the church. Afterward, he comes over to talk to me, asks where I'm from. My jeans, flannel shirt, and Guggenheim hat must appear odd to this formal Englishman. I have the presence of mind to ask him what books to read, and he writes down for me *The Herefordshire School of Romanesque Sculpture*, by Malcolm Thurlby. Finally, the older English people crowd back onto the

bus—off to the next church—and as if to a friend, they wave to me: good-bye, good-bye . . .

I later learn from reading Thurlby that the Herefordshire School of Romanesque sculpture was a group of twelfth-century masons and sculptors who came together for a brief time to work on the area churches as part of an architectural boom of the times. Hereford rivaled Yorkshire as a prolific center for sculpture in medieval England; remote as southwest England might seem from great centers of Romanesque art, the Hereford builders had associations with cosmopolitan culture.[44] Norman lords made pilgrimages to Santiago de Compostella, Spain, and to western France and to Paris, to connect with the international Romanesque style. These well-traveled lords became patrons of the construction of new churches.[45] Other stylistic influences came from a diversity of places: Scandinavia, Italy, and, in England, various Celtic traditions and Anglo-Saxon art.[46]

Figure 9.17. Kilpeck Sheela on a corbel table next to an animal mask, Church of St. David and St. Mary, Herefordshire, England, 12th century.

The best example of the Herefordshire School is the Kilpeck Church. Remarkably well preserved, the church has hardly changed in 850 years, yet in its time it was considered "absolutely up to date" in the eclectic architectural styles of the period.[47] The Kilpeck Sheela can be found in her original setting on a corbel table. But she is not alone up there in the bizarre world of Romanesque sculptures. Her companions include animals, masks, musicians, and mythical creatures. All attest to the unusual license given the artists who created the corbel carvings in a strange amalgamation of Celtic, Anglo-Saxon, Scandinavian, and French Romanesque themes. A walk around the church reveals the beautiful south door, with a Tree of Life tympanum, snakes ascending and descending on pillars (see figure 9.18), intricate Celtic scrollwork, a door arch with a Green Man, a phoenix in a cocoon of frankincense and myrrh, and more diverse corbel figures: an Agnus Dei (lamb of god), four rams, dragons above angels, beasts devouring sinners, a manticore, lions, an upside-down ibex, beak heads, Viking animal heads, a hound and a hare in harmony, a kissing couple, a pig, knights, a pair of doves, a basilisk that can kill with a look—and among them, the Sheela na gig.

The old dilemma remains: How do we interpret such decorative carvings? Do these images represent the vitality of the ever-renewing life force or a fallen world caught in the struggle between good and evil? Undoubtedly, the Church of St. David and St. Mary at Kilpeck was built as a testament to Christianity, yet just as clearly the church incorporates much pagan imagery. Certainly on the day of my visit, the tour group was informed by their guide that all the carvings reflected the teachings of the Roman Catholic Church and embodied a Christian worldview drawn from the Old Testament and the New. One by one, our guide explained the symbolic meanings of the various sculptures, and the one clear message he believed they delivered: we mortals are flawed by sin and need to keep on a straight and narrow path to reach salvation. And yet, in these sculptures, lively pagan themes abound.

One source drawn on for the creation of the church carvings was the popular twelfth-century bestiary, *The Book of Beasts,* which describes the nature and habits of "each creature real or mythical." The book was derived

Figure 9.18. Kilpeck pillars flanking the south door, Church of St. David and St. Mary, Herefordshire, England, 12th century. Do these snakes represent the defeat of the devil or the renewal of nature?

from classical works such as Aristotle, as well as from early English literature and oral traditions.[48] John Michell, in his book *The Traveler's Key to Sacred England,* makes the observation that Kilpeck has many pagan, non-Christian surprises. One outstanding example can be found on the south door tympanum: the carving of the "Tree of Life, the Irminsul of Nordic mythology. This was the chief symbol of the pagan religion, as the cross is of Christianity"[49] (see figure 2.6). The Christian corbel figures are also mingled with pagan and Celtic mythological symbols and sometimes are "uncompromisingly sexual in imitation of the vital energies in nature."[50] In his monograph on the Kilpeck church published in 2000, James Bailey raises a question about the symbolic nature of the snakes on the outer columns of the south door. They might reflect the defeat of the temptation of evil, but it is equally possible that they reflect the Celtic belief in the vitality of nature and the renewal of life in the spring, just as the snake is reborn through the sloughing off its skin.[51]

Malcolm Thurlby, in *The Herefordshire School of Romanesque Sculpture,* calls us back to the image. He finds it ridiculous that "theoretical considerations become so all-consuming that some even dispense with the image!"[52] He chides us not to forget that "we are dealing with works of art which are intended to have a visual impact."[53] A visual impact this Kilpeck Sheela certainly does make. She is a startling sight—a bald, nude woman with genitals longer than her torso. Large hands pull at the perfect oval of her vulva. All the while, she bears an expression of welcome in her eyes wide open to wonder as, with self-assurance, she offers up her sex.

PART III

—◦—

Image

10
The Power of Images

The image of the Sheela na gig is rooted in the soil of Europe, traceable back through Celtic influences to the classical figures of Baubo and the Gorgon Medusa, back even earlier to the Neolithic frog goddess, and finally back to the images of vulvas found in Paleolithic caves. But the startling image of a female displaying her sex is not an anomaly of European religious art; it manifests as a reoccurring theme across time and space in non-European representations. So universal, in fact, is this feminine image that it has been abstracted over the centuries into the diamond glyph seen in textiles around the world (not to mention in the Paleolithic Blombos Cave engravings, which are echoed in the 2013 Scottish discovery of the Ness of Brodgar lozenge-decorated stone from the fourth millennium BCE).[1] Female divinity is also widely symbolized as a downward-pointing triangle, suggesting woman's ontological primacy.[2] On every continent of the planet, there are found in the visual arts and in mythical narratives expressions of goddesses and heroines parting their thighs to reveal sacred powers. So rooted in our psyches is this image that it seems as if the icon of the vulva is the original cosmological center of the human imagination.

Kālī

As history and prehistory demonstrate, the image of the Sheela na gig originates in the primal energies of death and creation. The wellspring of her potency is her sex, the source of all; her vulva is the entrance to the cosmic womb. Outside of Europe, on a different continent and from a different culture, the most influential manifestation of the Dark Goddess of destruction must surely be Kālī. While the past several decades have seen a revival of fervent interest in the Sheelas, enlivening a broader awareness of their importance, in India devotion to Kālī has never waned. Her image appears both in iconography and in sacred texts (see figure 10.1). Still venerated today, she comes from an unbroken lineage of goddesses—born from Durgā, the goddess (Devī) who embodies Śakti (Shakti), the universal rhythm of generation, annihilation, and re-creation. Like the Great Goddess of Old Europe, Śakti is the primordial creative feminine power underlying all existence, "the womb from which all things proceed and to which all things return."[3]

As might be expected from two dark goddesses like Kālī and the Sheela na gig, their iconography and purposes often overlap. Both have menacing appearances; black-skinned Kālī dances in cremation grounds, just as many Sheelas dwell on churches among the tombs of the dead and, sometimes, are carved on gravestones. Yet Kālī can generate new worlds, as when she stands and often dances on the corpse of her consort, Shiva, and brings him back to life. Some Sheelas, like the Kiltinan Church Sheela (figure 1.3) and the Ballynahinch Castle Sheela (figure 1.5), appear to dance a jig, and their swollen vulvas testify to their regenerative capacities. Ferocious Kālī's lolling tongue (like the Gorgon Medusa's) is a universal symbol of apotropaic power.[4] At least six Sheelas have such tongues, doubling the avertive energy of their sexual display. But always and most important, their force flows from their femaleness.

Just as with the Sheelas, Kālī's beginnings go back to prehistory with the image of the vulva. In Ajit Mookerjee's energizing book *Kali: The Feminine Force,* the author points out that the name Kālī has been in use "generically since antiquity."[5] In the Kaimur region of central India there exists a monument devoted to the female principle of Śakti, constructed out of layers of thin rock in the shape of triangles, the symbol par excellence of the female sex. It dates back to the Upper Paleolithic and is "known locally as the shrine of Kalika Mai (Mother Kālī)."[6] This structure is reminiscent of the triangular shrines dedicated to the fish goddess Lepenski Vir in Old Europe. Traditions of the divine feminine dating back to 3000 BCE can be found in the Indus-Sarasvatī civilization. Like in Neolithic Europe, goddesses probably predominated in "the indigenous religious beliefs."[7]

Figure 10.1. Contemporary drawing of Kālī, Madhubani, India, an example of religious art produced by Indian women, with paint made from flowers and paper treated with cow dung. A strong floral motif indicates her generative powers. Kālī stands on Shiva's heart to cool her murderous rage. *(Collection of Starr Goode)*

Controversy remains about this claim, but the prevalence of terra-cotta statues of the Great Mother is undeniable. Later, such female deities were likely absorbed into the Indo-European Vedic pantheon, as seen in sacred texts like the *Rig Veda*.[8]

Mookerjee observes that if the Goddess "to some extent went underground" with the dominance of the patriarchal Aryan culture, she regains her primal position as the Śakti in classical and medieval Hinduism.[9] Kālī makes her textual debut ca. 400–500 CE in the *Devī-Māhātmyam* (Glory of the Goddess), which tells the stories of the various battles between the Śakti and male demons. The Indic gods have to call on the feminine force to vanquish these demons because of their own powerlessness to restore equilibrium to the disordered world that they themselves have created. In Miriam Robbins Dexter and Victor H. Mair's invaluable work *Sacred Display: Divine and Magical Female Figures of Eurasia,* the authors describe how "Kālī becomes a major figure in the *Devī-Māhātmyam* . . . one of the earliest and most significant tantric hymns to the goddess Devī in her many manifestations."[10]

In the chaos of the great battle to restore order, out of urgent necessity, Kālī springs forth from the brow of Durgā. Thus, her power is born solely out of the Śakti, purely out of the divine feminine, with no relation to a husband-god. Unfettered, she acts out of the essence of herself, an annihilating energy capable of destroying "the most arrogant and truculent man-beasts," brutal forces that have for a long time oppressed the world.[11] The formidable Kālī emerges wielding a sword and a noose while draped in a tiger skin. She swiftly decapitates the *asuras* (demons) Chaṇḍa and Muṇḍa, and for this victory Durgā awards her the name of Chāmuṇḍā (see figure 10.2).

The image of Chāmuṇḍā Kālī is comparable in her haglike emaciation to any Sheela na gig. Her entire appearance is a feat of the human imagination. She seems an animated skeleton with her sunken eyes, toothless mouth, and desiccated breasts sagging down to a hollowed-out abdomen. Traditionally, her eight arms may hold instruments of slaughter, a severed head, a thunderbolt, a cobra, and a skullcup full of blood. Adorned by a necklace of skulls, she sits or sometimes dances on the corpse of a defeated

Figure 10.2. Chāmuṇḍā Kālī, Orissa, eastern India, sandstone, 9th century CE. A fearsome form of the devouring Kālī. *(Image © The Trustees of the British Museum)*

demon. She is an agent of death, yet her body vibrates with energy, as if at any instant she may rise up and finish her dance of destruction so as to plant the seeds of regeneration.

Kālī assumes different shapes as befits the model of a goddess who destroys and creates. In the Indic tradition, a goddess may adopt a frightening form or a benevolent one to fulfill various purposes, but all manifestations originate from the substance of the one Devī (see figure 10.3).[12] June McDaniel, in her essay "Kali: Goddess of Life, Death, and Transcendence," notes that Kālī is a "strange and mercurial figure" who can be portrayed as both a terrifying black hag dancing where the dead are burned *and* the beloved universal mother Kālī Ma protecting her devotees from danger.[13] In her manifold capacities, she gives birth to worlds, preserves them, and consumes them again in a continuous dance of opening and closing.

In another episode of the *Devī-Māhātmyam,* the death-wielding

Chāmuṇḍā becomes one of the Saptamātrikā, the seven *matrikas,* or mothers, who materialize out of Durgā's forehead. In "Durga: Invincible Goddess of South Asia," Laura Amazzone clarifies Chāmuṇḍā's role as that of a protectress. This reflects the likely apotropaic origins of the Saptamātrikā as female energies that guarded villages from illness and natural disasters.[14] Though Chāmuṇḍā's ferociousness is shown in the lethal weapons she uses to fight the demons, on a psychological level such weapons "are not to be used for violence, but are symbols of liberation," to cut away and free us from what is destructive or unhealthy in our lives.[15]

In an antinomy similar to that of the Sheela na gig, Chāmuṇḍā the destroyer can also be Chāmuṇḍā Mata, or Mother, from whom all beings are born (see figure 10.4). The Chāmuṇḍā Devī Temple sits on an isolated hill in the medieval city of Chamba, with majestic views of the valley, the Ravi River, and the distant Himalayan mountains. Renowned for its calming atmosphere, the temple dates back to the sixteenth century CE.[16] Throughout the temple, carvings depict scenes from the *Devī-Māhātmyam.* Chāmuṇḍā Mata

Figure 10.4. Chāmuṇḍā Mata, Chamba City, Himachal Pradesh, northern India—a wooden relief from the old temple dedicated to the Goddess. *(Photograph courtesy of OPIS Zagreb)*

herself is rendered in wood with a powerful doubling of her image. Gone are the weapons, as she displays the greatest source of power—her vulva. In a tantric acrobatic feat, her hands hold her thighs wide apart in an openness worthy of any Sheela.

The powerful nature of Kālī is revealed through the myriad qualities she assumes—destructive, creative, brutal, protective. Old and new, she is an ancient figure of life and death, and yet she represents a tradition of the divine feminine still very much alive today.[17] At the very instant Kālī first manifests from the dark brow of Durgā, as the *Devī-Māhātmyam* describes for us, the skies are filled with her primal roar. Mookerjee points out that this is not a savage cry, and he turns to the insights of C. G. Jung to explain the phenomenon: "The impact of an archetype . . . stirs us because it summons up a voice that is stronger than our own. Whoever speaks in primordial images speaks with a thousand voices."[18]

Lajjā Gaurī

Much beautiful art has been inspired by divine female exhibitionists. From the second to the twelfth century in our era, erotic sculptures known as Lajjā Gaurīs were created and worshipped in temples across India. In their most elemental form they invoke the ancient, almost universal symbolism of the frog. Their froglike (i.e., Sheela-like) display posture is known as *uttānapad*, and most often they have a lotus-flower head (see figure 10.5). In this pose, the soles of their feet turn up sideways, and upbent arms rest

Figure 10.5. Lajjā Gaurī, Naganathakolla, Nāganātha Temple, Bijapur District, Karnataka, India, Badami Museum, late 7th century CE. One of the most refined Lajjā Gaurīs, carved in red sandstone. *(Courtesy of Wikimedia Commons)*

on knees. Except for being adorned with jeweled girdles, anklets, armlets, bracelets, and necklaces, they are naked.[19] Personified as a *pūrṇa kumba*—a filled (*pūrṇa*) pot or womb (*kumba*)—these figures convey the sense of a "brimming vase of fortune."[20] Here is a display figure overflowing with beneficence. As an image carved in relief with soft curves and a lush roundedness, she incarnates all the affirming powers of the cosmic life force. Resonating with her full display, she has been described by scholars as the vast, primordial Mother who sustains the universe and "is most truly, actively herself when spreading [her legs] wide."[21]

In her definitive *Forms of the Goddess Lajjā Gaurī in Indian Art,* Carol Radcliffe Bolon documents over 130 figures, each sculpture unique. This suggests that as with the creators of the Sheelas, these artists too followed no text but instead used their own imaginations.[22] Although details may vary from figure to figure, a consistency appears in the iconographic use of both genital display and the lotus flower (see figure 10.6). These images play off one another, for the lotus, India's most sacred plant, resembles a yoni in the richness of its petaled form. In the Lajjā Gaurī, the lotus, a vegetative symbol of the generative power of life, does not float on the surface of the water, as in nature, but blossoms as a head atop her body. Thus the Lajjā Gaurī contains two centers of creativity: the lotus and the yoni. These confirm the essence and the power of the Goddess as the source of the boundless abundance of "all that is born and of all that is to be born."[23]

The shrines housing the Lajjā Gaurīs are frequently located outside major temples or at remote sites with springs nearby. The Yoni Pūjā (the making of offerings) performed with a Lajjā Gaurī often involves pouring water over her wide display, acknowledging her as the carrier of the waters of life. Her body is the pūjā altar. Ghee, as an ablution, might also be rubbed on her yoni.[24] As can be seen by the worn notch of her vulva on many scuptures, she is intimately touched by devotees, much as the Sheela na gigs were (and are).[25] Just as she blesses the shrines themselves, the Goddess grants good fortune to her admirers through her unlimited generosity. The practice of Yoni Pūjā to Lajjā Gaurī persists to this day.

Figure 10.6. SoHo Lajjā Gaurī. Walking down a street in New York City, I behold a goddess on the sidewalk. The art gallery inscription calls her a yoni Hindu deity from Jaiselmore, India. She holds her lotus blossom head from which buds hang down.

Tantric Goddesses of Nepal

Motifs of female erotic display embellish the richly decorated temples of Nepal. Art historians have associated these carvings with the Sheela na gigs.[26] At the seventeenth-century Bhimsen Temple in Durbar Square, Kathmandu, remarkable exhibitionists can be found on its pagoda towers.[27] A World Heritage Site, the square abounds with royal palaces, images of divinities, and temples adorned with erotic imagery, making it one of the most popular places in Nepal.

The Bhimsen Temple is known for its spectacular artwork. Amid the sculptures of entwined couples engaging in the tantric practice of ecstasy, at the base of a large pillar sits a single female. An acrobatiste of formidable flexibility, she makes the classic Sheela gesture—holding open her labia to reveal a capacious vulva (see figure 10.7). A truly advanced yogini, she offers a glimpse of the Śakti, who creates and sustains the universe. A self-satisfied bliss radiates from her serene countenance.

Figure 10.7. Bhimsen Temple display figure, Durbar Square, Kathmandu, 17th century CE. A solitary meditation.

222
IMAGE

In Sanskrit, the word *yoni,* as well as meaning the female genitals, also refers to the cosmic womb.[28] Philip Rawson, in his masterwork *The Art of Tantra,* makes the fundamental point that "the inner sexual energy of humanity is identified in India with the cosmic energy"; in tantra, the female vulva, or yoni, is "an emblem of the creative source of reality."[29] This is a spiritual stance far from the medieval Christian view of the female sex as a gateway to sin. Rawson acknowledges that the Indian figures connect quite naturally to Sheela na gigs, but that the idea of making Yoni Pūjā to a displayed female form has been "degraded in Western culture."[30] We have lost a sacred connection. As Rawson writes, European Paleolithic cave art was rooted in the imaginative idea of "a generically female creative womb" that was the generatrix of all life.[31] He believes that this symbolic meaning of the human vulva as an all-embracing creative energy is what Indian tantra seeks to preserve.[32]

African Protectresses

Heading west to the continent of Africa, we find in Mali and Gabon a tradition of villagers carving guardian images onto the doors of their granary huts. Inside these structures, not only food but ritual objects are kept. Among the Dogon people of Mali, such wooden doors can have a complex mix of human and animal carvings as protectors. But on many of the doors in Gabon the image of a single female is enough to fulfill the task of protection. Certainly, more information about these figures needs to be revealed; they most likely date from the nineteenth century CE or earlier.[33] In their two-volume *Encyclopedia of Africa,* Kwame Anthony Appiah and Henry Louis Gates Jr. offer only this bit of information: "The Fang of Gabon and the Dogon of Mali use guardian images to protect sacred ancestral relics. . . . [They] carve elaborate doors that ritually protect community food supplies and sacred objects."[34]

Centered on a granary hut door from Gabon, a numinous female hunkers down in the classic frog goddess stance (see figure 10.8). Her open legs reveal the source of her spiritual power. She seems to be in a trance, yet confident of her abilities to guard the grain stores and the contents of the room. Like

Figure 10.8. Granary hut door, Gabon, Africa, wood. Her winged headdress denotes her status as a sacred guardian spirit, a goddess, and her diamond glyphs go back to the eighty-thousand-year-old carvings found in the Blombos Cave, South Africa. *(Gaulkberry Collection; photograph courtesy of Xochi Maberry Gaulke)*

the Sheelas, these figures have apotropaic powers; they protect the entrances against animals and thieves. Unlike the Sheelas, they are not set nearby doors but *are* the doors themselves.

The bodies of these African protectresses bear prominent designs of diamonds or lozenges to magnify their potency. These can appear on the inner thighs, both shoulders, and the forehead, and the largest one is placed on the abdomen. As previously noted, the diamond glyph is a universal symbol of femaleness, found in weavings around the world.[35] Elizabeth Wayland Barber, in her definitive work on textiles, *Women's Work: The First 20,000 Years,* confirms that the lozenge shape imitates the vulva and is "generally taken as a powerful fertility symbol."[36] Each of the diamond glyphs carved on the African figures is constructed of nine smaller discrete lozenges, thereby amplifying their power by creating symbols within the symbol. They may also represent the nine months of pregnancy. A single dot marks her pubic triangle.

Similar patterns can be seen in Old Europe as far back as the seventh millennium BCE, where the lozenge and triangle with one or more dots were found "on the pregnant belly or other parts of the pregnant goddess."[37] Marija Gimbutas believes that the origins of the glyphs of the lozenge and triangle "probably are schematized configurations of the vulva and the pubic triangle and relate to the life source."[38] A dot above the vulva may represent "the seed inside the womb or field."[39] Not only does the Grain Mother, the Gabon figure, watch over the food stores of her people, but her body is the field where the grain grows. Her magical abilities ensure the future.

Caribbean Goddesses

Moving further west, across the Atlantic Ocean to the Americas, the Taíno Indians of the West Indies worshipped as *zemís,* or spirits, two supernatural females, Itiba Cahubaba and Atabey. Both were always portrayed with parted legs to show their sex. The Taíno were known for their relatively peaceful culture and matrilineal descent. In 1492, this people experienced the malefic fate of being the first tribe to come in contact with the European invaders, who commenced to decimate them and their culture. But images of these goddesses remain as artifacts, found in the caves and stones of the land, and in the psyches of a thin thread of descendants of the original Taíno natives.

Itiba Cahubaba is a matrika, the progenitor Great Mother of the Taíno race, whose origin lies in her full-lipped vulva, centered between her outstretched legs (see figure 10.9). This posture creates a triangular shape considered "a classic form" commonly found in other matrika images throughout the Americas.[40] In another sign of her potency as an ancestress, the hands rest on her royal pregnant belly. Traditionally, Itiba Cahubaba represents the

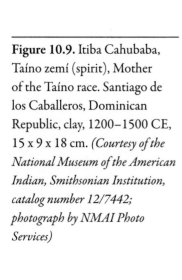

Figure 10.9. Itiba Cahubaba, Taíno zemí (spirit), Mother of the Taíno race. Santiago de los Caballeros, Dominican Republic, clay, 1200–1500 CE, 15 x 9 x 18 cm. *(Courtesy of the National Museum of the American Indian, Smithsonian Institution, catalog number 12/7442; photograph by NMAI Photo Services)*

226

earth opening up and giving birth to all life. In one version of her myth, she "succumbs in childbirth, begetting with her sacrifice the humanity and universe of the Taíno."[41]

Itiba Cahubaba's name lends itself to various translations, revealing the worldview of the translator. Words matter. She has been called "Great Bleeding Mother," "Ancient Bloodied Woman," "Blood-Bathed Old Earth Mother."[42] I prefer the awe engendered by Cuban-American artist Ana Mendieta's translation: "Old Mother Blood."[43] To collaborate with the "artistic and spiritual legacy" left by her Taíno ancestors, Mendieta carved ten life-size figures of Taíno goddesses on cave walls at a remote site outside of Havana.[44] Itiba Cahubaba, the final image of the series, was created in the red interior of a womblike cave in order to touch on what Mendieta called the inner knowledge of the Taíno culture.[45]

Atabey, in the Taíno pantheon, reigns as "Mother of the Waters" (see figure 10.10). She controls the fresh waters of rivers and lakes, which are part of her realm as an earth goddess.[46] She is also the parthenogenetic mother of Yúcahu, the supreme vegetative deity of the Taíno, who is the spirit of cassava, the tribe's main crop.[47] Although Atabey was sometimes commemorated in small amulets worn by pregnant women, her most enduring image appears on a megalith in a circle of standing stones at the Caguana Indigenous Ceremonial Park (Parque Ceremonial Indígena de Caguana) in Puerto Rico. In this large petroglyph she is seen squatting down in a flexed-leg posture of a frog, also denoting parturition. Her arms are raised; her naked vulva touches the ground. Her feet and hands look webbed, amphibian-like. Similar to the Egyptian frog goddess Heket, Atabey protects the unborn fetus floating in the waters of the womb and watches over mothers during childbirth. And similar to the waters of the Nile rising, when the heavy rains come in these Caribbean isles, the frogs begin their songs. These mating calls announce the planting season, the time to plant the cassava.[48]

Archaeologists believe that Caguana was once a communal site for "ritual, political and social activity that involved the whole community," and, most important, they gathered to play *batéy,* a much-loved ballgame.[49] The rectangular ballcourt is ringed by a series of standing stones carved with Taino zemís depicting their mythological universe. Centrally located in the

Figure 10.10. Atabey, Taíno zemí, "Mother of the Waters." She wears a formal headdress and holds a ball or solar disk in each hand. *(Courtesy of Getty Images; image by Dorling Kindersley)*

ceremonial center is a petroglyph dedicated to Atabey. In a recent effort to reclaim the cultural significance of this national historic landmark, the petroglyphs underwent a restoration. During this process, Atabey's vulva was inexcusably expunged. Hard to be an earth goddess with no female sexual organ.[50] Despite this censure, the image of Atabey has found a place in the popular imagination of many contemporary West Indians, ranging from the aesthetic depths of artist Ana Medieta's figure of Atabey to images of the goddess on T-shirts and refrigerator magnets.

Heraldic Goddesses of Ecuador

In the ancient Americas, the largest concentration of art depicting female sacred display once existed in Manabí Province, Ecuador. Atop the coastal hills of Cerro Jaboncillo (Hill of Evergreens), a "great" number of stone stelae were found carved with bas-reliefs of supernatural women in forthright exhibition of their sex.[51] Over a hundred years ago, archaeologist Marshall H. Saville, in three separate expeditions to Ecuador, discovered what the native people already knew—the extensive archaeological ruins of the Manteña culture among the remains of hundreds of *corrales* (enclosures) and mounds that covered several square miles.[52] Such phenomena make the site unique and "one of the most important regions in South America."[53] This civilization thrived for a thousand years, from around 500 until 1530 CE, until the Spanish conquerers arrived.

Although some details may vary, the basic iconography of the carvings remains consistent. The figure sits in bas-relief at the center of the composition, with arms raised, hands clenched, and legs opened to reveal a prominent vulva (see figure 10.11). Framing her head, terraced geometric designs border the top of the stone. She is consistent with the "purest" form of the heraldic woman motif—pronounced genitalia symmetrically flanked by two animals (spiral-tailed monkeys) or by objects (floating solar or lunar disks).[54] In one instance of true conceptual art, her hands become the animals, assuming bird shapes. She may or may not have breasts; her feet or hands or thighs may be exaggerated in size, but like the Sheelas, her vulva is always on display. Among all the artifacts found in thousands of acres of ruins—animal and human figures, columns, pottery, sculptures, stone seats—Saville considered these female stelae the most noteworthy images.[55] And, almost certainly, all the human figures carved on the stones are women.[56]

Such arresting images exude a powerful beauty. Not surprisingly, mystery surrounds the sacred stone females of Ecuador. First and foremost: What do they mean? The late anthrolpologist Frederick J. Dockstader, in his *Indian Art in South America,* analyzes their function as being "similar to that of gravestones in our own culture."[57] Not surprisingly, Jørgen Andersen also sees similarities between the "formidable" stelae of the Manabí and the Sheelas in

Figure 10.11. Stone stele exhibitionist, Cerro Jaboncillo, Manabí, Ecuador, 19 x 17.5 inches. The image is visually striking in its contrasting shapes of the circle of her head, the square of her torso, the triangle of her vulva, and the billowing curves of her enormous thighs. *(Courtesy of the National Museum of the American Indian, Smithsonian Institution, catalog number 010451.000; photograph by NMAI Photo Services)*

that both are "monstrous" symbols of death combined with the life-giving vulva.[58] On a different note, archaeologists Colin McEwan and Florencio Delgado-Espinoza contend that the Ecuadorian sculptural corpus was part of "seasonal initiation and fertility ceremonies."[59]

Douglas Fraser, in his learned study "The Heraldic Woman," puts forth an impressive survey of scholarly thought about the female stelae of Cerro Jaboncillo. At first, Marshall Saville, in not much of an interpretive stretch and in the patriarchal fallback position of his time (1867–1935), calls these numinous figures "idols." Other modern scholars believe the art represents a moon goddess or the Earth Mother, a symbol of procreation and abundance.[60] Saville himself later compares the Manabí woman to the Mexican Mother Earth goddess Tlazolteotl, and Fraser too believes the Manabí image supports "the view that she represents the Great Earth Mother from which all life is reborn."[61]

Clearly, these females are more than ordinary. They appear to possess a repository of wisdom, as if emanating ancestor energies from the Beyond that will help the tribe's survival. Scholar extraordinaire of sacred feminine images from cultures all over the globe Max Dashú points out that the stone carvings at Cerro Jaboncillo of women boldly displaying their vulvas "have clear shamanic overtones" reinforced by the "fantastic lizard-beings carved on the obverse side of the stelas."[62] Looking at the weight of evidence provided by exhibitionist figures from all over the world, it is not much of a leap to say that such art draws on the seemingly endless powers of the vulva to protect, destroy, and create.

Two more points: First, much as I appreciate Saville's pioneering work in bringing to public awareness the archaeological treasures of Manabí in all his meticulous descriptions of the artifacts, he never once employs the word *vulva*, let alone *genitalia*. This supposedly objective scientist, clinically detailing down to a tenth of a centimeter the figures before him, never mentions the vulvas that are almost half their lower bodies. All he can say is: this is a female. Surely such a reticence influences his sense of their full meaning and shows an entrenched patriarchal blindness or perhaps a fear of female sexuality. Next, I must mention the other stunning find in these coastal hills—U-shaped stone seats upheld by handsomely carved animal or human figures. Again, Saville's patriarchal bias interprets that they must be seats of power for male chieftains.[63] However, the only depiction of anyone sitting on these remarkable stone seats is carved on a stele—and that image is of a female in sacred display of her vulva![64]

In September 2012 an article in the Ecuadorian press stated that the National Museum of the American Indian in Washington, D.C., had agreed to return the Saville collection of thousands of artifacts (including the stelae and stone seats) to Ecuador. Sadly, a museum spokesperson for their repatriation program states that such a plan does not exist.[65]

Dilukái, the Palau Exhibitionist

Crossing the waters to the far side of the Pacific, the image of the female in sexual display appears throughout Oceania. However varied the circumstances of the motif of a woman with legs splayed to show her sex, however

Figure 10.12. Dilukái, Republic of Palau, Caroline Islands, wood and paint, late 19th–early 20th century, 26 x 38 x 8 inches. She is wearing a red *báchel* (a prestigious ceremonial necklace worn by women) around her neck, and a *deruál,* a valuable armband made from turtle shells on her arm; these adornments signify her importance. *(Image © The Metropolitan Museum of Art; courtesy of Art Resource, NY)*

original the forms created from the imagination of the artists of any particular culture, it is rather astonishing to see how consistently the powers of the vulva are perceived. On Palau (now called Belau), in the western Caroline Islands, south of the Philippines, the tradition of the *dilukái* endures, alive to this very day.

This imposing figure guards the entrance of the *bai,* a ceremonial house for unmarried men. She presses her knees open to achieve the widest imaginable revelation of an enormous pubic triangle (see figure 10.12). Known as the "most famous" displayed female figure in Micronesia, she is carved in high relief from wood, then painted.[66] Sometimes she is flanked by phallic males in profile, smaller figures who move toward the erotic female center. Other times she sits, a solitary figure on the bai, as shown in a photograph taken nearly a hundred years ago (see figure 10.13).

Figure 10.13. Dilukái gable figure, Republic of Palau, Caroline Islands. This 1919 photo shows the dilukái figure conspicuously placed on the gable at the end of a bai. *(Courtesy of Trust Territory Archives, Pacific Collection, University of Hawaii, Manoa Hamilton Library; photograph from Kramer)*

Always, she must be placed on the eastern gable of the entrance to the bai to fulfill her function of cosmic fertility. She must also face the rising sun to absorb the life-giving solar light. While she remains the cental motif on the facade, often depicted about her are other symbols of fecundity such as sun disks, inexhaustible trees that pour forth fruits, and birds that herald the dawn.[67] On a bai meticulously reconstructed at the Ethnologisches Museum in Berlin, a dilukái sprouts an elaborate Tree of Life growing up out from her spine. She is the source of this magical breadfruit tree, a popular cultural image that has come today to stand for Palau and its natural resources.[68]

As with the Sheelas, the dilukái possesses many dimensions to her powers. The "wonder-working" energies of sexual display are invoked to protect anyone entering the bai, the well-being of the villagers, and the fertility of the taro fields.[69] In fact, the whole bai represents the body of a giant female ancestor, and the Palau people "associate entrance and departure from the men's house with death and rebirth."[70] The vulva can be perceived as "the mysterious divide between nonlife and life."[71]

In the dilukái, the themes of apotropaia and fertility entwine once again. Douglas Fraser remarks that these combined powers stem from her exhibitionism, her primal sexual display.[72] Jørgen Andersen sees this pairing as a function of primitive art, a category in which he includes the dilukái and the Sheelas, "who may be considered as mainly apotropaic, but occasionally lend themselves to fertility beliefs."[73] The supra-ordinary dark vulva of the naked dilukái is also connected to the widely practiced Palauan tradition of tattooing a *V* shape on a woman's mons veneris. Women could not be married or provide for the community until thus tattooed, which was intrinsic to the aesthetics and eroticism of this matrilineal culture.[74]

When the Spanish missionaries claimed these islands at the end of the nineteenth century, they tried to ban many native traditions like tattooing as a kind of witchcraft. A top priority was to paint over the dilukái or remove them from the gables and urge the natives to throw the figures into the sea. A Palauan reports this history: "That carving was the first thing that went when the missionaries came, because they thought that it was uncouth. You don't have women's parts displayed in public."[75] But this desecration didn't sit well with the native people, who chased the missionaries off to other parts of the islands. Under the repressive influence of colonial thinking, the dilukái has sometimes been described as an immoral woman said to be used as a warning against promiscuous behavior—much like what the Catholic bishops said about the Sheelas. No scholarship of any depth should rest on such a superficial, sexist interpretation of this sacred, supernatural female.

After so much reporting of the erasure of the vulva, an image of divine feminine force, it is a pleasure to announce: the dilukái lives! Can't fly out to Palau? A trip to downtown Long Beach, California, will reveal a life-size

dilukái (see figure 10.14). She reigns calmly in a sculpture garden in the midst of noisy urban traffic; behind her is a Catholic church and elementary school. The figure is part of an exhibit of the Pacific Island Ethnic Art Museum, which reports no trouble whatsoever with their neighbors despite her prominent position easily seen from the busy street. She is not tucked away in some obscure corner under a palm tree; in fact, she has a six-foot leg span and proudly displays her impossible-to-miss vulva and clitoris. The dilukái was carved in Palau according to tradition from a breadfruit tree and then shipped to the museum. Here she resides in an accepting public space popular with local mothers who like to bring their children to lunch at this urban oasis.[76]

Figure 10.14. Dilukái of Pacific Island Ethnic Art Museum 7th Street Sculpture Garden, Long Beach, California. A favorite spot for mothers to relax with their children.

■ ■ ■

We have visited the visual art of cultures in India, Africa, the Americas, and Oceania in pursuit of an image. Yet in chronicling the sacred display of these numinous females, we have touched on only a few manifestations of this primal image so essential to human experience. A visit to Max Dashú's Suppressed History Archives website, the product of four decades of research, is a revelation of the myriad forms of the Goddess. A universal symbol of the ever-renewing life force is concretized in the figure of a female parting her naked thighs, performing not a shameful act, but a holy one. In a *cri de coeur,* art historian Philip Rawson, in *Primitive Erotic Art,* puts forth a damning analysis of arrogant Western attitudes toward so-called primitive people, which have led to whole populations being "destroyed without compunction."[77] Fueling this lethal self-righteousness is "Western sexual neuroses, especially those from which Christian missionaries suffer."[78]

Such an assumption of moral superiority has engendered another great crime: the mutilation of untold numbers of works of sexual art, which Rawson laments as "so appalling as to numb one's mind with shame at our civilization's mania for destruction."[79] This assault has come at a cost to the West. Instead of learning from the nourishing roots of this primitive art and its gifts of imagery based on feelings and sensations, modern Western life seems to prize efficiency and objective fact above all else. This primitive art, or, more precisely, primary art, touches on what Rawson names as the source "of our thoughts and language, not only about sex itself, but about our world, its creation and our own psychic energies."[80] What better depths for the human imagination to rise up from than images of the vulva as the creative source of all?

Stories of the Power of Display

We now turn from visual representations to narrative ones, finding tales from around the world of the ritual display of the female genitals. Earlier chapters have touched on the many powers of female sexual display in Irish cultural traditions as well as in classical times, with Baubo and the Bubastis festival in Egypt. This anasyrma, this daring exposure of the vulva, has been a tactic employed by women to stop death and let life flower. All in all, the wondrous vulva can restore equilibrium to what is out of balance. For thousands of years, in myth and custom and perception, its energies have been embodied by supernatural females and ordinary women like you and me, even to this day. Once again, the following narratives are but a few such accounts.

In the realm of myth, we have noted, in chapter 4, the story of how the Irish warrior Cú Chulainn flew into a blood rage full of murderous desires that could only be quelled by the display of the vulvas of a battery of naked crones. (Perhaps the greatest archetype of wounded male pride is that killing machine Achilles, who deserted his comrades because of his anger. Perhaps he would have benefited from the calming sight of a vulva!) First-century Greek scholar Plutarch, in a section of his *Moralia* called "The Bravery of Women," tells the story of the warrior Bellerophon, who rode the winged horse Pegasus, child of the Gorgon Medusa. In the myth, when he felt a prick to his honor, he waded into the sea and called on Poseidon to avenge him. He prayed to the god not only to destroy the Lycian people but to flood their land as well:

> A wave surged and inundated the land; it was a terrible sight, when the sea, following him, rose on high, and completely concealed the plain. Then, when the men begged Bellerophon to hold it back, and could not persuade him, the women, lifting up their undergarments, came to meet him; and when he, out of shame, went back again [toward the sea], the wave too, it is said, withdrew along with him.[81]

When all pleas of the men to the crazed Bellerophon failed, it fell to the women to save the people and the land. Only they could avert the annihilation called for by this aggressive male through the greater force of their female nakedness.

In addition to striking fear in the heart of a warrior, the uncovered vulva has also been employed to defeat demons in two French fables. Persistent European belief in its apotropaic powers appears in a sixteenth-century story told by Rabelais. In it, the old wife of a farmer sends the devil "running for his life by opening her legs and displaying the token of her femininity."[82]

It is a popular story, and images of this routing of the fiend were reproduced on drinking mugs in the seventeenth century.[83]

A century later, in "The Devil of Pope-Fig Island," from Jean de La Fontaine's *Fables,* a demon suffers a similar humiliation. Perretta, the young housekeeper described in the verses as a sprightly, clever lass, comes to the aid of her village, which has been attacked by the evil one. With every confidence in the world, she decides to use her secret weapon to undo him. An illustration for the story details the ensuing scene (see figure 10.15): With an ease shown in her knowing smile, the young woman holds up her skirts to unveil an overwhelming sight. Mouth agape with shock, the devil recoils in fright, his gaze caught by her sex. The horror etched on his face challenges medieval inquisitors' accusations of women having sexual intercourse with Satan.[84] La Fontaine's tale is drawn no doubt from older folk traditions of the protective force of the vulva, whether displayed by a crone or a maiden. Here, the young heroine invokes the time-honored power of the vulva.

Not only men and demons withdraw from the exhibition of female genitalia, but also animals, who with their keen instincts know when they are outmatched. Russian folklore recounts the tale of a bear that appears out of the forest but flees when a young woman raises her skirts before him.[85] The same event is told again, but this time by a Swedish doctor traveling in Lappland, who reports having witnessed a confrontation between a bear and a woman. Once again, a young woman raises her "tunic" and the beast leaves her alone, shuffling "off among the thick firs."[86] She has the sense to do this because she knows her mother had once exposed her sex to a bear, whereupon the animal quickly retreated back into the woods.[87]

Humans, devils, animals—what is left for the avertive powers of the vulva to tame? Only the elements, most especially the ocean. This primordial source of life has an energetic affinity with the vulva, entrance to the womb and carrier of the waters of life. In the folk traditions of many cultures, when women stand on the shore and raise their skirts before the sea to present their naked vulvas, this is not a gesture of threat or contempt but one of deepest respect. In "Universals in Apotropaic Symbolism," art historian and ethnologist Christa Sütterlin interprets the custom in ancient Japan of females exposing their genitals before sea storms not as a sign of aggression but rather as an

Figure 10.15. The devil deterred, an illustration by Charles Eisen for the *Fables* of La Fontaine, 1896. The devil is no match for the force of this sight. *(Courtesy of Wikimedia Commons)*

The Power of Images

act of appeasement.[88] Perhaps the great Sea Mother is calmed by a reciprocal image of the feminine. Science and medical journalist Catherine Blackledge begins her book *The Story of V: A Natural History of Female Sexuality* with this statement: "There is a Catalan saying: *'La mar es posa bona si veu el cony d'una dona'*—'The sea calms down if it sees a woman's cunt' [not considered here a derogatory word]. This Catalan belief in the power of the vagina is, in fact, the source of the good luck custom of fishermen's wives displaying their genitals to the sea before their men put out on the water."[89] The longevity of this belief in the equilibrating powers of sexual display was recorded by the first-century Roman philosopher and historian Pliny, in his *Natural History*. He writes of hailstorms, whirlwinds, and lightning being stilled and driven away by the anasyrma of naked women.[90]

The multifaceted energies of the exposed vulva manifest not just to deter destruction but also, in a seemingly opposite function, to bring about a renewal of nature with the return of the sun and a delight in life through the spirit of play. We have seen how Baubo's comic lewd gesture plucked Demeter out of the depths of her grief, and how the generative powers of the Grain Mother's laughter restores the dying earth. In an entirely different culture a world away, a parallel myth occurs in Japan. The story was first written down around 710 CE in the *Kojiki,* the Record of Ancient Matters, the oldest extant chronicle in Japan, a collection of the myths about the nation.[91] In this story, Amaterasu, a Shinto sun goddess, has retreated into the feminine sanctuary of a cave, disgusted at the lethal antics of her violent brother. Engulfed in darkness, the rice fields begin to die. Eight hundred deities gather before the sealed cave to chant and pray for the return of the sun goddess. But nothing will budge Amaterasu from her lair, and the gods are at a loss of what to do. Then Ame-no-Uzume no Mikoto (Terrible Female of Heaven) begins her dance.[92] Her feet drum a rhythm on an overturned tub. As the energies rise, Ama-no-uzume lifts her kimono in the direction of Amaterasu, and the crowd erupts in laughter. Drawn by the irresistible sounds of pleasure, the sun goddess emerges from her cave, and life blossoms again.[93]

We find similar content but in a different cultural form in the myth "The Ritual Baring of Hathor."[94] The story dates back over three millennia to the

Egyptian Late Kingdom (1160 BCE). The gods Horus and Seth are locked in a fierce power struggle for the kingship of Egypt, creating continual disturbances throughout the universe.[95] During the dispute, the monkey god Babai taunts the aged sun god Rā by shouting at him that his shrine is empty, meaning his time of worship has passed.[96] With a sore heart, Rā retreats to lie down in his garden. After a time, Hathor, as the beneficent Lady of the Southern Sycamore, comes to her father, Rā, master of the universe. In a gesture to lift his sadness, "she uncovered her nether parts before his face, and the great god laughed at her."[97] As his laughter erupts from this diverting spectacle, the god is relieved of the weight of his sorrow and can resume his place in solving the debate. Once again, a potent female, yet with a heart as light as a feather, steps in at the crucial moment to bring the cosmos back into balance by unveiling her sex. Through the gesture of ritual anasyrma, the joy of life returns.

One of the greatest benefits of sacred display is that it can help nature flourish. Many Western countries have had an enduring belief in the fertilizing ability of women walking naked through the fields.[98] European peasant women enacted the custom of exposing their vulvas to the growing flax, while saying: "Please grow as high as my genitals are now."[99] Marija Gimbutas confirms this instinctive bond: European "pre-industrial agricultural rites show a very definite mystical connection between the fertility of the soil and the creative force of women."[100]

This is not just an anomaly of the West. In the Marquesas Islands of Polynesia, gratitude for a bountiful harvest is expressed in the rite of the *ko'ika to'e haka,* the clitoris dance.[101] At the conclusion of the harvest festival, this traditional dance is performed by young women who raise their skirts in a celebratory salute to their own sexual capacities and to bestow blessings on the land for continued fruitfulness. In another part of the world, in modern Africa, Miriam Robbins Dexter and Victor Mair describe a rainmaking ceremony performed by the Ihanzu, a people in north-central Tanzania. When all else fails in times of drought, fecund women—women who have already given birth to children—perform a dance until the clouds appear. They sing obscene songs and display their nakedness with such intention that "the ancestral spirits rejoice and the rains come."[102] When all the energies of the earth, humans, and spirit align, wholeness is restored.

Lest we think such activities reside only in the realm of myth or in the ritual practices of certain tribal peoples, ordinary women in everyday life have called on a reliable power within their bodies. Employing nothing more than the raising of their skirts, women have stopped the violence of wars, protected the environment from degradation by multinational corporations, challenged colonial oppression, and faced down tyrants. Such is the apotropaic power of the displayed vulva, a direct image of the primal force of creation, greater in these instances than the forces of meaningless destruction.

Two incidents from China demonstrate the determination of women to employ their vulvic powers in the service of peace. Writer Lu Xun heard an account from his nursemaid of how in the nineteenth century rows of older women stood atop the city walls and repelled invaders by uncovering their vulvas. This stopped the attackers from firing their guns and cannons, or supposedly it would make the weapons blow up if they were used.[103] The nursemaid knew of the event because she herself was one of those bold women! In Yunnan Province in southwest China, a Lisu woman enacted a similar custom in the late eighteenth century. During a major battle between two tribes, a woman (once again from a vantage point of height) climbed a cliff, took off her long skirt, and waved it, a signal for the battle to stop. The fighting immediately ceased, and the men dispersed to their villages. The Lisus have a longstanding tradition that women can stop a war "if a woman of either side waves her skirt and calls for an armistice" (see figure 10.16).[104]

Two more incidents, this time from Nigeria: In 1929, in the famous Women's War, the Ogu Umunwanyi, Igbo women from the Aba region protested against a proposed tax on the market women (see figure 10.17). They discarded their everyday clothes to transform into a unified energy field of rebellion. Ornamenting their bodies only with leaves and with sacred ritual objects, they protested colonial oppression by the British. Fueled by the power of their nakedness and the sense that this was a matter only the women could handle, "the women sang, danced, ridiculed, burned and looted; destroyed hated native courts, cut telegraph wires, marched on the houses of chiefs

collaborating with the colonialists, and forced them to flee."[105] Because of their heroic actions, colonial authorities dropped plans to impose a tax on the local tradings of these market women.

The second incident occured seventy years later in Nigeria. On July 8, 2002, six hundred rural peasant women between the ages of twenty and ninety took over the Chevron-Texaco oil facility in Escravos, Nigeria (see figure 10.18). For ten days, the unarmed women maintained control over the facility, trapping seven hundred male workers inside and halting the production of half a million barrels of oil a day. By what power did these women achieve this seeming miracle? By threatening to strip naked in public! As every other means of protest had failed, the women united across

Figure 10.17. Aba women of Nigeria. Their 1929 uprising was the first major challenge to British colonial authority and set a precedent of feminist and anticolonial protest. *(Courtesy of Wikimedia Commons)*

ethnic boundaries to use their last resort—the power of their femaleness. Anthropologist Terisa Turner explains the enormity of the symbolism behind this threat by the Niger Delta women: "We all come into the world through the vagina. By exposing the vagina, the women are saying: 'We are hereby taking back the life we gave you.'... Men who are exposed are viewed as dead. No one will cook for them, marry them, enter into any kind of contract with them or buy anything from them."[106]

The Naked Option: A Last Resort, a film by Candace Schermerhorn, tells the story of why the women confronted one of the largest and wealthiest oil companies in the world. The environmental devastation caused by oil mining led to the loss of their livelihoods. The inability to feed their families drove the women to risk their very lives. The peaceful occupation ceased when Chevron-Texaco agreed to the women's demands that the oil giant

hire their sons and develop their impoverished communities by constructing schools and electrical and water systems. Inspired by this seige in Escravos, women from different tribes occupied four other Chevron-Texaco flow stations in other parts of Nigeria.[107]

In 1985, on the island of Luzon in the northern Philippines, a myth-in-the-making was enacted by the Kalinga women. At that time, the Marcos dictatorship, with World Bank funding, was forging ahead with a plan to build four huge hydroelectric dams in the heart of Kalinga tribal land. As Filipina anthropologist Mariflor Parpan reported in 1985 to the Non-Governmental Forum in Kenya, such a project would have put underwater the Kalinga land "from the tip of one mountain to the tip of another mountain," displacing a hundred thousand people.[108] Despite elders speaking out to save "the land which is sacred and beloved, from whose womb spring our Kalinga lives," all

Figure 10.18. Nigerian women's protest, 2002. In the 21st century, women united to halt the lethal injustices of one of the world's most powerful corporations. *(Photograph courtesy of The Naked Option, www.nakedoptionmovie.com)*

legal efforts and appeals were rebuffed by the government.[109] When an engineering team arrived, protected by almost a battalion of soldiers, their survey of a mountain disturbed ancestral graves. The Kalinga women knew then that they must act.

According to Parpan, one day the women made flanking formations around the men:

> They were dressed only in their native wraparound skirts, the *Kahin*. . . . At a signal, they removed their skirts. They undressed right before this group of men! And then, they used the heavy skirts to thrash at the men and pin them to the ground . . . they removed all the survey implements and guns . . . and they removed the men's clothes, right down to their socks. . . . You see, we have a cultural taboo—not to lay eyes or hands on women. . . . So they knew that their men would be disarmed immediately if they were in front of women who were naked.[110]

The women then hid their spoils in the forest while the embarrassed men stole home only after it became dark. The women showed great courage by risking their lives and by displaying their nakedness to strange men. As author and artist Léonie Caldecott puts it in "Dance of the Woman Warrior," these women were "unshaped by the game of violence and the struggle for supremacy," and their unarmed nakedness gave them a "holy power to heal discord."[111] The Kalinga women demonstrated an uncompromising spirit by stopping an action that would have killed them as a people, and so they defeated the globalization efforts of the World Bank and a corrupt dictator.[112] The bank withdrew its funding, and the dams were never built.

More recently, in August 2012, during the Republican National Convention held in Tampa, Florida, women did not expose their vulvas but became them. To empower women by bringing attention to the Republican "war on women," Code Pink, a women-initiated grassroots peace and social justice movement, called on women to "bring your vagina" to the convention (see figure 10.19). In a witty bit of theatrical display they donned body-sized pink vagina costumes (actually vulvas, to be anatomically precise) and held signs reading, "Vagina: Can't say it? Don't legislate it." This, of course, refers to Michigan state representative Lisa Brown, who was banned from speaking

Figure 10.19. Code Pink vulva street theater. Another message to Congress from the women of Code Pink. *(Courtesy of Rae Abileah, Code Pink)*

on the House floor by Republican House leaders for giving a speech they called "vile" and "disgusting."[113] Legislator Brown had dared to use the word *vagina* while speaking in opposition to a measure that would limit women's access to health care and take away their reproductive rights. In an interview for the *Daily Beast,* Code Pink cofounder Medea Benjamin shared the group's vibrant strategy for the protest at the Republican National Convention:

> We were the dancing vaginas. One of the things we have found is the surest way to make the police go away is try to get your picture in front of them wearing a vagina. The whole horse brigade will leave. It is so funny that they get very intimidated by our vagina costumes. They also laugh and take their own photos of us. That's what we try to do—make our points, but in a way that's not too angry or dull. We try to be creative and satirical and try new ways to get the message across.[114]

In drawing on the creative energy of the vulva, the Code Pink activists wanted the Republicans to see that women were not going to silently endure their rhetoric against them, like soon-to-be-defeated Representative Todd Akin's comment about "legitimate rape" not causing pregnancy.* At the time of the peaceful protest, organizer Rae Abileah (alluding to the Occupy movement opposing the 1 percent corporate elite) pointed out that women are "the 51% of the 99%."[115]

The power of the image of a displayed vulva manifests in many diverse cultures and throughout time. Its figurative and literal use in visual art, myth, and social action reveals the panoply of its energies, ranging from an apotropaic repelling of violence to the blessing of good fortune to the elemental nurturing of life. All in all, its continuum from destruction to creation endures as a most organic metaphor for the mysterious experience of being alive. How compelling is the figure of the open female nude! How is it that this image of female display became so central to the human imagination?

---

*Women strike again at a Republican National Convention! On July 17, 2016, in downtown Cleveland, one hundred women stood naked and held round mirror disks up to the rising sun to reflect their protest against the war on women.

11
The Creative Source

When contemplating female display, the question arises: By what process does this image appear all over the world and throughout time? Contradictory theories have been proposed by archaeologists, art historians, anthropologists, and mythologists. Does the image appear in geographically diverse cultures through diffusion—that is, through a transfer of traditions via trade routes and the migration of people? Or is such an image a universal pattern of energy present in the psyches of all humans?

Douglas Fraser, in "The Heraldic Woman: A Study in Diffusion," rejects any archetypal basis for the creation of this art. Instead he traces the transmission of the display motif from the Mediterranean and Near East to the Far East to the Pacific Islands, and finally to the Americas.*[1] But even he admits a lack of evidence to explain the appearance of the image in all its extensive cultural manifestations.[2] Researcher Max Dashú, in her extensive body of work on goddess figures, holds a different view. She writes that diffusion alone cannot "explain the transhistorical and intercontinental recurrence of certain themes."[3] In addition, scholar Christa Sütterlin claims that apotropaic images are universal symbols that rise independently in the minds of humans in widespread cultures. Whereas Fraser finds that no "psychological necessity binds this image together," Sütterlin believes that genital display reflects "a psychological level in humanity not bound" to any specific culture.[4] She recognizes an archaic perseverance in the apotropaic display of the vulva that transcends any

---

*Note that Fraser's essay focuses on heraldic women—that is, displayed females flanked by two other beings.

historical factors—the motif reappears as "a common pattern in human communication."[5]

Certainly there are instances of cultural diffusion (for example, along the heavily traveled Silk Road), yet Fraser's categorical denial of any independent invention of the displayed vulva seems an extreme position. He rejects any idea of it being a symbolic image drawn from nature to address the "universal problems faced by mankind [*sic*]."[6] But the vulva *is* a force of nature, and humans do have an inherent urge to make images. Sütterlin sees the possibility that the image may have been created simultaneously from a "universal response" to common human problems traceable to biological roots.[7] Does it not make sense that so basic, so primal an experience as the vulva in birth, sex, and internment into Mother Earth for rebirth would be rooted in our imaginations?

But what is the imagination? What does it mean to call the displayed vulva an archetypal image, especially in this postmodern culture that eschews any such universals as a meta-narrative and therefore false? What meanings and mysteries are behind this image? Is such a representation merely a manifestation of biological instincts or an instinct of the spirit?

The Dynamics of the Imagination

A good place to start this exploration is to look at the forces that generate an image. We perceive the outer world in images through our five senses and then interpret all the impulses that the sense organs send to the brain via images.[8] The other source of images comes to us from our inner world. As Jung explains in *The Structure and Dynamics of the Psyche,* the function of consciousness is to integrate the images from these two worlds—that is, "not only to recognize and assimilate the external world through the gateway of the senses, but to translate into visible reality the world within us."[9] No work of art, let alone any enduring image, was ever generated solely by the conscious mind, but only with that other independent pole of the personality, the unconscious mind.

Many artists and creative thinkers have pondered the source of the imagination. Irish poet and mystic William Butler Yeats, in *The Second Coming,* is troubled by "a vast image out of *Spiritus Mundi,*" the breath or spirit of the world. Yeats apprehends that each individual human mind is connected to this collective memory out of which symbols arise and return. In his essay "The Philosophy of Shelley's Poetry," Yeats writes that anyone with an experience of the mystical state of the soul will share "the sudden conviction that our little memories are but a part of some great Memory that renews the world and men's [*sic*] thoughts age after age, and that our thoughts are not, as we suppose, the deep, but a little foam upon the deep."[10] Yeats believes it is our common link to the Spiritus Mundi, to this vast collective mind, that makes the images in poetry resonate with feeling and meaning between poet and reader.

Biologist Edmund Ware Sinnott, in his short essay "The Creativeness of Life," offers a universal conception of creativity. As does the poet, the scientist too turns to the creative operations of the unconscious to explain the imagination, hoping to convey some sense of the mystery involved. Sinnott emphasizes that the whole unconscious is presumably "filled with a throng of images and fantasies."[11] He conceives the greatest power of this mind to be an ability to fashion its "floating fantasies" into patterns, and through this quality, into the living stuff of expression.[12] This organizing of energies provides not random changes but imaginative ones that supply images to the conscious mind of what is needed by life at any particular moment. Thus, the creative power, he states, is *the most important factor* in human evolution. For Sinnott, imagination is the basic formative quality of life. The scientist then wonders if there is not perhaps a spiritual order at work here in these processes.

Turning again to Jung for a third view on the dynamics of the imagination, he too holds it as a foundational force. Like Sinnott, Jung considers imagination to be "the creative source of all that has made progress possible to human life."[13] Jung also believes that in addition to our physical instinctive roots, humans inherit collective psychic ones. And as the imagination operates through all these parts of our psyche, its influence can be felt simultaneously "in the contents of the conscious mind and of the unconscious, in the collective as in the individual."[14]

Jung differentiates the unconscious mind into the personal unconscious and (in one of his best-known concepts) the collective unconscious. The personal unconscious consists of forgotten or repressed contents explainable by a person's life. However, in Jung's hypothesis, the collective unconscious is transpersonal; it does not develop through individual experience but, as mentioned above, is a psychological inheritance shared by all humans. The collective unconscious contains the whole cultural and spiritual heritage of our evolution and is part of the structure of the human psyche.[15] But since it is unconscious or unknown, it is hard to convey exactly what it is. Jung theorizes that as far as we can say anything about it at all, the collective unconscious appears to consist of mythological motifs or primordial images that are innate and universal, common to humanity at all times and in all places.[16] Using a term from Western traditions, Jung calls these basic psychic structures *archetypes,* derived from the Greek words *arkhe,* "first," and *tupos,* "a model"—thus, an original pattern. One primary example would be the Great Mother. Theodor Abt, in his illuminating Jungian perspective on the nature of images, *Introduction to Picture Interpretation,* notes that the archetypes are "organizing factors in the human psyche which form and structure human ideas and feelings."[17] They arrange psychic elements into images, and the unconscious manifests through these archetypal images or symbols into our conscious awareness.

Symbols live in two worlds: the visible (it's a vulva) and the invisible (the mysteries of life and death). They create a bridge between the conscious and the unconscious minds, a bridge from the known to the unknowable (a living reality beyond our field of understanding). Such images carry for us a quality of the depths, of intense emotions felt through contact with their numinous power, what Yeats called the "resonance of poetry." They make the world come alive and let us experience that we are parts related to a greater whole. Symbols point to possibilities; there is no final answer as to their meaning. As French scholar and mystic Henry Corbin, whose life work was devoted to the imagination, wrote: "The symbol announces a plane of consciousness distinct from rational evidence; it is a 'cipher' of a mystery, the only means of saying something that cannot be apprehended in any other way; a symbol is never explained once and for all, but must be deciphered over and over again."[18]

Because symbols exist simultaneously in two different realms, they can reconcile the opposite qualities of our limited conscious awareness and the overflowing, seemingly endless unconscious.[19] Their meanings have a quality of paradox. We have seen this with the image of the Sheela na gig and with many of the other display figures: they are both terrifying and beneficent; they can bring new life and take back the dead. Leave it to pugnacious playwright David Mamet to comment on this incompatibility. He makes the wry observation that artists aren't driven to "create art" or to "help people" or wonder "what is it good for?"; they create because "they are driven to lessen the burden of the unbearable disparity between their conscious and unconscious minds, and so to achieve peace."[20]

The Universal Power of the Feminine

Now, to circle back to the crux of the matter: Why this conversation on the origins and essential qualities of images? What does all of this have to do with the Sheela na gig, with cross-cultural representations of displayed females? First, it is to bring us around to the existence of common ideas or energies. The universal motif of the vulva (whether depicted abstractly or in the figure of a displayed female) can rise up independently in the minds of artists from different cultures not in contact with one another. Migration patterns of cultural diffusion do occur but do not sufficiently explain the ubiquity of this reoccurring symbol. It is part of human nature. (Of course, even an image that has spread to different locations as a result of diffusion at one time had its origins in an archetype as some inner necessity of expression.) Secondly, this conversation on images serves to recognize the universal power of the feminine. This primal energy, unbounded by time and space, is behind the creation of uncountable representations of the vulva.

While images of female sexual display from cultures around the world can vary in detail and take on local coloring, none lose their central focus on the powers of the vulva or the essence of its symbolic meaning. Sheela na gig, Baubo, Gorgon, Kālī, Chāmuṇḍā, Lajjā Gaurī, the Kathmandu exhibitionist, the Gabon door guardian, Itiba Cahubaba, Atabey, the Manabí stelae, the dilukái—all are archetypal expressions of the yoni of the Great Mother.

Regardless of the name she goes by, with her vast and seemingly paradoxical powers she is the source of fertility and gives birth to and sustains the world. She takes back the dead, and she renews life. She guards entrances. She is the beauty and joy of the world. She can be a beloved universal Mother or a terrifying hag.

And yet there is no end to the meaning of these display figures. They are wild, dangerous, free. Their quintessence cannot be boxed in by one final explanation. Alive like all of nature, they also contain the opposite quality, that of death. These manifestations of the Goddess give us knowledge of the reality of life and its basic pulse: change. The symbol of the vulva rendered in art helps us experience the world as unified, meaningful, and alive.

Symbols may be the oldest way humans interpret reality. Not language, not tools, but creating images is at the root of what it means to be a human being—it is a fundamental activity of our species. Evidence of figurative representation goes back hundreds of thousands of years, as seen in the rudimentary carving from Berekhat Ram, Israel, or the nearly eighty-thousand-year-old triangles from the Blombos Cave in South Africa (figure 7.1). But around forty thousand years ago an explosion of creativity occurred in that wondrous gift bequeathed to us from our ancestors, the Paleolithic cave art. This concentrated burst of image-making announces the dawn of the human spirit.[21] Those lucky enough to be allowed inside the Chauvet Cave remark on the feeling of aliveness of the images of the animals and the lingering presence of the artists as seen in the outlined handprints announcing: *We are here* (see figure 11.1).

It is beyond the scope of this book to analyze the cause and effect of why this Ice Age revolution in artistic expression took place. Whether through some recent development of the cerebrum anterior part of the brain, or some tip of the iceberg of long-existing artistic practices finally breaking through, in any case, in some new grand way, something happened. No previous scattered symbol-making activity can match the full-blown symbolic representations of what Randall White, lead archaeologist at Abri Castenet, calls the "organized symbolic systems shared across space and through time" seen in the Upper Paleolithic caves.[22] Was the new level of

symbolic thinking in this era a psychological phenomenon? An emerging self-awareness was becoming differentiated from its source, the matrix of the unconscious. Due to this separation, human consciousness could turn and reflect on itself and thus form a new creative relationship with the infinitude of the inner world. Symbols could now flow between these two aspects of the mind.

As seen in rock art not only in Europe but in Africa, Asia, Australia, and North America, images can be derived not only from sense perceptions of the outer world but also with contents from the inner world to create pictures never seen before by the outer eye (see figure 11.2).[23] Another outstanding example is located in the deepest chamber of the Chauvet Cave. The original drawing is a black pubic triangle symbolic of female powers (figure 7.8). Added later to this image are two animals flanking her. Life-size, she has the same legs as many of the Paleolithic goddess figurines, full and tapering down to a footless point, but now the sexual triangle is the lower part of a human body, while a lion shares her right leg and a bison her left. We see these animals in profile; the vulva is full frontal at the center

Figure 11.1. Stenciled hands, rock shelter, Carnarvon Gorge, Queensland, Australia. Handprints in rock art occur in many cultures around the world. This Aboriginal art appears on the gorge's sandstone walls. *(Photograph courtesy of Don Hitchcock, www.donsmaps.com)*

Figure 11.2. A rock goddess, Anbangbang Shelter, Kakadu National Park, northern Australia. Several figures stand in awe before an ancestress revealing the energy of creation. The Kakadu rock shelters contain one of the world's greatest concentrations of rock art sites, with over twenty thousand years of Aboriginal occupation. *(Photograph courtesy of* Voices of the First Day *and the Aboriginal Arts Board)*

of the composition as the generatrix of all life. This is not a sight from the outer world but a cosmological image of origins that reveals a communication with both the outer and inner worlds. Jungian analyst Theodor Abt calls such a picture the "experience of something spiritual from the inner world entering human consciousness," as it combines representations of the outer world (a vulva and animals) and "the inner realm of fantasy" (a vulva-lion-bison imagined being).[24]

Sanctuaries of the Sacred Feminine

It can be no accident that the Upper Paleolithic imagination found its greatest expression inside caves. While acknowledging the multitudes of goddess figurines carved during this era, it is inside caves—literally the womb of the Earth Mother—where our ancestors created galleries of art. What passion must have given them the courage to enter the dark with only their animal-oil lamps, to touch their way through passages of great distance, feeling the contours of the cave walls until pathways opened into great caverns. All this was an adventurous quest to discover the most alive places where the energies of the animals and of their great Creatrix were emerging from the veil of rock. To know the places where the spirits of the cave resided and then to create images of horses, lions, bisons, and vulvas on those exact sites allowed their powers to enter the world.[25]

Paleolithic cave art is grounded in the imaginative idea of a universal creative womb as the generatrix of all life.[26] Indeed, the very structure of the caves, with their entrances, passages, and caverns, mirrors the primordial vulva, vagina, and womb of the Goddess. Just to enter the cave is to be inside a place of origin, an act of transformation. As the "magician-mother," the Goddess gives birth to all the life pictured on the cave walls and, in season, calls all forms back to her.[27] In parietal art, the image of the pubic triangle of the Great Mother symbolizes the source of life and simultaneously the tomb to which the dead return, so that they may be born again.

Such a sanctified environment could only have served to enhance the atmosphere of the ceremonies conducted there. What can we know of the rites that took place in the sanctuary of the Paleolithic caves? Probably the very act of making the art was an ecstatic process. Some patriarchal scholars are quick to limit the purpose of the caves to "hunting magic." However, renowned Paleolithic scholar and archaeologist André Leroi-Gourhan, in analyzing thousands of paintings and sculptures from numerous caves, comments on the centrality of female images in the caves. He observes that for Paleolithic women and men what constituted "the special heart of the caves is clearly the panels in the central part, dominated by animals from the female category and female signs."[28] By contrast, masculine animals and signs were "arranged around feminine signs, or they featured only peripherally in the narrow entrances toward the sanctuary or in the narrow tunnels at the back."[29] Leroi-Gourhan notes that the panels provide evidence of being frequented, and he believes that the most important parts of rites must have been performed before them.[30] Parietal art expert J. Robert-Lamblin sees the Chauvet Cave not as a place to inhabit but rather a place to enact ritual, and accordingly the chamber of the Salle du Fond "resided over by the female figure [the engraved vulva] was a temple to the origins of life."[31]

Marija Gimbutas describes the Paleolithic caves as "sanctuaries for the enactment of seasonal rites, initiation rituals, and other ceremonies related

Figure 11.3. "The Wall of One Thousand Vulvas," sandstone walls, rock shelter, Carnarvon Gorge, Queensland, Australia. One of the interpretative signs at the site states: "The most common engraving found here is of the human vulva. Engravings of vulvas are common along the cliffs of the Great Dividing Range in this region." *(Caption title and photograph courtesy of Don Hitchcock, www.donsmaps.com)*

to a participation in the sacred cycles of life."[32] Even in the Upper Paleolithic, the Goddess personifies the ever-renewing round of life in all of its manifestations. Her time is cyclical, not linear, and rituals to her must have expressed awe at the wonders and terrors of being alive, at the nurturing and devouring aspects of nature entwined in one being. Our ancestors perceived the powers of the feminine to be the creative source of reality in this world and in the world beyond. At this heightened dawn of the human imagination, the image of the vulva resonated as the center of their mythical world. In this ancient culture, no symbol responded more completely to their deepest concern: that life will come again.

Most of us will probably never be allowed into the Chauvet Cave and can only dream what it would be like to move through the chambers, look upon its treasures, and reflect on the lives of our Paleolithic forebears. But in 2008 *New Yorker* staff writer Judith Thurman had the privilege of entering the cave. The account of this twenty-first-century woman concludes with these impressions: "Halfway home to the mortal world, I asked Alard [her guide] if we could pause and turn off our torches. The acoustics magnify every sound, and it takes the brain a few minutes to accept the totality of the darkness—your sight keeps grasping for a hold. Whatever the art means, you understand, at that moment, that its vessel is both a womb and a sepulchre."[33]

■ ■ ■

In the 1960s, archaeologist Marija Gimbutas started her great work of decoding the symbols she kept discovering on the tombs, temples, frescoes, reliefs, sculptures, figurines, pottery, and pictorial painting of Neolithic Old Europe. In time she came to understand this coherent system of images to be the language of the Goddess. She realized too that the "main theme of Goddess symbolism is the mystery of birth and death and the renewal of life, not only human but all life on earth and indeed the whole cosmos."[34] Gimbutas writes that as she traced these images back to their origins in the Paleolithic, and forward to historical times, what struck her was "not the metamorphosis of the symbols over the millennia but rather the continuity from Paleolithic times on."[35]

The power of the image of the vulva is rooted in our instinctual nature and the primordial motifs of our inner life. The sacred display of the vulva has an unbreakable thread back to the beginning of human culture. Of course, we cannot understand a Sheela na gig or any other female figure of display solely through the intellect; it is inadequate to deal with the fullness of a symbol, to render it alive. The beauty of her image comes from the feeling that she engenders in us (see figures 11.3 through 11.7). Throughout time, we humans have employed the vulva as a symbol of the primary processes of life: coming into being, passing away, returning. There is no more enduring image.

Figure 11.4. Porta Tosa, Milan, Italy, 12th century. Once guarding over a gate of the city walls, she is now housed in the Castello Sforzesco. In one hand she holds a dagger by her genitals, and in the other, a serpent. Her power was too much for a 15th-century cardinal, who ordered the removal of the figure. *(Photograph courtesy of Giovanni Dall'Orto)*

Figure 11.5. Black Sea Sheela. A life-size sculpture in a park in Sochi, Russia, site of the 2014 Winter Olympics. *(Photograph courtesy of Casey Revkin-Maugér)*

Figure 11.6. Hawaiian lava-rock carving. This double display of vulva and tongue in a Hawaiian petroglyph was found at the Puako Archaeological Preserve on the Big Island. *(GSA Collection, Goddess Sites and Images, from the* Re-Genesis Encyclopedia *database; photograph courtesy of Eahr Amelia Joan)*

Figure 11.7. Ancestress, marlstone, Tambelar village, western Sumba, Indonesia. With a monstrous expression and Sheela-like gesture, death and regeneration are embodied in this Bronze Age grave figure, a representation of a mythical female ancestor. *(Accession # IIc 12671; photograph by Peter Horner, © Museum der Kulturen, Basel, Switzerland)*

12

The Return
of the Goddess

Can an image still be alive if it hasn't been created since the passing of the era of the Sheelas over three hundred years ago? Did the energy behind the Sheelas die, or did it abide underground like a rhizome, waiting to break out into our current age of disconnection and despair? Can a seemingly dormant archetype be revivified? How is the Sheela part of the psychic event of our era, the return of the Goddess? And if she has returned, why, and to what end? What can she offer us? Why do we need this image?

The image of the Sheela na gig embodies the numinous power of the Dark Goddess over the mysteries of life and death. These primal energies cannot be controlled. Such a representation challenges the efficient running of the machine of state. The Sheela symbolizes what terrifies patriarchal society, with its increasing oppression under the guise of "order"—the chaos of nature and female sexuality. We, in the industrialized West, live in a culture that emphasizes goal-oriented linear thinking at the expense of symbolic thinking in images. The meaning of the displayed vulva of the Sheela cannot be safely contained by dry mental interpretations but must be felt through the web of associations from the dark richness of the unconscious. How, then, can the much-needed compensatory images of the sacred be valued?

The Loss of
the Numinous Imagination

One of the fundamental crises of our culture is a lack of connection to images that originate from the deepest, most transformative part of ourselves. Yet ironically we are bombarded with images as a result of our plugged-in lifestyle. The shadow side of the Information Age is the consumption of escapist images from a virtual reality that leaves us more disconnected from any grounding in our own creativity. We are adrift with a mass of empty images that do not function as images traditionally have done: to construct a bridge between this world and the immense inner world of the Beyond. In an essay appearing in a recent issue of the journal *Parabola*, "Imagination and the Void: To Be or Not To Be," author and teacher Patrick Laude takes on the issue of our contemporary way of relating to images: "One must wonder what may remain of the power of creative imagination when such a passive, hardly conscious relationship with images has settled in and become second nature."[1] These media and virtual images construct a world of unreality to mesmerize and sedate us with entertainment. Such diversions, Laude states, mask "an industrialized world of tedious, mechanical, senseless activity."[2] Scholar Max Dashú believes this consumer culture has rendered our imaginal lives "bound, twisted, displaced, and appropriated" by media conglomerates.[3] They feed us spectacles of illusion. How far this is from the imagination's ability to connect us with the whole of reality to foster the feeling of being alive.

Another troubling problem has been described by Jungian analyst Theodor Abt. The general trend in education over the last several hundred years toward goal-oriented rational thinking makes "the understanding of chains of cause and effect the dominant way of looking at reality."[4] The originality of symbolic thinking in images that see beneath the surface into another world has declined. In a recent interview in the *Los Angeles Times*, innovative theater director Peter Sellars expresses his alarm at the devaluation of creativity in schools. Science is emphasized over the humanities, which have been "systematically removed from the menu of most Americans."[5] He believes this has resulted in a less compassionate civilization: "Right now we are in such deep, deep, deep waters, and the only solutions are going to be the creative ones."[6]

An additional destructive notion is the idea that creativity exists just for the gifted few. To the detriment of our fullness as human beings, this idea ignores our natural heritage. Inherent to the human personality is the desire to create images and to receive them from the psyche, then to discover their meaning. Countering this devaluation of the imagination in the classroom is an oft-printed essay written almost forty years ago, "Everyman with a Blue Guitar: Imagination, Creativity, Language," by English professor James E. Miller. In it, Miller makes an impassioned cry for "a radical revision of the curriculum and classroom practice" to create enlivened classrooms where imaginative energies are available to every student.[7] In his experience as a teacher he does not see the world as divided into creative and uncreative people, but rather that imagination and creativity are faculties and attributes of everyone.[8] Finally, Miller turns to the work of biologist Edmund Ware Sinnott, who makes a singular point: it is not reason but the great flight of imagination that has been the greatest force in human evolution.[9]

What is the psychological cost of this separation from the creative center of ourselves? We think we are no longer part of nature but superior to it—that science has conquered nature. In truth, we are in the grip of a suicidal urge to make more efficient machines to poison every element that sustains life and to destroy the beauty of this planet. Jung, in his last writing on symbols, completed ten days before his death, delivers a final warning. He cautions us that we do not realize how much our rationalism has dehumanized us by destroying our ability to respond to numinous symbols and ideas: "Today, for instance, we talk of 'matter.' We describe its physical properties. . . . But the word 'matter' remains a dry, inhuman, and purely intellectual concept, without any psychic significance for us. How different was the former image of matter—the Great Mother—that could encompass and express the profound emotional meaning of Mother Earth."[10] When the sacred realm is split off from matter, we feel ourselves to be isolated in the cosmos, lost without a devotion to nature.

This loss of consciousness is calamitous to all life. Acting with a short-sighted greed, patriarchy believes the world to be a dead thing, an object to be consumed without restraint. As mythologist Joseph Campbell puts it, with this view of the universe a human being is no longer born as a child "to flower in the knowledge of his [or her] own eternal portion but as a robot fashioned to serve."[11] Cultural historian and ecotheologian Thomas Berry asks: Without roots in the earth and cosmos, how are we to activate the psychic energy that is required to transform the major ecological issues confronting us?[12] With spirit placed outside the natural world and rationalism displacing the inner world of the imagination, how are we to experience a delight in life to sustain us through its vicissitudes? Pioneering biologist Rachel Carson observes that the "more clearly we can focus our attention on the wonders and realities of the universe about us, the less taste we shall have for destruction."[13]

No one has stated more clearly the ramifications of this war on nature than Pulitzer Prize–winning writer Chris Hedges. In a recent essay, "The Implosion of Capitalism," he too connects the heedless devastation of the earth with our loss of the luminous imagination. Hedges exhorts us to wake up from a lethal amnesia in order to face the fact that our social structure is at a dead end, or else soon "we all go down together."[14] Succinctly, he diagnoses our current condition of corrupting the air, water, and soil of where we live; waging one useless war after another; and creating a privileged elite bent on returning the rest of us to a state of feudalism. Where is the meaning and value of life when its most basic elements are reduced to commodities, to cash products?

Hedges, too, laments the emphasis in schools on what is considered "practical" by the corporate state while cutting the arts and humanities, which are regarded as "impractical." These disciplines have the power to transform us through their celebration of the creativity of human culture. While the clear, cold line of reason has its place, Hedges points out its limits: "Reason makes possible the calculations, science and technological advances of industrial civilization, but reason does not connect us with the forces of life. A society that loses the capacity for the sacred, that lacks the power of human imagination, that cannot practice empathy, ultimately ensures its own destruction."[15]

Ironically, the power of reason as provided by the near-unanimous body of science that gives hard evidence of global warming is denied by multinational corporations that exploit the earth because such an acknowledgment may limit profits. At a recent congressional hearing on a new peer-reviewed report that surveyed 1,372 climate scientists and reaffirmed the major findings of the Intergovernmental Panel on Climate Change (IPCC), Republican senators refused to go against their corporate donors, dismissing the current science as "offensive" and "irrelevant."[16]

Many informed scientists, scholars, and artists concerned with the fate of the earth have called for a restoration of an older vision of life held by premodern societies. Such cultures saw the world as alive with spirit infusing matter; they honored ambiguity, mystery, and the imagination as a bringer of essential knowledge.[17] This knowledge of the sacredness and interdependency of all life permeated Native American culture and is found in the roots of Western civilization, in Old Europe. The new story is to awaken to the old story.[18]

The Legacy of
Patriarchal Warrior Societies

Our current nightmare began over five thousand years ago in the violence of war when male-dominated tribes with a pantheon of martial gods invaded the peaceful, egalitarian Goddess-centered cultures of Old Europe. In her essay "War Is Man's Business," cultural and art historian Elinor Gadon points out that by the time of Homer's *Iliad*, a paean to the apotheosis of glory through slaughter, warfare had become institutionalized. "This warrior ethos ratified the barbaric action of kings whose territorial ambitions drew them ever more deeply into the compulsion to conquer and enslave other peoples."[19]

We need to rebuild the earlier vision of community based on cooperation rather than exploitation. Chris Hedges believes this foundational shift will be as necessary for our survival "as changing our patterns of consumption, growing food locally and ending our dependence on fossil fuels."[20] Scholar and social activist Riane Eisler recognizes this revision as a return to a partnership model rather than a dominator one. Anthropologist Victor Turner uses the term *communitas,* "community," or what he calls human kindness; he sees this force as the "essential and generic human bond, without which there could be no society."[21]

Lest one think such notions are pie-in-the-sky utopian illusions, new studies by scientists have shown that cooperation, not competition, made the survival of the human species possible. Unfortunately, a complete misreading of evolutionist Charles Darwin by nineteenth-century industrialists led to a rapacious social code of "survival of the fittest" and has justified a concentration of wealth in the hands of an elite few. Darwin's 1871 book *The Descent of Man* actually argues that "those communities which included the greatest number of the most sympathetic members would flourish best, and rear the greatest number of offspring."[22] Darwin also pointed out that "the social instincts lead an animal to take pleasure in the society of its fellows, to feel a certain amount of sympathy with them, and to perform various services for them."[23]

In the essay "Survival of the . . . Nicest?" historian of science Eric Michael Johnson reports on peer-reviewed research by psychologist Michael Tomasello, co-director of the Max Planck Institute for Evolutionary Anthropology. Synthesizing three decades of research, Tomasello has developed a comprehensive evolutionary theory based on human cooperation. Tracking the effect of climate change on food supplies in the African savannahs, Tomasello concludes, "Individuals now had to coordinate their behaviors, work together, and learn how to share."[24] Calling contemporary corporate financial structures out of sync with our evolutionary roots, Tomasello fears such practices "may not be good for our long-term success as humans," and he too calls for a "return to the collaborative environments that the human species has long called home."[25] We need to cultivate what social thinker Jeremy Rifkin calls the emerging "empathic civilization" to avert planetary breakdown.[26]

To those who question such findings, one might ask, when looking at our deteriorating ecosystem and worldwide economic system in collapse, how has this exploitative social structure been working out for the health of the planet and the well-being of its inhabitants? This is why we need the image of the Goddess now. The war on nature began as a war on the feminine, and it continues to this day. In the West, the lineage that generated figures such as the Sheela na gig originated from older traditional cultures that celebrated the ever-present cycles of nature in all its light and dark aspects: creation and destruction and renewal. The spiral dance of life belies the myth of linear progress from maternal to paternal domination and the necessity of andro-cratic culture. This inaccurate view of prehistory was first put forth by unin-formed nineteenth-century thinkers with a limited knowledge of the past, along with a decided patriarchal bias.

Founder of the Institute of Archaeomythology Joan Marler, in an essay on the beginnings of patriarchy in Europe, gives an incisive overview of that problematic scholarship. Works like *Ancient Law* (1861) by Sir Henry Maine or *The Origin of Civilization and the Primitive Condition of Man* (1870) by John Lubbock describe the "male rule within the patriarchal family as the pinnacle of civilized evolution, elevated from the *natural* (associated with women and indigenous societies)," which are thought of as primitive and savage.[27] This notion of cultural evolution was upheld in the influential 1861 work of anthropologist Johann Jakob Bachofen, *Mother Right*.[28] Such theories were expanded in the twentieth century by the prominent archae-ologist V. Gordon Childe in *Social Evolution* (1951), in which he considers Paleolithic and Neolithic cultures barbaric.[29] In essence, male dominance is thought to be the basis of human society and the origin story of Western civilization.

But what is a civilization? Marija Gimbutas writes movingly in the pref-ace of *Civilization of the Goddess,* one of her last great works: "I reject the assumption that civilization refers only to androcratic warrior societies. The generative basis of any civilization lies in its degree of artistic creation, aes-thetic achievements, nonmaterial values, and freedom which make life mean-ingful and enjoyable for all its citizens, as well as a balance of power between the sexes."[30] It is no secret that we now live in a patriarchy, but it was not always so. Thanks to Gimbutas's foundational work, we see the evidence of the refined culture of Old Europe that flourished between 6500 and 3500 BCE and in Crete until 1450 BCE. Its way of life was based not on domination but on attunement with the creative energies of nature imagined as the body of the Great Goddess. As seen in the numerous goddess figurines and vulvas carved on cave walls dating back over thirty thousand years, this flowering of religious symbolism was part of an uninterrupted imagery from the Upper Paleolithic.

Given the entrenched patriarchal mindset of our current world, Gimbutas points out that archaeologists and historians "have assumed civilization implies a hierarchal political and religious structure, warfare, a class stratification and a complex division of labor. This pattern is indeed typical of androcratic (male dominated) societies" but not true of the societies that preceded them.[31] The peaceful civilization of Old Europe was destroyed by successive waves of invasions by Kurgan nomadic pastoralists from north of the Black Sea steppes. With its patriarchal social system, the Kurgan assault on Old Europe introduced new beliefs and behaviors such as a hierarchical social structure, weapons, worship of sky gods, bride stealing, cattle raiding, heroism in combat with a dagger-wielding warrior elite, and the worship of male warrior gods.[32]

By no stretch of the imagination can this overthrow of one culture by another be seen as progress from a primitive society to a more advanced one. Compared to a brutal warrior culture where women were subservient, Old Europe took pleasure in a higher quality of life, one of uninterrupted peace. Gimbutas describes this civilization as having created "towns with a considerable concentration of population, temples several stories high, a sacred script, spacious houses of four or five rooms, professional ceramicists, weavers, copper and gold metallurgists, and other artisans producing a range of sophisticated goods. A flourishing network of trade routes existed that circulated items such as obsidian, shells, marble, copper, and salt over hundreds of kilometers."[33] The violent, patriarchal Indo-European society did not evolve out of the matrilineal, egalitarian, artistic culture of Old Europe but rather did its best to destroy it. The spread of this dominator model was not an advance but a catastrophe, which we endure to this day.

The legacy of Old Europe tells us something very liberating to know: war is not at the root of human culture. No Paleolithic cave painting portrays any use of weapons against other humans, nor can the remains of any such weapons be found in Old Europe or in the Indus Valley.[34] Of the nearly 150 paintings that still exist in the temples at Çatal Hüyük in Neolithic Anatolia, not a single one depicts any scenes of conflict or fighting, war or torture.[35] Furthermore, in Old Europe the evidence of cemetery grave goods shows no subservience between the sexes but rather "a condition of mutual respect."[36] Archaeologist Krum Bacvarov of the National Institute of Archaeology in Bulgaria found that "there are few grave goods in early Southeast European and Anatolian Neolithic burials—no exceptionally rich graves which would indicate an unequal distribution of wealth."[37] Thus such burials show no evidence of hierarchy.

Scholars of the divine feminine Anne Baring and Jules Cashford, in their monumental *Myth of the Goddess: Evolution of an Image,* note the consequences of changing cosmologies. The moral order of the Goddess was focused on the epiphanies of human, animal, and plant life manifesting from the unmanifest (the Goddess as source of all), whereas the moral order of the patriarchal culture was based on "the paradigm of opposition and conquest," with nature as something "other" to be conquered.[38] The worldwide expansion of patriarchy over the millennia has nothing to do with a superiority of culture in ideas or artistic expression or spiritual content or human relations, but rather focused on a superiority of physical force. As a founder of the field known as modern matriarchal studies, Heide Göttner-Abendroth points out in "Notes on the Rise and Development of Patriarchy" that this hierarchal social structure based on domination and the ceaseless search for enemies "constantly creates chaos like wars, conquests, oppression, revolutions, and civil conflicts, all of which have been laboriously choreographed by the rulers of their day. In its relatively short history, patriarchy has proved to be extremely turbulent and unstable, as shown by quickly changing 'world empires' with their high consumption of human lives."[39] Here in America, we need only look at our recent past, to the fate of the native peoples of this continent, to see such destruction; or we can just look back at the twentieth century—a century, as the poet Sylvia Plath put it, of "wars, wars, wars."[40]

Yet it is not just brute force that acts as an anchor for oppressive cultures, but also the use of the power of images. Cosmological images can legitimize political systems. Different cultures use the imagination, but in service of what? What energy animates the sacred images? A dour war god or a great Creatrix? In her work as an anthropologist, Peggy Reeves Sanday has found that images create cosmological orders that can act as the ultimate authority in societies. She believes that to understand the spiritual and social forces that shape a culture, certain questions must be asked: "Which sex is imbued (naturally or socially) with the reproductive powers that recharge the sources of supernatural fecundity? What is the gender of the dominant symbols tying the archetypal to the social?"[41]

In our modern Western world, God the Father now rules as Creator of the universe, usurping the much older image of the body of the Goddess as the source of all. It is not simply a question of exchanging one image for another. Each symbol radiates the contrasting values of different worlds that are either living in partnership or striving for domination. Symbols shape reality and structure experience through differing concepts of what it means to be human.[42] The cosmological foundation of patriarchy is reflected in seventeenth-century philosopher Thomas Hobbes's view of the human condition: "a warre of every man against every man."[43] Pioneering feminist scholar Carol P. Christ captures the essence of patriarchy in her definition of it as "a system of male dominance, rooted in the ethos of war which legitimates violence, sanctified by religious symbols."[44]

Many images of male warrior gods from the Bronze Age forward have served to reinforce this violent system. The new, young, warrior-heroes-gods (Zeus, Marduk, Baal, Indra, Yahweh, and Horus, to name but a few) often murder the earlier "chaotic" goddesses in their forms as dragons or serpents in order to kill off "the old order of deities."[45] Such mythological actions are mirrored in the precepts of ancient Greek philosopher Pythagoras when he writes, "There is a good principle that created order, light and man and a bad principle that created chaos, darkness and woman."[46] Thus women, symbolizing the chaos of sex and nature, must be subdued. The brutal consequences of this misogyny reached a grim apotheosis in the medieval witch burnings that lasted into the eighteenth century. The *Malleus Maleficarum* (Hammer of the Evil-Doing Women), a fifteenth-century handbook on how to torture women to death, stated: "All witchcraft stems from carnal lust, which in women is insatiable."[47]

Feminist philosopher Simone de Beauvoir's revolutionary book *The Second Sex*, banned by the Vatican when published in 1949, comments on the privilege patriarchal religion bestows on males while it denigrates women:

"For the Jew, Mohammedans, and Christians, among others, man is Master by divine right; the fear of God will therefore repress any impulse to revolt in the downtrodden female."[48] Images of gods that reflect the "divine right" of male superiority lead to laws and customs that sanction men to control the sexuality of their wives (often to ensure male heirs). What fundamentalist religion does not have as its basis the desire to have power over women's bodies and a fear of women's sexuality as something dark, overpowering, evil? In June 2013, a multicountry analysis published in *Scientific American* reported that violence against women is at epidemic proportions.[49]

The current war on women's reproductive rights is nothing new, nor is the worldwide sex-slave trade and the continuing lack of gender and social equality. Former U.S. president Jimmy Carter has said without equivocation that violence against women and girls is the most serious and unaddressed violation of human rights on earth. He calls attention to catastrophic injustices through his work at the Carter Center, in his book *A Call to Action: Women, Religion, Violence and Power,* and in a recent TED talk, "Why I Believe the Mistreatment of Women Is the Number One Human Rights Abuse." In parts of the world to this day women are being tortured, beheaded, burned as witches, and stoned to death for infidelity. With the unconscious assumption that male is universal, an assumption that taints the interpretation of symbols, is it any surprise that the power of the female sex inspires so much fear?[50]

The Urgency of
the Return to the Goddess

In her influential essay "Why Women Need the Goddess," Carol P. Christ makes it clear why we need a change of religious symbols by reclaiming the image of the Goddess. This is because, as she points out, "a symbol's effect does not depend on rational assent"; it can socialize us without our conscious awareness and even against our own interests.[51]

Accordingly, such images can cause us to live with oppressive political structures that are upheld by the prevailing symbol system of the culture. We need an image of the divine as female to empower women and to re-sacralize nature, so that all humans may find their rightful place in the circle of life. In strong contrast to the beliefs of Western religion and culture's image of the weak female dependent on males, Carol Christ sees "the simplest and most basic meaning of the symbol of Goddess is the acknowledgment of the legitimacy of female power as a beneficent and independent power."[52]

Looking at a twenty-first-century culture that has just such a symbol of the Divine Mother at its cosmological center, one can see the effects this image has on the women and men of that society. Peggy Reeves Sanday's book *Women at the Center: Life in a Modern Matriarchy* gives a vivid account of her two decades of fieldwork with the Minangkabau of West Sumatra, the largest and most firmly established matrilineal society in the world today. The spiritual center and the ultimate authority of the culture rests in the archetypal figure of Bundo Kanduang, the mythical Queen Mother of the Minangkabau (see figure 12.1). She integrates all members of different clans under the ancient tradition of *adat matriarchaat* or *adat ibu*—women's customary law.[53] Women elders, when performing life-cycle ceremonies, carry the title of Bundo Kanduang, which also carries the meaning "our own mother" of each clan and one's own biological mother. Matrilineal descent has the status of divine law. The cosmological order is based on female-oriented symbols and places senior women, along with their brothers, at the center of "social, emotional, aesthetic, political, and economic" daily life.[54]

The unifying image of Bundo Kanduang gives the Minangkabau a common commitment to their women's customary law, which is grounded in maternal values of nurturance and generosity. In terms of gender relations, women and men are not ranked but linked, connected in partnership rather than domination.[55] The social structure of this matriarchy is not the reverse of patriarchy, which is based on violence and political control, but has as its foundation the archetypal image of the Great Mother. From this foundation rises the sovereignty of women as mothers and elders to conjugate—"to knit and regenerate social ties in the here-and-now and in the hereafter."[56] Sanday reclaims the word *matriarchy* as meaning not women ruling over men but "mothers from the beginning," based on the etymology of the Greek root *arche* as "beginning," "origin," "source."[57]

The Minangkabau are not a tribe existing in isolation and therefore

Figure 12.1. Bundo Kanduang. Her image unifies the world's largest matriarchy. *(Photograph courtesy of Michael J. Lowe)*

able to preserve their ancient customs; they live very much in our modern times, with schools, banks, business acumen, and satellite dishes connecting them to the outside world. Nor is this a utopia free from the sorrows of loss inherent in being alive or the conflicts that arise in human relationships. The Minangkabau take pride in their love of diversity. Differences of opinion are accepted, and through a lengthy process of discussion in village councils consensus is negotiated. Because of its ethos of maintaining peaceful relations through politesse and consideration for the feelings of others, "wielding power by using force or adopting an attitude of dominance by either men or women" would be antithetical to the adat matriarchaat.[58] The Minangkabau have safeguarded their culture by recognizing the tension between power (*kuasa*) and good relations (*tali budi*) and balancing them through their female-centered customs that emphasize the accommodation of differences.[59] By holding to their values, the Minangkabau have also survived the external forces of usurpation by foreign kings and the proselytizing wave of Islam with their women's customary law intact.

In the West we have come to accept male aggression as based in biology and as natural as male hegemony rather than understanding the effects of social conditioning. Under such constraints of subjugation women have endured much suffering. However, in the Minangkabau culture, rooted in a respect for the feminine with the image of Bundo Kanduang at the center of their spiritual and daily life, there is little or no violence toward women. Sanday, during her many stays in West Sumatra, was "unable to identify a single case of rape" among the Minangkabau.[60] When the anthropologist asked why this was so, informants told her that "whatever the biological basis of male sexual aggression might be, Minangkabau customs overrode such tendencies."[61] This is the power of images to shape human behavior for better or worse through their influence on custom, law, and religion. In her essay "Trapped in a Metaphor," Sanday points out that our patriarchal culture often justifies male aggression as just basic instincts, but what interests her is the "ways in which metaphors trap people in a self-absorbed cycle of violence or free them to work for the common good."[62]

For example, the energy behind the Minangkabau symbol of Bundo Kanduang cultivates in men qualities of kindheartedness and compassion. What is often called the Minangkabau "state myth" tells the story of how the Queen Mother, as the source of wisdom and center of the universe, educates her son in the way of the adat so as to bring him "under its civilizing influence."[63] The power of male aggression is subdued by the moral authority of the divine queen. Sanday, in her fieldwork, was "struck by the degree to which Minangkabau men freely show vulnerability and emotional dependence. Young men often walk hand-in-hand in public places, physically demonstrating their mutual feelings for one another."[64] These men channel aggression not in feats of physical bravado as in the West, but through its diffusion "in feats of magical, religious ecstasy or it is worked out through endless verbal discussion and negotiation within the village council" of male clan leaders.[65]

Human beings are not just biologically programmed animals. Symbols create a cultural environment that shapes the quality of our response to our instincts. Images inform moral values and can show us that we are not always at the mercy of reactive drives that erupt into behavior—we also possess a miraculous capacity for choice. As Sanday emphasizes, it is through the recognition of choice "that we can hope for change in our own society."[66]

Another book that provides hope for a different world is *Societies of Peace: Matriarchies Past, Present, and Future,* edited by Heide Göttner-Abendroth. This collection of papers from two world congresses on modern matriarchal studies provides evidence from archaeology, anthropology, philosophy, and sociology to document cultures around the world that still follow matriarchal customs in part or whole (and exposing once again the false myth of the universality of patriarchy). From the Iroquoian model of woman power to the Masuo people on Lugu Lake in the Himalayas, the Shipibo people of the Upper Amazon, and the Asante of West Africa, scholars investigate gender-egalitarian societies from the past to the present. The work also offers a sorely needed model of more peaceful societies based on matriarchal social and spiritual practices by which men as well as women can thrive.

Another community based on matriarchal principles exists in present-day Colombia. Nashira is an ecovillage located in the Cauca River Valley, on the very land where two thousand years ago the Malagana culture flowered with its worship of an Earth Mother figure and many female deities.[67] On this site, low-income Colombian women are creating a better quality of life for themselves and their families through housing, farming, and communal markets. Angela Dolmetsch, one of the founding mothers of Nashira, calls it a work in progress, "where generosity, solidarity, respect for the environment and maternal values are creating a happy and sustainable community. It is a social experiment, which as it expands, could change the world."[68]

The catastrophic degradation of Mother Earth, savage economic inequalities, and the sheer human misery rising from perpetual wars point to the unsustainable destructiveness of the patriarchal system. Hierarchal power relations cement its violence, a violence that pushes us closer to the edge of extinction. The matriarchal principles of respect for difference, taking care of those in need, and reverence for the web of life are just the antidote to the alienation of these fractured times. When the whole world is the offspring of the womb of the Great Mother, everything is sacred, not made for exploitation. With such a cosmological center, everything is in relationship.

Looking at our own Western heritage, it is important to realize that the images of the Goddess from Old Europe were not entirely done away with by the invasions of androcratic warrior cultures—that even through patriarchal times the energy of the Goddess did not completely die out but went underground. After all, in Europe she reigned throughout the Paleolithic and Neolithic and most of the Bronze Age in Mediterranean Europe.[69] Her great epoch lasted for tens of thousands of years, a much greater time than the comparatively brief history of the Christian era. She has been the most enduring image in the archaeological record of the ancient world.[70] Despite the demonization of her regenerative powers, the Goddess lives on in our blood memories as an indelible imprint on the Western psyche. Even with the forces of domination, the spirit of partnership persists, without which human society cannot exist. Nor can we exist without nature. Marija Gimbutas offers a lyrical description of the living Goddess in twentieth-century Lithuania, her native land: "There still flow sacred and miraculous rivers and springs, there flourish holy forests and groves, reservoirs of blossoming life, there grow gnarled trees brimming with vitality and holding the power to heal; along waters there still stand menhirs, called 'Goddesses,' full of mysterious power."[71] Gimbutas asserts that images and symbols carrying the energies of the Goddess "could have disappeared only with the total extermination of the female population."[72]

Our natural heritage of a deep-rooted gynocentric past still survives in societies like the Minangkabau and in the depths of the psyche, that storehouse for memories of human experience. Rising up from the layers of the imagination, the Goddess reappears in the conscious minds of women and men. Over thirty years ago, Carol Christ commented on this phenomenon: "The Goddess symbol has emerged spontaneously in the dreams, fantasies, and thoughts of many women in the past several years."[73] And in the last half of the twentieth century, accompanying the second wave of feminism, the women's spirituality movement began, and multifaceted images of the feminine principle entered contemporary culture.

Little wonder that she has returned, given the current conditions of the war on women, the war on nature, and the war on the imagination. It is as if the dire needs of our times have called her back, as if she has returned for us to look beyond the outworn images of patriarchy to restore balance to our world so out-of-balance. Joseph Campbell, in his foreword to Marija Gimbutas's *The Language of the Goddess,* also sees the necessity for a reemergence of the divine feminine: "One cannot help but feel that in the appearance of this volume at just this turn of the century there is evident relevance to the universally recognized need in our time for a general transformation of consciousness."[74] As Riane Eisler notes in her cultural transformation theory, there is a possibility now, despite resistance, for a paradigm shift from our systems of disequilibrium to the direction of a partnership model.[75]

Jungian analyst Betty De Shong Meador, in "Ripe Time: An Inquiry into Gimbutas' Appeal," believes that the constellation of images of the Goddess rising out of the unconscious psyche is an idea whose time has come.[76] While feminism fought for equality for women in the outer playing fields of daily work and relationships, symbols of the Goddess give us what we have lacked for millennia—an inner representation of female divinities that celebrates our bodies, our sexuality, and our creativity. Meador sees that the great urge felt by a diverse mix of people to bring back the rejected feminine, to bring back a sacred being in the body of a female, has "reached a critical mass and spilled out into the collective consciousness."[77] For Gimbutas, the cyclical nature of reality has brought the Goddess back, giving us hope for the future by "returning us to our most ancient human roots."[78]

13
The Secret
of the Sheelas

The Sheela na gig is a manifestation of the Dark Goddess, and the modern florescence of the figure shows her to be part of the spirit of our times. Her image gives us what we need. She alone has dominion over her female body, which she displays in such a fearless manner. She embodies the wholeness of nature in its creative and destructive forces, with her open vulva—the portal of life as well as an image of return in death, ripeness centered in the dry body of a crone. The figure arises from the deepest parts of the imagination; no woman who walked the earth ever looked like a Sheela na gig.

As an image of a supernatural female, the Sheela reclaims the sacred powers of the feminine to give life and to take it back again for regeneration into a new form. Originally, it appears that those artists and country folk who placed her on churches and castles thought that she could protect life and guard against evil forces. Barren women rubbed her tumescent vulva for fertility magic, and pregnant women turned to her in their hour of need. Belief in her healing powers survives to this day. Later, even when patriarchal zealots tried to destroy the figures, she could not be done away with. The primal energies animating her image could not, cannot, be annihilated. Many Sheelas still survive intact upon their stone walls.

The Return of the Sheela

Maureen Concannon, in her book *The Sacred Whore: Sheela Goddess of the Celts,* makes the case for the psychological significance of the Sheela. As a symbol, she has reappeared in Western consciousness as a "signal that the human psyche is responding" to an urgent need to restore the repressed feminine.[1] As a transformative archetype of sex, birth, and death, three of the most powerful experiences of life, yet "loaded with taboos during the patriarchal period," the autonomous Sheela can serve to bring back the balance in our time.[2] Concannon also makes the telling observation that recently more and more Sheelas are being discovered, "appearing, as if miraculously, at ancient sites and on medieval buildings."[3] Our awareness has awakened, come alive to their presence; we see what we could not see before.

In the 1960s and 1970s, with the great social upheaval of the multifaceted women's movement, curiosity about the Sheelas blossomed. In 1977, art student Jørgen Andersen's dissertation on the medieval architectural figure became the first book entirely devoted to the Sheela na gig—*The Witch on the Wall.* This work helped to inaugurate the present-day return of the Sheela. Even though no longer rendered in stone and placed on sacred and secular architecture, the Sheela image in our time is reborn through contemporary artists in music, poems, paintings, sculptures, and tapestries, and by scholars in essays, books, and websites. More people are visiting the actual, in situ Sheelas themselves thanks to the expanded catalog of known Sheelas in Jack Roberts and Joanne McMahon's 2000 book *Sheela-na-Gigs of Ireland and Britain: The Divine Hag of the Christian Celts—An Illustrated Guide.* An updated catalog of known Sheelas can also be found in Barbara Freitag's 2004 book *Sheela-na-gigs: Unravelling an Enigma.* These resources make it much easier to find the surviving Sheelas than it was years ago when this writer had to rely on Andersen's 1977 update of Edith Guest's 1935 less-than-precise directions. And because of the growing fascination with the figure, as mentioned above, previously unknown Sheelas continue to be discovered on architectural sites in Ireland and Great Britain. In the last decades, the Sheela na gig has become a cultural phenomenon, with a bookstore in Galway, Ireland, named after her; an Irish Sheela na gig comedienne, Jeanne Rathbone; and an English rock band Sheelnagig—never mind her replication in jewelry, T-shirts, and small plaques found in shops throughout Ireland and England.

The Emergence of
the Feminist Sacred Art

Individual artists, the bearers of the new in any age, have experienced a new theme emerging in their work—the Goddess. In an era that seems bent on destroying the natural world, here comes the symbol par excellence of the power and soul of nature. This visionary impulse has disrupted the previously dominant views of history and art, which have denied the contributions of women. The rebirth of the Sheela na gig as a fitting subject for contemporary artists is part of this new story, one based on the female body but no longer a passive, fetishized object of male desire. Artist and educator Faith Wilding speaks to why there are so many vulvas in the work of feminist artists: "We are inventing a new form of language radiating a female power which cannot be conveyed in any other way at this time."[4]

Perhaps the most famous artistic expression of this aspect of the spirit of the women's movement is Judy Chicago's *The Dinner Party,* a communal celebration of female artistic expression and achievement. First exhibited in 1979 at the San Francisco Museum of Modern Art, *The Dinner Party* has been permanently housed at the Brooklyn Museum since 2007. Chicago created her masterpiece because the "general lack of knowledge of our heritage as women was pivotal in our continued suppression."[5] The center of *The Dinner Party* is an immense ceremonial table in the shape of an open triangle, a symbol of equality and, from Paleolithic times, the symbol of the feminine. Arranged with thirty-nine elaborate place settings for notable women in history going back to the goddesses of prehistoric times, each place has a ceramic plate with a petal-like design of a vulva in open display. Yet every design is singular so as to invite the spirit of the individual guest.

Women have lined up to see Chicago's monumental work, which was described by the *Village Voice* as the "first epic feminist artwork."[6] However, upon being first exhibited in 1979 it was controversial to say the least. Conservative (male) members of Congress castigated this celebration of female power as "weird sexual art"; Congressman Robert K. Dornan derided it as "ceramic 3-D pornography."[7] *The Dinner Party* also challenged the canon of patriarchal modernism and the invented forms and themes of "male genius" previously held as a universal standard. Modernist art critics, threatened, considered Chicago's work to be domestic kitsch, as it used "women's crafts" such as embroidery and china painting. Postmodern feminists claimed the artwork reduced women to a passive role and locked them into an essentialism (biology determines destiny) much as patriarchy had done. Such an analysis narrows the dynamic energies of the multivalent vulva and misunderstands the vivifying effects of uncovering the suppressed history of the Great Goddess. The quintessential point is that for many artists, the muse is back.

The work of another pioneer of this revolution in art, Mary Beth Edelson, employs wit, exuberance, and the female body to create her vision of a transformed world. Since the early 1970s, through a wide range of mediums, Edelson has questioned entrenched male-dominated dogma about what are suitable subjects for art. As an artist she says she has used her body as a "construction site" to redefine fixed cultural norms that limit female identity, to restore "a living mythology that cuts across many areas—political and spiritual."[8] To that end, Edelson's art has given us new images of femaleness, often through collages overlaying the bodies of contemporary women with ancient figures like Medusa, Baubo, and the Sheela na gig—all sisters in a lineage rooted in the power of their female sex. Referring to the impact of the return of the Goddess in her own work, Edelson writes of the symbols encompassing multiple forms of the divine feminine: "Reaching across the centuries we take the hands of our Ancient Sisters. The Great Goddess alive and well is rising to announce to the patriarchs that their 5,000 years are up—Hallelujah! Here we come."[9]

Nothing better embodies Edelson's visual dialogue between her body and the Goddess than a series of photographs taken during ritual performances. She later drew over the photographs to construct symbolic images that reclaim a forgotten heritage as well as create a contemporary aesthetic.[10] Priestess and Goddess meet in the artist's body. In her work *Rites of Passage* (see figure 13.1), it is as if a modern Sheela with a Medusa head radiating snakes of flame has come down off her wall to part her legs once again amid the stones. Through sexuality and spirituality, fire and stone, the artist renews herself, channeling the Sheela-like energies of destruction and

creation. Edelson knows firsthand the cost of such transformation: "How many twists and turns this Goddess odyssey has taken over the years—and how utterly unforeseeable were the punishing and ecstatic events that knowing Her brought my way."[11]

One of Edelson's great art-making gifts is her sense of fun. What a relief to experience the lightness of humor, so effective in penetrating the viewer's consciousness. Here Edelson directly uses the Sheela figure in another of her themes, the trickster archetype whose power of wit can upend entrenched

Figure 13.1. *Rites of Passage,* drawing on photograph, part of Woman Rising/Sexual Energies series; Mary Beth Edelson, 1975. *(Courtesy of the artist)*

285

The Secret of the Sheelas

realities. In many of her pieces, the artist makes the most of the playful qualities of that most recognizable of Sheelas, the Kilpeck (figure 2.5), with her impish expression and mesmerizing vulva. *Sheela of the Tree* shows a Sheela with a face-splitting grin cleverly utilizing a hole in the trunk for her self-exposure in a blend of nature and art (see figure 13.2). What mischief might she be brewing?

As the archetypal Fool, Sheela of the Tree can expose subversive truths but still keep her head. The Sheela's shameless display of her sex disrupts social assumptions about female identity. Edelson's use of the Sheela image shatters patriarchal claims about the natural processes of reality by exposing that so-called reality as an ideology mediated by the dominate culture.[12] As the title of one of Edelson's exhibitions drolly observes, "There Is Never Only One Game in Town." For the artist, the construct of the Goddess "offered a

Figure 13.2. *Sheela of the Tree,* bronze, 16 x 14 x 6 inches; Mary Beth Edelson, 1982. She has a large vulva of empty space and a tongue à la Medusa and Kālī; her eyes are wide open to delight. *(Courtesy of the artist)*

framework for dismantling the master's house with women's tools."[13] Or as she expands the point in her own inimitable way: "The master's tools will never dismantle the master's house. To which I say: Let's get some other tools! Fuck his house—who goes there anyway?"[14]

The artist intuitively aligns the Sheela with another disruptive merry prankster of the vulva, Baubo. In classical times Baubo's body could be a visual pun of the face as vulva, and through the laughter caused by her bawdy raising of her skirt she revives the dead world. Edelson connects the Sheela and Baubo as sisters of display in layered drawings, collages, watercolors, and paintings (see figure 13.3). In *Sheela Surprises Her Groom,* the Sheela's head tilts in a deceptively submissive gesture because beneath the bridal veil stands Baubo—a sexual surprise indeed for the patriarchy (see figure 13.4). In "Humor and Masquerade: The Transformative Art of Mary Beth Edelson," art critic Alissa Rame Friedman writes that the hybrid figures of Sheela/Baubo illustrate that the female body can create a meaning of its own to challenge "contemporary stereotypes regarding the 'essential' nature of woman."[15]

In *Sheela/Buffie Johnson* (see figure 13.5), Edelson brings the powers of the Sheela na gig into the present by reconstructing her supernatural body out of the faces of contemporary women artists—Buffie Johnson, Michelle Stuart, Betye Saar, and Yoko Ono. Edelson holds these women to be sisters on the wild path of creative expression. With them, she is developing a brand-new culture from "our shiny new consciousness, and our eager hearts and excited minds."[16] Out of the oldest source comes the new. All smile and laugh except the solemn Yoko Ono, who sings into a microphone, the image doubling as the Sheela's labia. In contrast to patriarchal religious hegemony, here the women have direct access to the divine; they *are* the divine. For Edelson, throwing off "the baggage of centuries of sexist and fossilized theology" allowed her to awaken to the greater self, now imagined as sacred femaleness.[17] This sense of an electrifying freedom is found in her statement for women: "I am, and I am large, and I am my body, and I am not going away."[18]

Prominent radical artist Nancy Spero also uses the Sheela na gig as a signature icon in her art. She says the primary focus of her art became "to see

Figure 13.3. *Life Savers,* painting on canvas, 8 x 6 feet; Mary Beth Edelson, 1989. Against a backdrop of chevrons, the ancient symbol of the Goddess, Baubo stands on the solid foundation of a Sheela, whose display is shaped like a life preserver. Another life preserver hangs above it all with the word *Tricksters. (Courtesy of the artist)*

SHEELA SURPRISES HER GROOM

Figure 13.4. *Sheela Surprises Her Groom,* transfer, watercolor, ink, 12 x 10 inches; Mary Beth Edelson, 1974. A blending of the two figures of the Sheela and Baubo, who gaze in opposite directions, with Baubo's hair ribbons acting as a bustier and Sheela's hands grabbing Baubo's coiffure as if lifting a skirt. *(Courtesy of the artist)*

Figure 13.5. *Sheela/Buffie Johnson,* collage; Mary Beth Edelson, 1976. Her torso is a body of eyes with an intent female gaze. *(Courtesy of the artist)*

what it means to view the world through the depiction of women," not a male idea of a woman's body, but woman-as-protagonist in charge of her own fate.[19] Well known for her epic scrolls made of long, continuous sheets of paper (early in her career Spero repudiated oil painting on canvas as too masculine a medium), she created an ensemble of female figures who run, tumble, and dance exuberantly across the panels, or who just remain still. Her artwork constructs a timeless simultaneity of images drawn from Paleolithic cave art and Greek, Egyptian, Indian, and pagan goddesses, as well as from art history and contemporary media. Described as the "High Priestess of Hieroglyphics," Spero calls herself omnivorous in her repertoire of characters but admits nevertheless that the Sheela is one of her "star" figures that she uses "over and over."[20]

Indeed, so incessant was the mysterious energy of the Sheela figure that the artist claims she "couldn't get rid of her in my mind."[21] In one of her paper scrolls titled *Propitiatory,* Spero juxtaposes diverse figures like Artemis, a modern athlete, a Sumerian goddess, the Egyptian sky goddess Nut, Australian rock-art dancers, and repeated images of the Cavan and Burgesbeg Sheela na gigs. Is this singular creation an act of propitiation by the artist that these energies may vivify our present-day consciousness? Spero often returns to that most visually striking figure in her repertoire, the Kilpeck Sheela, used in such pieces as *Coffee Table Sheela, Sheela and the Dildo Dancer, Sheela Dancing, Sheela Totem I, Sheela Na Gig at Home* (see figure 13.6), and *Chorus Line. Chorus Line* is a witty piece showing nine identical Sheelas (nine muses?) linked arm-in-arm in a colorful row of display. How the self-delight portrayed there lifts one's spirits! In *Sheela & Wilma,* the Kilpeck Sheela is alternately aligned with a dancing figure from a Saharan cave painting who is skeletal yet bears unborn babies curled inside her body.[22] Thus the medieval Sheela is coupled back to an ancient African figure who also carries the energies of death and life.

Jeremy Strick, director of the Museum of Contemporary Art in Los

Figure 13.6. *Sheela Na Gig at Home,* handprinting on paper, underwear, clothesline, clothespins, video; Nancy Spero, 1996. What is a supernatural female doing in the quotidian setting of women's work, the wash hung out to dry on a clothesline? Can one domesticate a goddess? *(© The Estate of Nancy Spero, licensed by VAGA, New York)*

Angeles, calls feminist art "the most influential international movement of any during the postwar period."[23] At the heart of this body of work is a genre of goddess art that draws from the iconography of powerful female forms found in ancient matristic cultures. Jenny Klein, professor of gender studies and art history, calls it a fact that feminist spirituality "was the single most important idea to inform the radical politics of a number of artists working in the 70s."[24] She salutes the bravery of the women artists who through their creation of insurgent images "were willing to risk everything in order to challenge the injustice of a male-dominated system."[25]

Against the cultural feminism that emphasized the value of female connections and a spiritual embrace of the Goddess,[26] in the 1980s a backlash emerged from the "third wave" of feminism, which was based on postmodernist or poststructuralist theories that social identity is constructed through language and semiotics. These critics stressed the necessity of academic discourse over personal experience and assailed feminist sacred art as naive despite the depth of archaeological evidence revealing the legacy of the Great Goddess reaching back to prehistory. Then these critics alleged the worst crime of all: essentialism. They said that art based on the female body trapped women in a biological determinism of innate femaleness. The fear was that women, as in the old, malefic trope, will once more be defined as nature and body, while only men possess the quality of mind to create culture. Finally, theory-driven feminists dismissed this art as simply a reversal of roles: "Instead of the male supremacy of patriarchal culture, the female (the essential female) is elevated to primary status."[27]

This is a failure not only of analysis but of imagination. It betrays an ignorance of the vast functions of the Goddess that lie beyond motherhood, and an inability to see beyond hierarchical structures. For contemporary artists, a return to the Goddess acknowledges the energies of her sacred body as the creatrix of nature, culture, and cosmos, concomitant with the powers of destruction and the spiral dance of renewal. When these artists use the female body of the Sheela na gig, which is rooted in primal forces, the resulting images are meant to shatter social patterns of sexism—not to confine but to break free of rigid gender roles. The problem is domination, as research activist Max Dashú points out in "Essentialism or Essence? Out from the

Land of Theory." She writes that the so-called essentialism of the gendered symbolism found in Goddess art is not about biology but a "transformative reclamation" given the "long history of deprecating the body—especially the female body."[28] In the 1977 inaugural issue of *Chrysalis*: *A Magazine of Women's Culture,* editors Mary Beth Edelson and Arlene Raven stated that the aim of this radical art was not "a retreat to an idyllic prehistory, but rather a projection of a post-patriarchal spiritual consciousness."[29] Through the power of images, women artists have used this past to envision an egalitarian future. Goddess art is not about the disastrous mistake of separating ourselves from nature but about experiencing anew the depth of our relation to the living world.

Contemporary artists continue to produce work grounded in a matriculture. During the spring of 2013, the Museum voor Moderne Kunst Arnhem in the Netherlands launched the exhibition Female Power: Matriarchy, Spirituality and Utopia, dedicated to the works of younger artists as well as second-wave feminists like Mary Beth Edelson, Nancy Spero, and Ana Mendieta. Like their activist predecessors, a new generation of women artists from around the globe are once again tapping into the visual strength of female spiritual traditions. Curator Mirjam Westen writes that their work inscribes women in history and art history so they may "never again be hidden away under the folds of time."[30]

Some works in the exhibit visit existing matriarchal communities, like Mathilde ter Heijne's *Export Matriarchy* (installation of a house from the matrilineal Mosuo people in China) and Cuny Janssen's *My Grandma Was a Turtle* (using photographs of the Turtle clan of the matriarchal Delaware tribe in Oklahoma). Pinaree Sanpitak focuses on the female form in *Anything Can Break,* consisting of hundreds of breast-shaped clouds covering an entire ceiling. In her other works Sanpitak abstracts the vulva in paintings, textile art, and even culinary performances. A review of her recent show at the Los Angeles County Museum of Art describes her work as placing "the female presence at the very core of the culture."[31]

The first comprehensive exhibition to assess the international foundations and legacy of feminist art, WACK! Art and the Feminist Revolution, opened in 2007 at the Museum of Contemporary Art in Los Angeles. (The exhibit later traveled to New York and Washington, D.C.) Holland Cotter, art critic for the *New York Times,* called the show "a thrill": "One thing is certain: Feminist art, which emerged in the 1960s with the women's movement, is the formative art of the last four decades. Scan the most innovative work, by both men and women, done during that time, and you'll find feminism's activist, expansionist, pluralistic trace."[32] One entered the exhibit as an initiation, with the presence of—what else?—a startling red vulva. The eponymous *Abakan Red* by Magdalena Abakanowicz is an enormous suspended sculpture of sisal weaving dyed a rich vermilion. With its ovoid shape and partable lips, one could pass through it to enter a mysterious interiority.

The motif of entering the portal by which life comes into this world was famously employed by Niki de Saint Phalle in her 1966 sculpture *She: A Cathedral* (see figure 13.7). Its title points to the enormity of the worlds

Figure 13.7. *She: A Cathedral;* Niki de Saint Phalle, 1966. After passing through her vagina, one encounters rooms such as an aquarium (uterus), a music room (stomach), and a milk bar (breast). *(Photograph by Hans Hammarskiöld; courtesy of Moderna Museet, Stockholm)*

contained within a female body. The huge installation (eighty feet long and thirty feet wide) consisted of a colorfully painted reclining woman with legs parted. Her vulva became the new entrance to the Moderne Museet in Stockholm. This work generated a large public reaction in magazines and newspapers throughout the world, prompting such questions as "Well, what IS a woman's place?" In 1988, artist and author Cristina Biaggi created architectural plans for *The Goddess Mound.* Her vision of a sacred site was inspired by Maltese and Scottish temples and tombs from the Neolithic period that symbolize the Great Goddess. This outdoor sculptural structure focuses on internal space; its design celebrates every woman's life-giving force (see figure 13.8).

Micol Hebron, a twenty-first-century interdisciplinary artist and professor of art, is not afraid to have her work focus on images of the female body or to have such work be called essentialism. In her work as an artist and a scholar, Hebron reclaims the term *essentialism* not with the pejorative

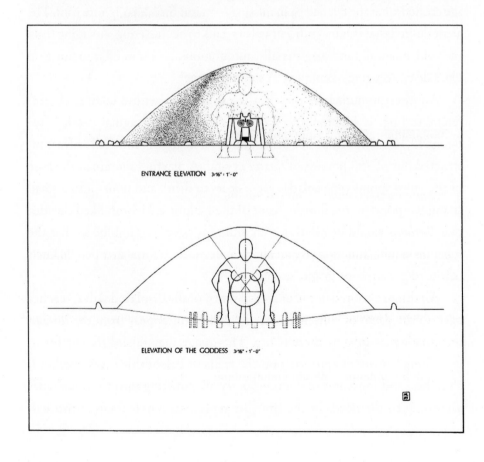

Figure 13.8. Drawing of *The Goddess Mound,* by Cristina Biaggi, 1988. (The exterior earth mound measures 25 feet high and 74 feet in diameter; the interior negative shape of the Goddess is 22 feet high and 14 feet wide.) Enter her sacred vulva and meet the Goddess! This space of dark mystery evokes prehistoric caves and the possibility of rebirth. *(Courtesy of the artist)*

anti-intellectual connotation given by post-structuralist theorists but in the liberating spirit of radical feminist art. In a world still dominated by patriarchal notions of power, she describes her work as creating alternative representations of the female body and anatomy. In 2010, to explore something different, something closer to her own bodily experience, she created a solo exhibition, titled Essential, consisting of five large-scale photographic artworks of vulvas as images of empowerment.

A more recent show, Sisterhood Is Powerful, at the Jancar Gallery in Los Angeles, consisted of portraits of female genitalia in various mediums such as glittery canvases and etched brasses. A striking ten-foot-tall photorealistic drawing of a vulva greeted people as they entered the gallery (see figure 13.9). The work is named *Judith*, after three dynamic females: artist Judy Chicago, scholar Judith Butler, and the mythical figure Judith who beheads invading general Holofernes. Hebron had wondered what her contemporary experience would be like if she saw vaginal forms as often as she saw phallic forms, so she created what she felt had been missing—an impossible-to-ignore yoni. The artist desired that this magnificent vulva seems to be "hovering, emerging from the void, magically and magisterially, autonomous. . . . I wanted it to function like a deity. A heroic monument. A sublime force."[33]

Another monumental yoni in the exhibit, but with a completely different feeling, is Hebron's *Barbara* or *The Vageode* (vaginal geode) (see figure 13.10). The sculptural installation is a nearly six-foot-tall vulva constructed out of 250 pounds of quartz crystal. A playful fountain at the base of the vulva spouts piña coladas for visitors to drink and pours into a small triangular pond on the floor in front of the sculpture. Hebron liked the idea that *Barbara* would be offering a life fluid for people to imbibe so that the vageode would "function like an altar, or an oracle, a form that people knelt before to get answers, magic, sustenance."[34]

All this art, rooted in the universal motif of the displayed vulva, reaches back to the dawn of consciousness and cannot disappear from the human imagination as long as there is life. The image may take different forms in its long history of appearing on the walls of Paleolithic caves, medieval churches, and museums of contemporary art. Shifting into various shapes according to the needs of the time, its representation is focused through

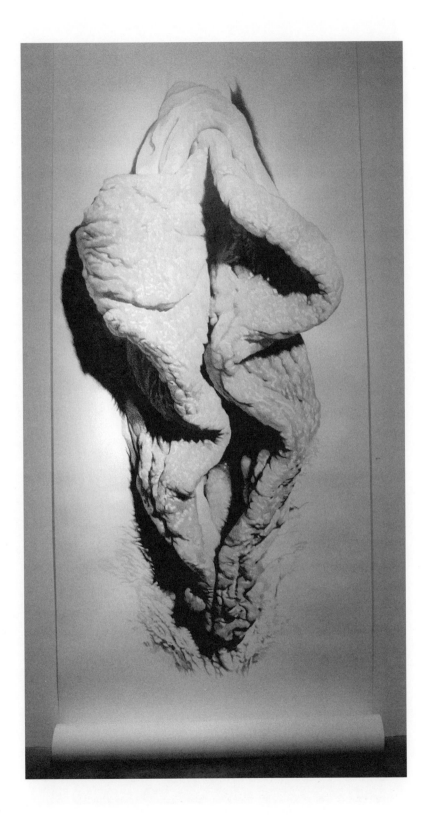

Figure 13.9. *Judith,* graphite on paper, 12 x 4.5 feet; Micol Hebron with Siobhan Hebron, 2011. The labia folds and textures evoke an almost spiritual sensualness. The excess paper lies in a roll on the floor to symbolize a passage from the invisible to visible. *(Collection of Eugenia Butler, courtesy of the artist)*

Figure 13.10. *Barbara* or *The Vageode,* mixed media installation (quartz crystal, gold leaf, shag carpet, piña-colada cocktail); Micol Hebron, 2011. *Barbara* is named after the artist's late mother—beautiful and unattainable now. *(Courtesy of the artist and Jancar Gallery)*

the lens of an individual artist's sensibility, but the primal energy behind the image is indelible. The American-born Sheela na gigs of Mary Beth Edelson and Nancy Spero may veer from the original intentions of the medieval stone carvers, but the symbolic value of the Sheela's iconography resonates with the spirit of our age.

A New "Vagenda"

The return of the Sheela as part of the return of the vulva heralds a new zeitgeist of reverence for the female body, part of what has been called the "fourth wave" of feminism. Words like *vulva, vagina,* and *uterus* have entered into the cultural conversation from a new viewpoint. No one has more admirably contributed to reclaiming these words than playwright Eve Ensler, in her Obie Award–winning play *The Vagina Monologues,* which has been produced in 140 countries in multiple languages.[35] She has also founded a global women's campaign called One Billion Rising: Rise Release Dance, which on Valentine's Day 2014 (which Ensler renames V-Day or Vagina Day) brought close to one billion women and men in two hundred countries out onto the streets to dance to protest violence against women.[36] According to United Nations figures, one in three women on the planet will be beaten or sexually assaulted; Ensler has come to see that "violence against women is the methodology that sustains patriarchy, then you suddenly get that we're in this together. Women across the world are in this together."[37]

A 2011 article titled "The Naming of Parts: A New Frankness about Vaginas" reported on the new "vag art" created by young female artists and craftspeople taking up themes from the heyday of feminist art in 1970s. The article detailed how renegade potter Carrie Reichardt assumes an activist alter ego, Super Vag. Through her performances, she dispels messages that tell women that somehow their bodies need fixing: "I think it is not just the porn industry that vaginas need reclaiming from but from the very misogynistic society we live in."[38] In 2012, Rhiannon Holly Baxter and Lucy Cosslett launched *The Vagenda,* a blog that asks real women everywhere to demand a media that reflects who they actually are. The pair just published their first book, *The Vagenda: A Zero Tolerance Guide to the Media.* Artist Nicola Canavan, through her website and celebratory workshops, wants to create a community of courageous and fearless women to join her in the act of Raising the Skirt. She is creating what she calls an "anasyrma army," a circle of women who use sacred display to embrace the power in their bodies.

Even well-established artists have been caught up in this new spirit. In June 2015, British sculptor Anish Kapoor, a former Turner Prize winner, installed a gigantic (sixty meters long and ten meters high) steel vulva/vagina in the gardens of the French palace of the Versailles. The artist stated that the controversial sculpture signified the vagina of Queen Marie Antoinette taking power. Sadly, reactionary forces still abound, as *Queen's Vagina* was soon attacked by vandals, who sprayed it with yellow paint.

Recently in London, the Shoreditch Sisters Women's Institute, founded nationally in 1915, gathered women to make a quilt comprised of individual hand-sewn vulvas to support a campaign against female genital mutilation (see figure 13.11). They have received sewn panels from as far away as France

Figure 13.11. *Shoreditch Sisters Vulva Quilt*. Women quilt together to celebrate the beauty of their femaleness. *(Courtesy of Shoreditch Sisters Women's Institute)*

and the United States. Shoreditch sister Tara Scott, age twenty-four, says the group uses women's art practices such as needlework techniques in a subversive way to rescue female genitalia from "an airbrushed representation, or surgically altering it in any way. In that way we are also campaigning against the popularity of labiaplasties."[39]

A similar goal was a motivating force behind British artist Jamie McCartney's monumental sculpture *The Great Wall of Vagina* (see figures 13.12 and 13.13). This nine-meter-long, ten-panel polyptych consists of four hundred plaster casts of vulvas of women ranging in age from eighteen to seventy-six. Five years in the making, the *Great Wall* includes mothers and daughters, identical twins, transgendered women, as well as a woman pre- and postnatal. As the artwork celebrates awe at the variety of female display, McCartney hopes his sculpture will help foster self-acceptance among women and to fight the rising numbers of cosmetic labial surgeries.

Figure 13.12. *The Great Wall of Vagina;* Jamie McCartney, 2011. A monumental work of art that affirms the female body as it is through an aesthetic presentation of diversity. *(Courtesy of the artist; image © Jamie McCartney)*

The Secret of the Sheelas

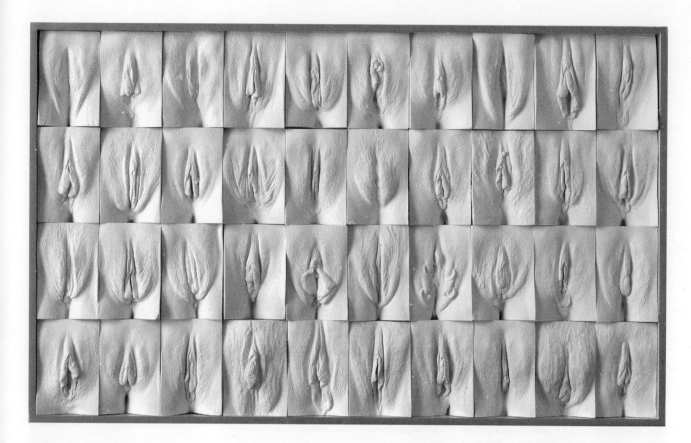

Figure 13.13. *The Great Wall of Vagina,* panel 9; Jamie McCartney, 2011. A close-up of thirty vulvas displaying their uniqueness. *(Courtesy of the artist; image © Jamie McCartney)*

Artist Charles Sherman's *Kreatia Kali* shows that the archetypal pattern of the displayed vulva may take many forms (see figure 13.14). From her pitiless gaze to her feathery vulva, the image embodies cosmic forces that affect all life. She holds dark and light birds to contain the opposites in her human/bird form. A primordial figure, yet utterly modern, she combines the real and the imagined.

The Sheela on Her Native Soil

Coming back to the present-day reemergence of the Sheela na gig, what of her appearance on her home turf, in Ireland? With its Neolithic stone monuments and pagan Celtic roots, Ireland's long suffering as a colony under British domination, the nineteenth-century famines, and the entrenched institutional power of the Catholic Church, Ireland has its own unique history. So how do contemporary Irish artists take up the image of the Sheela na gig?

Figure 13.14. *Kreatia Kali,* asphalt on canvas; Charles Sherman, 1984. A modern display figure as a Lady of the Beasts and bird goddess, having a nonhuman head and a womb of dark breasts. She symbolizes the forces of creation (Kreatia) and destruction (Kali). *(Collection of Starr Goode)*

Irish feminists seeking freedom from fixed gender identities must contend with traditional representations of the iconic feminine, such as Mother Ireland and the Virgin Mary. Over the last few centuries the complex figure of Mother Ireland evolved as a unifying symbol for the nationalist cause, in some ways recalling the old Celtic goddess of sovereignty. However, Mother Ireland as representing a nation dispossessed, with no rights, had little power other than to provide inspiration for Gaelic poets and patriots demanding justice as she endured the sufferings inflicted on her as an occupied colony.[40] The Virgin Mary as the immaculate, as in the Immaculate Conception, the Mother of God, has had a strong hold in this predominately Catholic country, with shrines and grottoes throughout the land dedicated to her. Church and state combined in the 1937 Irish constitution, written after Ireland finally won her independence from Britain. The supremacy of a woman's role as mother was enshrined in the Republic's constitution; the idea that a woman's place is in the home became the cornerstone for the new state.[41]

Three recent essays on the Sheelas analyze the consequences of the fusion between nationalism and Catholicism (originating in part as a resistance to British colonialism) for Irish women.[42] This fusion, in the words of poet Eavan Boland, creates a feminine that "becomes the passive projection of a national idea."[43] In chronological order, the essays are "Representations of History, Irish Feminism, and the Politics of Difference" (1991) by Molly Mullin; "'I Won't Go Back to It': Irish Women Poets and the Iconic Feminine" (1995) by Lia Mills; and "'Wide-open to Mirth and Wonder': Twentieth-Century Sheela-na-Gigs as Multiple Signifiers of the Female Body" (2007) by Luz Mar González-Arias. Each work addresses female icons that idealize women, while Irish national policies have largely excluded them from public life, ignored them as artists, and simplified them as chaste yet maternal. González-Arias notes that such a lifeless non-corporeality is an "erasure of the female body."[44] A foundational question for all feminists is: Who controls our bodies? But another question is this: After millennia of living under patriarchal divisiveness, what images of the feminine can act as a remedy for static, passive icons to restore us to wholeness, to our full humanity?

Sheela na gigs! What figure could offer a greater contrast to repressive patriarchal traditions? Molly Mullin points out that the image of the Sheela na gig has become almost emblematic of Irish feminism as a force for hope and change.[45] The Sheela has been resurrected from the Irish past to manifest in the imaginations of visual artists, poets, and musicians and in articles and books by scholars. Yet the struggle to select which images actually represent this past is far from over. This can be seen in a singular use of the Sheela that occurred during the Dublin Millennium, a celebration of the city's thousandth year. The official poster, titled "Faces of Dublin," thought to stand for a thousand years of the city's history, did not have a single image of a woman! Nothing new here in the exclusion of women from history. To counter this misogyny, artist Cathleen O'Neill created a poster called "The Spirit of Woman," with women's faces relevant to the millennium celebration featuring a decorative border of Sheela na gigs. While O'Neill says she was only trying to reclaim "a positive woman's symbol for the Millennium," the *Irish Times* reported that some people still found this alternative version of history emboldened with the Sheelas to be scandalous.[46] When O'Neill contested patriarchal notions of Dublin history, she made visible the evidence of women's contributions framed by the Sheelas' unapologetic sexual display.

O'Neill's poster art also challenged the power of male dominance in its construction of gender.[47] Self-described "feminist court jester" Nell McCafferty, a journalist, weighed in on the poster controversy in a column that featured a graphic of a Sheela wearing a nun's veil. Protesting institutional and cultural censorship, McCafferty wrote, "If you have not by now heard of *Síle na Gig*, you cannot tell your arse from your elbow. Then again, given the nature of Catholic-controlled education in the Republic of Ireland . . . it is possible that that is precisely what you cannot do."[48] Mythical and religious images like Mother Ireland and the Virgin Mary have been used to legitimize the social order's claims of the so-called natural inevitability of women's submissive role. The subversive use of the Sheelas by contemporary Irish women unravels this rigid narrative. With a trickster energy, her image upends sexual taboos to unveil the many-faceted powers of the female body.[49] Poets and artists are moving out of the shadow of the invisible woman to take up the vivifying figure of the Sheela na gig.

The poem "Female Figure," by Susan Connolly, appeared in the book *Áit Bhríd* (Brigid's Place) alongside four other pieces by other poets writing on the Sheela na gigs.* The book was created in part as a response to the systematic exclusion of Irish women in literary publications. For example, the three-volume *Field Day Anthology of Irish Writing* (1991) covered a millennium of work, yet an all-male editorial team virtually excluded women writers. In 2002, to remedy this controversial denial of women's voices, Cork University Press published the *Field Day Anthology of Irish Writing: Irish Women's Writing and Traditions.*

Connolly's poem "Female Figure" takes a new look at an old figure when the poet gives the Sheela an active voice in the opening stanza:

> *Mouth fixed*
> *in a wide grin,*
> *puffed out*
> *cheeks*
> *fingers to lips—*
> *am I saying something bad?*
> *No! after*
> *centuries of*
> *darkness*
> *I tell*
> *the truth.*[50]

Here the poet plays with the idiomatic phrase "fingers to lips"—we know which lips the Sheela is really touching. And in a reversal of meaning, this is not a gesture of silence but a sign of speech. These lips, the lips of her sex, speak words that originate from a startling source. Such speech disrupts a phallocentric discourse that would silence her, and her words restore the female body as a visible agent of culture.[51] Ironically, the poet then touches on male fears of the female sex ("am I saying something bad?"). She decisively dismisses such conventional concerns with an emphatic "No!" Despite

---

*Men too (such as Scottish poet Robin Robertson and Irish poets Michael Longley and John Montague) have been enticed by the Sheela as a subject. And in his poem "Sheelagh na gig," Nobel Laureate Seamus Heaney intuitively compares her to a tadpole (shades of the frog goddess!).

enduring the "centuries of / darkness," of demonization, of mutilation, her body, as bodies do, tells "the truth."

In the next stanza, the Sheela shares the truth of a mutual need in her relationship with women. They come to "look" and "talk" to her of their "desire-need." Could this mean not only women now, but all those women who over generations did not neglect her, who kept the knowledge of her powers? They brought their desire-needs to the Sheela na gig, stood before her to seek relief from suffering. They touch her just where she touches herself. In her constancy, she has kept:

> *Fingers to*
> *lips I speak*
> *my need of*
> *you.*

If they need her, she too needs these women; their devotion quickens her. As the poem unfolds, with a spirit of joy she "laughs" because she has prevailed as a "witness" and "survivor" of the events of time that sought to destroy her. Her astonishing figure persists.

The Sheela ends her poem in a triumph over the stultifying traditions of the old order:

> *Caught in stone*
> *I celebrate*
> *all who tell*
> *the truth—*
> *over centuries*
> *of darkness.*

Now in a community of women, she celebrates all who speak the light of truth to dispel the darkness of oppression. Whatever the interpretations of the Sheela's original meaning, the poet presents to Irish women the daring physicality of the Sheela figure as an alternative to the asexual icons of Mother Ireland and the Virgin Mary.

Whereas "Female Figure" could be about almost any Sheela, in the poem

"Sheela-na-gig" Connolly appears to be writing specifically about that most imposing of Sheelas, the Cavan Sheela (figure 1.2). Possessing twin sets of lips, her tongue protrudes from thick facial lips that echo her swollen, open vulva—another instance of the poet connecting speech to the sex of the Sheela. Her very existence speaks out a challenge to male-dominated constructs of Irish womanhood. Scholar Luz Mar González-Arias believes that the "protagonist of this poem rescues the voices of those female bodies that had been hidden since the end of female spirituality in Ireland."[52]

The poet questions the meaning behind the stone figure as an image "of what?" Her answer to this question in the last stanza moves from the exterior to the interior, from a description of an outer gesture to inner imaginative associations. The poem's ending transports us back to the beginning of matriarchal spirituality:

> *Clutching*
> *her vagina*
> *with both hands*
> *place-of-the-snake*
> *womb-of-the-mother*
> *mother-of-us-all*
> *sheela-na-gig*[53]

There is no period at the end of this poem because there is no end to this lineage. In a few lines of poetry, Connolly has compressed forty thousand years to reveal the Paleolithic roots of the Sheela's wide-open display. The primal Great Mother eclipses any state-church patriarchal dogma about gender. The Neolithic snake goddess, sexual and ever-renewing even in death, aligns with the creative, destructive, and regenerative powers of the womb. This is the indelible force behind the image of the Sheela na gig.

Irish artist Carmel Benson also associates this range of energies with the Sheela in her reimaginings of the figure. She says that works like her oil painting *Sheelagh Shrine* concern "generation, birth, sexuality, departure."[54] A frame within a frame within a frame, the painting draws us to its center, which depicts the antinomies of life and death (see figure 13.15). This shrine

Figure 13.15. *Sheelagh Shrine,* oil on board, 22 x 24 cm; Carmel Benson, 2004. A reclining figure at the center of the composition, she is face, breasts, and hands pulling at vulva. *(Courtesy of the artist)*

portrays not just a sacred heart but three separate panels: breasts, vulva, and mouth, all a luscious red, ripe with the creative life force. Beneath this triptych lies a horizontal Sheela, hands touching her vulva, but with tight, straight legs she seems to be a stiff nude of death, like the Cycladic goddesses or some of the wooden supernatural bog figures of Scotland, Britain, and Ireland. Benson made this shrine after traveling around Ireland and seeing many Sheelas' mutilated vulvas, and after her mother's painful death from "cancer of the womb."[55] The background of pink washes the *Sheelagh Shrine* with a feeling of love for the sanctity of the female body.

Like other contemporary female Irish artists, Benson sees the vital essence of the Sheelas as a necessary antidote to the passive images of women produced by the patriarchal ideology of the Catholic Church. Benson celebrates the iconography of the Sheela na gig as reaching back to what she calls an image of the great Earth Mother, an image that rejects phallocentrism.[56] In a series of lithographs, *Squatting Sheelagh, Crouching Sheelagh, Leaping Sheelagh,* and *Floating Sheelagh,* Benson transforms the stone figures by re-creating them in vivid colors. In the course of the artist's Sheela odyssey, she says, "Naturally, I visited the poor Sheelas buried in the bowels of the National Museum at that time as though they had been interred for some awful offense. I wanted to 'liberate' these images in some way. Hence, the very bright colors of my own Sheelas."[57]

Crouching Sheelagh (see figure 13.16) has an about-to-burst-out-of-the-frame fullness, much like the powerful physicality of the Cavan Sheela. Mouth and vulva are twinned by their red color and tumescence, once again linking speech to the female sexual organ.[58] Clearly, with her overt sexuality, this figure does not fit into any silent, submissive gender identity that has been imposed on Irish women. In *Sei Kieran, Sheelagh Travels,* Benson gives the complex figure of the Seir Kieran Sheela, now blue, a background of colorful patterns of diamond shapes in pink, blue, red, orange, and gold (see figure 13.17). It is as if the Sheela has traveled back to the most ancient image that humans associate with the vulva, the lozenge.

As with many of us, artist Fiona Marron has had her own voyage of discovery with the Sheelas that "inexplicably linked" her to something greater than herself.[59] In her article "Meetings with Remarkable Sheela na Gigs," she recalls a revelatory trip to the basement of the National Museum, where "at least twenty Sheela na gigs in all their vulva glory stared at me. . . . My eyes kept being drawn to the vulvas, those dark secret caves."[60] This fateful encounter inaugurated several years of searching for Sheelas, vivid dreams about the figures, and intense meditative work in her studio. Marron felt that in her own way this creative devotion was "setting the Sheelas free."[61] With titles like *Voice from the Rock, Speaking Stones, Raising Her Voice,* and *Singer of the Sagas* that invoke the faculties of hearing and speaking, we have another instance of an artist whose work imbues the Sheelas with life and a voice. In *Singer of the Sagas 5,* the Seir Kieran Sheela's inward gaze is highlighted by a vibrant blue aura (see figure 13.18). From these depths, out of the rounded *O* of her lips, comes forth a song of "joy and strength

Figure 13.16. *Crouching Sheelagh,* lithograph, 60 x 45 cm; Carmel Benson, 1996. A reimagining of a medieval Sheela. *(Courtesy of the artist)*

Figure 13.17. *Seir Kieran, Sheelagh Travels;* Carmel Benson, 2003. The Seir Kieran Sheela na gig set against a background of contemporary North African textile work is juxtaposed against a different culture, that of the primal foundation of Mother Africa. *(Courtesy of the artist)*

and also quiet endurance."[62] She sings the stories of her people. Visually balancing the holes, or cup marks, above her vulva is an ancient Irish spiral of unfolding energy.

Although her paintings portray the distinctive personalities of individual Sheelas, Marron sees a thematic unity in their physical expression of the ground of being. Her series on the archetype of the Cailleach, the hag of death, reminds us "of where we have come from and where we are going."[63] All life arises from and sinks back into Mother Earth. Marron calls the hag "the most powerful" of her Sheelas (see figure 13.19).[64] Death and sex: loss demands replacement. From here, where else is there to go but to *Suideachán– The Birth Chair* (see figure 13.20)?

Whether it be the patriarchal ideal of pliant docility or, more recently, the emphasis on unhealthy thinness, women's bodies often remain imprisoned in

Figure 13.18. *Singer of the Sagas 5,* print, 76 x 56 cm; Fiona Marron, 1992. Her open mouth and the whirl of energy at her feet, mirror the many openings about her sex. *(Courtesy of the artist)*

oppressive models altogether impossible to fulfill. Is it any wonder that Irish artists have turned to the startling, uninhibited image of the Sheela na gig to burst free from such male stereotyping of the feminine? Women must contend not only with the patriarchy out there, but with internalized patriarchy. In the view of the scholar Luz Mar González-Arias, the creative reimagining of this medieval female figure can "encourage contemporary women to stop perceiving their own corporeality as a heavy, awkward and shameful burden of guilt."[65] In addition, this reclamation inspired by the Sheelas fits "into a

Figure 13.19. *The Crone,* mixed media, 76 x 56 cm; Fiona Marron, 1992. A bone-white figure standing with the stillness of death; the ripeness of her vulva promises new creation. *(Courtesy of the artist)*

global feminism recuperation of the body as an active participant in the creation of culture."[66]

In the documentary film *Mother Ireland,* journalist Nell McCafferty is asked to choose a new icon for Ireland. Mischievously, she replies, "If I had to pick a female image of Ireland, I would pick a Sheela na gig." In her newspaper column she urges the Irish people to "bring *Síle* home, into every

Figure 13.20. *Suideachán–The Birth Chair,* pastel, 76 x 56 cm; Fiona Marron, 1992. The artist describes this figure as a woman squatting in the birthing position, her swollen genitals in the moment just after or just prior to giving birth. *(Courtesy of the artist)*

Irish home, where she belongs."[67] Visual artist Louise Walsh, whose work has been inspired by the Sheela as a symbol of female empowerment, gives an account of a lecture she attended at the Irish Museum of Modern Art. It seems the keeper of antiquities of the Irish National Museum gave a dry talk, delivering "scientific" archaeological investigations, calling the Sheelas mere decorations. To say the least, this perspective highly angered the women in

Figure 13.21. Ballylarkin Sheela, County Kilkenny—the most serene of all Sheela na gigs. *(Replica of the Ballylarkin Sheela na gig by Starr Goode and Charles Sherman)*

the audience, who felt fiercely protective of the figures. Walsh recalls the response of those around her: "We know how they speak to us. . . . We need them. We want them. They are ours. They are our symbols."[68]

With the rise of the Indo-European and Semitic patriarchal culture, then later the Christian era, the transformative powers of the Dark Goddess have been demonized and forced underground, only to resurface in myth and art as the evil witch, the ugly old hag, or the Sheela na gig. But she can never be erased completely. The astonishing figure of a female displaying her powers is not an oddity of Europe's religious art but rather an archetype occurring all over the world. The medieval Sheela na gig, as a Dark Goddess, manifests as a universal motif in a particular form, in a particular time and place. But Sheela na gigs are not just historical artifacts. The image of the Sheela is alive today.

Humans use images to bridge the known to the unknowable. We need our imaginations to express the wondrous experience of being alive. The power of the image of the Sheela connects us to a wholeness that we can never completely understand, let alone illuminate its every secret (see figure 13.21). And in the end, that is what we are left with: the concrete image. Possible interpretations come and go, rise and fall. Whatever contradictory meanings we may project onto her, the image endures: powerful, mysterious, eternal.

Acknowledgments

I am deeply grateful for my wise and wonderful writer friends Miriam Robbins Dexter and Julie Mars, who read through my manuscript and helped make it better. My husband, Mark Rhodes, has also been an astute reader and supporter of my Sheela adventures over the years. Other accomplished artists and friends are Ruth Ann Anderson, who gave immense help with the images for this book as well as drawing the illustrations, and Anne Gauldin, who offered timely advice. I also want to thank Mandana Chambers for sharing her insights on symbols, Kathleen Forrest for seeing me through my years in the wilderness, Susan Boyle for her loving heart, Sue Maberry for her singular library skills, and Renée Brown, wherever she may be, for introducing me to the Sheelas. I hold in memory Patricia Monaghan, who did so much to get this book published.

Notes

CHAPTER 1.
HISTORICAL OVERVIEW

1. Kenny, "Irish Sheela-Na-Gig," 13.

2. Freitag, *Sheela-na-gigs,* 17; O'Donovan, Ordnance, 152–53.

3. O'Donovan, Ordnance, 152–53.

4. O'Connor, *Sheela na gig,* 5–7.

5. Kenny, "Irish Sheela-Na-Gig," 16.

6. Ibid.

7. FRSAI, "Figures," 78.

8. Guest, "Irish Sheela-na-gigs," 107.

9. Kenny, "Irish Sheela-Na-Gig," 13.

10. Andersen, *Witch on the Wall,* 22.

11. O'Donovan, Ordnance, 152–53.

12. Andersen, *Witch on the Wall,* 11.

13. Kelly, *Sheela-na-gigs: Origins,* 5.

14. Kelly, "Irish Sheela-na-gigs," 73.

15. Dinneen, *Foclóir Gaedilge.*

16. Kelly, "Irish Sheela-na-gigs," 73.

17. Ibid., 75.

18. O'Connor, *Sheela na gig,* 15; see also Kelly, *Sheela-na-gigs: Origins,* 5.

19. Freitag, *Sheela-na-gigs,* 57.

20. Lawlor, "Two Typical Irish," 5.

21. Oakley, *Lifting the Veil,* 88.

22. Dunn, "Síle-na-gGíoch," 70.

CHAPTER 2.
THE SHEELA AS SIN

1. Kelly, "Sheela-na-gig," 48.

2. Erlande-Brandenburg, *Cathedrals,* 13.

3. Weir and Jerman, *Images of Lust,* 138.

4. Ibid., 141; Kelly, "Irish Sheela-na-gigs," 76.

5. Weir and Jerman, *Images of Lust,* 138.

6. Erlande-Brandenburg, *Cathedrals,* 99.

7. Kelly, "Irish Sheela-na-gigs," 76.

8. Weir and Jerman, *Images of Lust,* 34–35.

9. Ibid., 122.

10. Ibid., 23.

11. Andersen, *Witch on the Wall,* 52.

12. Thurlby, *Herefordshire School,* 7.

13. Andersen, *Witch on the Wall,* 37.

14. Ibid., 39.

15. McMahon and Roberts, *Sheela-na-Gigs,* 36.

16. Kelly, *Sheela-na-gigs,* 6–7.

17. Kelly, "Irish Sheela-na-gigs," 77; Concannon, *Sacred Whore,* 109.

18. Concannon, *Sacred Whore,* 109, 115.

19. Roche, *Norman Invasion,* 80.

20. Kelly, *Sheela-na-gigs,* 7, 45.

21. Concannon, *Sacred Whore,* 109, 116.

22. McMahon and Roberts, *Sheela-na-Gigs,* 57; Concannon, *Sacred Whore,* 110.

23. Kelly, "Irish Sheela-na-gigs," 77.

24. Concannon, *Sacred Whore,* 64. Concannon's book is also an excellent history of the Celtic Christian Church.

25. Ocampo-Gooding, "Sheela-na-gig," 43.

26. Condren, *Serpent,* 152–53.

27. Andersen, *Witch on the Wall,* 61.

28. Ibid., 64.

29. Ibid., 65.

30. Weir and Jerman, *Images of Lust,* 48.

31. Kelly, "Sheela-na-gig," 48.

32. Andersen, *Witch on the Wall,* 47.

CHAPTER 3.
CELTIC CONNECTION

1. Henry, *Irish Art in the Early Christian Period,* 1.

2. Ross, "Celtic and Northern Art," 80.

3. Henry, *Irish Art in the Early Christian Period,* 17.

4. Ibid., 19.

5. Dexter, *Whence,* 5.

6. Ibid., 11.

7. Watkins, *How to Kill.*

8. Dunn "Síle-na-gGíoch," 80.

9. Ibid., 81.

10. Ross, *Pagan Celtic Britain,* 296; Henry, *Irish Art in the Early Christian Period,* 19.

11. Andersen, *Witch on the Wall,* 74.

12. Ross, "Celtic and Northern Art," 86.

13. Andersen, *Witch on the Wall,* 75.

14. Henry, *Irish Art in the Early Christian Period,* 101.

15. Ross, "Celtic and Northern Art," 83.

16. Concannon, *Sacred Whore,* 106.

17. Henry, *Irish Art during the Viking Invasions,* 192.

18. Andersen, *Witch on the Wall,* 81.

19. Ross, *Pagan Celtic Britain,* 148.

20. Andersen, *Witch on the Wall,* 111.

21. McKee, "Fury."

22. Henry, *Irish Art in the Early Christian Period,* 2.

23. McMahon and Roberts, *Sheela-na-Gigs,* 48; Weir, "Selected Monuments."

24. "Journeys through Grief."

25. Weir, "Selected Monuments."

26. Ibid.

27. Andersen, *Witch on the Wall,* 77.

28. Weir, "Selected Monuments."

29. Ross, *Pagan Celtic Britain,* 317.

30. Ross, "Divine Hag," 157.

31. Ross, *Pagan Celtic Britain,* 61, 66, 68.

32. Kelly, *Sheela-na-gigs: Origins,* 14.

33. Green, *Celtic Goddesses,* 164.

34. Gimbutas, *Language,* 214.

35. Andersen, *Witch on the Wall,* 76.

36. Ross, "Divine Hag," 140, 146.

37. Ibid., 146.

38. Green, *Celtic Goddesses,* 73.

39. Kelly, *Sheela-na-gigs: Origins,* 46; Concannon, *Sacred Whore,* 139.

40. Green, *Celtic Goddesses,* 84.

41. Translated by Miriam Robbins Dexter in Dexter and Goode, "Sheela na gigs," 65.

42. McMahon and Roberts, *Sheela-na-Gigs,* 69.

43. Battaglia, "Goddess Religion," 7.

44. Dexter and Goode, "Sheela na gigs," 65–66.

45. Lines 354–56 translated by Miriam Robbins Dexter in Dexter and Goode, "Sheela na gigs," 65.

46. Lines 537–41 translated by Miriam Robbins Dexter in Dexter and Goode, "Sheela na gigs," 65.

47. Ford, "Celtic Women," 430–31.

48. Dexter and Goode, "Sheela na gigs," 65–66.

49. Green, *Celtic Goddesses,* 84, 74.

50. Dexter and Goode, "Sheela na gigs," 65–66.

51. Ross, *Pagan Celtic Britain,* 297.

52. Ross, "Celtic and Northern Art," 104.

53. Dunn, "Síle-na-gGíoch," 81.

54. Green, *Celtic Goddesses,* 188.

55. Condren, *Serpent,* 65.

56. Guest, "Ballyvourney," 375.

57. Ibid., 378–79.

58. Ibid., 380.

59. Andersen, *Witch on the Wall,* 25.

CHAPTER 4.
MEDIEVAL MINDSET ON PAGAN SOIL

1. Battaglia, "Goddess Religion," 1.

2. Ibid., 2.

3. Green, *Celtic Goddesses,* 9, 14.

4. Ross, *Pagan Celtic Britain,* 271.

5. Gimbutas, *Civilization,* 301.

6. Battaglia, "Goddess Religion," 5.

7. Ibid.

8. Ibid., 6.

9. Perks and Bailey, "Stonehenge," 94.

10. Ibid., 96.

11. McMahon and Roberts, *Sheela-na-Gigs,* 52.

12. Coles, "Anthropomorphic Wooden Figures," 322; see also Freitag, *Sheela-nag-gigs,* 117.

13. Freitag, *Sheela-na-gigs,* 118.

14. Andersen, *Witch on the Wall,* 95.

15. Battaglia, "Goddess Religion," 7.

16. Ibid., 8.

17. Kelly, "Sheela-na-gig," 49.

18. Kelly, *Sheela-na-gigs: Origins,* 12.

19. Ibid., 45.

20. Andersen, *Witch on the Wall,* 71.

21. McMahon and Roberts, *Sheela-na-Gigs,* 57.

22. Kelly, *Sheela-na-gigs: Origins,* 12.

23. McMahon and Roberts, *Sheela-na-Gigs,* 58.

24. Rynne, "Pagan Background," 199.

25. McMahon and Roberts, *Sheela-na-Gigs,* 39.

26. Kelly, "Irish Sheela-na-gigs," 77.

27. McMahon and Roberts, *Sheela-na-Gigs,* 39.

28. Ross, *Pagan Celtic Britain,* 39, and "Divine Hag," 155.

29. McMahon and Roberts, *Sheela-na-Gigs,* 39.

30. Oakley, *Lifting the Veil,* 52–53.

31. Andersen, *Witch on the Wall,* 14; see also McMahon and Roberts, *Sheela-na-Gigs,* 62.

32. Wright, "Worship," 36.

33. Ross, "Divine Hag," 148, 149.

34. Ross, "Celtic and Northern Art," 104.

35. Andersen, *Witch on the Wall,* 107.

36. Feehan and Cunningham, "Undescribed Exhibitionist," 117–18.

37. McMahon and Roberts, *Sheela-na-Gigs,* 67, 60.

38. Concannon, *Sacred Whore,* 138; see also 138 for a full list.

39. Ibid., 115.

40. For a full list see Kelly, "Irish Sheela-na-gigs," 80.

41. Ibid.

42. For a full list see Concannon, *Sacred Whore,* 120.

43. Andersen, *Witch on the Wall,* 108.

44. Ibid., 104, 111.

45. Wright, "Worship," 48.

46. Gimbel, "Bawdy Badges," 78.

47. Ibid., 80.

48. Elworthy, *Evil Eye,* 34.

49. Shakespeare, *Love's Labor,* 21–22.

50. Elworthy, *Evil Eye,* 143.

51. Andersen, *Witch on the Wall,* 22, 26.

52. Ibid., 108.

53. Murray, "Female Fertility Figures," 99, and plates IX–XII.

54. Andersen, *Witch on the Wall,* 103.

55. Smith, *Mother,* 84.

56. Guest, "Ballyvourney," 380.

57. O'Connor, *Sheela na gig,* 11.

58. Ocampo-Gooding, "Sheela-na-gig," 154.

59. Freitag, *Sheela-na-gigs,* 70.

60. Ibid.

61. Ibid., 114.

62. Ibid., 89.

63. Ibid., 115.

64. O'Donovan, Ordnance, 154.

65. Lawlor, "Two Typical," 5–6.

66. Clibborn, "Ancient Stone Image," 571.

67. Ibid., 575.

68. Andersen, *Witch on the Wall*, 30.

69. Guest, "Irish Sheela-na-gigs," 117, 110.

70. Guest, "Ballyvourney," 374–84.

71. Guest, "Irish Sheela-na-gigs," 122.

72. Andersen, *Witch on the Wall*, 23; text translated from the German and Latin by Miriam Robbins Dexter.

73. Ibid.

74. Weir and Jerman, *Images of Lust*, 15.

75. Ibid.

76. Ibid., 146.

77. Guest, "Irish Sheela-na-gigs," 127.

78. Ibid.

79. Andersen, *Witch on the Wall*, 24.

80. Ocampo-Gooding, "Sheela-na-gig," 151–52.

81. Ibid., 153.

82. Andersen, *Witch on the Wall*, 24.

83. Kelly, *Sheela-na-gigs: Origins*, 40.

84. Guest, "Irish Sheela-na-gigs," 114.

85. Guest, "Ballyvourney," 381.

86. Andersen, *Witch on the Wall*, 88.

87. Gimbutas, *Language*, 61.

88. Andersen, *Witch on the Wall*, 31.

89. Ibid., 87–91.

90. Dexter and Goode, "Sheela na gigs," 68, translated from Old Irish by Miriam Robbins Dexter.

91. Fraser, "Heraldic Woman," 81.

92. Roberts, *Sheela-na-gigs*, 5.

93. Concannon, *Sacred Whore,* 129–30.

94. McMahon and Roberts, *Sheela-na-Gigs,* 13.

95. Freitag, *Sheela-na-gigs,* 70.

96. Starhawk, *Spiral Dance,* 20; see also Levack, *Witch-Hunt,* 127, and Freitag, *Sheela-na-gigs,* 87.

97. Weir and Jerman, *Images of Lust,* 14.

98. Ibid., 15.

99. McMahon and Roberts, *Sheela-na-Gigs,* 14.

100. Kelly, *Sheela-na-gigs: Origins,* 14.

101. Resonox, "Recalling the Sad Case."

102. Andersen, *Witch on the Wall,* 30.

103. Manning, "Sheela-na-Gig," 278.

104. Weir and Jerman, *Images of Lust,* 15.

CHAPTER 5.
THE SHEELA'S CLASSICAL FOREBEARS

1. Weir and Jerman, *Images of Lust,* 113.

2. Dexter and Mair, *Sacred Display,* 35.

3. Ibid., 37.

4. Weir and Jerman, *Images of Lust,* 113.

5. Mylonas, *Eleusis,* 291; see also Reif, *Mysteries,* 199.

6. Mylonas, *Eleusis,* 292.

7. Reif, *Mysteries,* 27.

8. Ibid., 89–90.

9. Gimbutas, *Language,* 319.

10. Lubell, *Metamorphosis,* 34.

11. Mylonas, *Eleusis,* 284.

12. Ibid., 234; Reif, *Mysteries,* 10.

13. Lubell, *Metamorphosis,* 31.

14. Mylonas, *Eleusis,* 287.

15. Lubell, *Metamorphosis,* 117.

16. Ibid., 26; see also Dexter and Mair, *Sacred Display,* 36.

17. Lubell, *Metamorphosis,* 12.

18. Murray, "Female Fertility Figures," 95.

19. Ibid., 99.

20. Ibid.

21. Ibid.

22. Gimbutas, foreword to Lubell's *Metamorphosis,* xiii.

23. Lubell, preface to *Metamorphosis,* xix.

24. Gimbutas, *Language,* xxiii.

25. Frothingham, "Medusa, Apollo," 350.

26. Dexter, "Ferocious," 26.

27. Frothingham, "Medusa, Apollo," 349.

28. Frothingham, "Medusa II," 13–14.

29. Monaghan, *O Mother,* 233, 241.

30. Marler, "Archaeomythological Investigation," 18.

31. Dexter, "Ferocious," endnote 7.

32. Murray, "Female Fertility Figures," 99.

33. Lubell, *Metamorphosis,* 112, 129.

CHAPTER 6.
THE DARK GODDESS OF THE NEOLITHIC

1. Gimbutas, *Language,* 252; Gimbutas, *Goddesses and Gods,* 177.

2. Gimbutas, *Achilleion,* 335.

3. Gimbutas, *Language,* 251.

4. Shakespeare, *Romeo and Juliet,* 2.3, 5–7.

5. Gimbutas, *Goddesses and Gods,* 159; see also Gimbutas, *Civilization,* 223, 243.

6. Gimbutas, *Civilization,* 244.

7. "Çatalhöyük Excavations."

8. Mellaart, *Çatal Hüyük,* 49, 77.

9. "Çatalhöyük Excavations."

10. Gimbutas, *Language,* 252–53.

11. Mellaart, *Çatal Hüyük,* 202.

12. Gimbutas, *Civilization,* 255; Mellaart, *Çatal Hüyük,* 78.

13. Gimbutas, *Goddesses and Gods,* 176, Gimbutas, *Civilization,* 256.

14. Gimbutas, *Living Goddesses,* 35.

15. Mellaart, *Çatal Hüyük,* 114.

16. Gimbutas, *Living Goddesses,* 56.

17. Gimbutas, *Civilization,* 285; Gimbutas, *Language,* 260, 157.

18. Lubell, *Metamorphosis,* 91.

19. Wilkinson, *Complete Gods,* 229.

20. Cooper, *Dictionary,* 107.

21. Archive for Research, *Book of Symbols,* 190.

22. Wilkinson, *Complete Gods,* 229.

23. Lubell, *Metamorphosis,* 94–95. Lubell writes that Heket as a frog-headed goddess was also part of a group of "heavenly midwives who assisted each dawn at the birthing of the sun god."

24. Murray, "Female Fertility Figures," 95–96.

25. Codrington, "Iconongraphy," 65.

26. Gimbutas, *Language,* 256.

27. Gimbutas, *Living Goddesses,* 29; see also Gimbutas, *Language,* 256.

28. Dashú, "Another View."

29. McMahon and Roberts, *Sheela-na-Gigs,* 107.

30. Gimbutas, *Language,* 319.

31. Ibid., 320.

32. Gimbutas, *Goddesses and Gods,* 177; see also Gimbutas, *Language,* 255.

33. Gimbutas, *Language,* 254.

34. Ibid., 254–55.

35. Gimbutas, *Goddesses and Gods,* 177, 178.

36. Gimbutas, *Language,* 256.

37. Ilieva and Shturbanova, "Some Zoomorphic," 309–10.

38. Ibid., 318.

39. Ibid., 319.

40. Chevalier and Gheerbrant, *Penguin Dictionary,* 411; Cooper, *Dictionary,* 108.

41. Franz, *Feminine in Fairytales,* 27.

42. Ibid., 28.

43. Gimbutas, *Language,* 256.

44. Gimbutas, *Civilization,* 243.

45. Gimbutas, *Language,* 210.

46. Gimbutas, *Civilization,* 244.

47. Gimbutas, *Language,* 210.

48. Gimbutas, *Civilization,* 244.

49. Solnit, *Men Explain,* 19.

50. Dexter and Mair, "Sacred Display," 8.

51. Mann, "Göbekli Tepe."

52. Ibid.

53. Ibid.

54. Dunn, "Síle-na-gGíoch," 71; see also Fraser, "Heraldic Woman," 45.

CHAPTER 7.
THE CAVE ART OF THE PALEOLITHIC

1. Appenzeller, "Art."

2. Henshilwood, d'Errico, Yates, et al., "Emergence."

3. Marshack, *Roots,* 109.

4. Gimbutas, *Language,* 185.

5. Eshleman, *Juniper,* 38.

6. Quoted in Lubell, *Metamorphosis,* 61.

7. Marshack, *Roots,* 297.

8. Eisler, *Sacred Pleasure,* 54.

9. Ibid., 55.

10. Lubell, *Metamorphosis,* 57.

11. Hughes, "Were the First?"

12. Gimbutas, foreword to Lubell's *Metamorphosis,* xiii.

13. Gimbutas, *Language,* 99.

14. Leroi-Gourhan, *Treasures,* 347.

15. Gimbutas, *Language,* 99; see also Leroi-Gourhan, *Treasures,* 123.

16. Thurman, "First Impressions," 62–63.

17. Soetens, "Source Goddess."

18. Le Guillou, "Discoveries," 1.

19. Ibid., 2.

20. Ibid., 4.

21. Cohen, "Prehistoric French Artistes."

22. Balter, "Engravings."

23. Ibid.

24. Cohen, "Prehistoric French Artistes."

25. Leroi-Gourhan, *Treasures,* 158.

26. Marshack, *Roots,* 317.

27. Leroi-Gourhan, *Treasures,* 174.

28. Marshack, *Roots,* 316.

CHAPTER 8.
ON THE TRAIL OF THE SHEELAS: IRELAND

1. Ross, "Divine Hag," 149.

2. Andersen, *Witch on the Wall,* 149.

3. Ibid., 22, 26.

4. Guest, "Irish Sheela-na-gigs," 120.

5. Ibid., 120; see also Freitag, *Sheela-na-gigs,* 138.

6. Freitag, *Sheela-na-gigs,* 78, 89.

7. Costello, "Co. Galway Sheela-na-gig," 312.

8. Andersen, *Witch on the Wall,* 99.

9. Camphausen, *Yoni,* 68.

10. McMahon and Roberts, *Sheela-na-gigs,* 13.

11. Abt, *Introduction,* 139.

12. Ibid., 123–24.

13. Goode and Dexter, "Sexuality," footnote 20.

14. Dexter, *Whence,* 89.

15. Siggins, "Heads and Tails," 47.

16. Ibid.

17. Siggins, "Rahara," 111.

18. Guest, "Ballyvourney," 382; Brenneman and Brenneman, *Crossing,* xi.

19. Siggins, "Heads and Tails," 47.

20. Ibid.; Siggins, "Rahara," 111.

21. Siggins, "Heads and Tails," 45.

22. O'Connor, *Sheela na gig,* 12.

23. Fethard Historical Society, "Short History of Fethard"; see also Andersen, *Witch on the Wall,* 148.

24. Guest, "Ballyvourney," 384.

25. Andersen, *Witch on the Wall,* 107.

26. O'Donovan, Ordnance, 150.

27. Ibid., 152.

28. O'Connor, *Sheela na gig,* 8.

29. Andersen, *Witch on the Wall,* 149; Cooke, "Kiltinane," 278.

30. Andersen, *Witch on the Wall,* 128; see also Cooke, "Kiltinane," 278.

31. Clibborn, "Ancient Stone Image," 571.

32. Guest, "Irish Sheela-na-gigs," 115.

33. Andersen, *Witch on the Wall,* 26.

34. "Early Christian Sites," 312–13.

35. Andersen, *Witch on the Wall,* 26.

CHAPTER 9.
ON THE TRAIL OF THE SHEELAS: GREAT BRITAIN

1. Andersen, *Witch on the Wall,* 22.

2. Ibid.

3. Weir and Jerman, *Images of Lust,* 23.

4. Ibid.

5. Murray, "Female Fertility Figures," 98.

6. Ibid., 99.

7. Martin, "Sheela-na-gig," 135.

8. Andersen, *Witch on the Wall,* 103.

9. Ibid.

10. Murray, "Female Fertility Figures," 99.

11. Colchester Castle Museum, 25.

12. Weir and Jerman, *Images of Lust,* 15.

13. Kelly, *Sheela-na-gigs: Origins,* 14.

14. Freitag, *Sheela-na-gigs,* 56.

15. Roberts, *Sheela-na-gigs,* 19.

16. Sheela na gig Project, "Easthorpe."

17. Ibid.

18. Murray, "Female Fertility Figures," 100.

19. St. Helena's Church pamphlet.

20. Andersen, *Witch on the Wall,* 39.

21. Ibid., 70.

22. St. Helena's Church pamphlet.

23. Ibid.

24. Andersen, *Witch on the Wall,* 69.

25. Ibid., 28, 140.

26. Ibid., 108.

27. Ibid.

28. Sheela na gig Project, "Copgrove."

29. Andersen, *Witch on the Wall,* 127.

30. Roberts, *Sheela-na-gigs,* 20.

31. Weir and Jerman, *Images of Lust,* 76.

32. Kelly, *Sheela-na-gigs: Origins,* 33–34.

33. Freitag, *Sheela-na-gigs,* 89.

34. Andersen, *Witch on the Wall,* 127.

35. Bignall, "Solving."

36. Andersen, *Witch on the Wall,* 141.

37. Freitag, *Sheela-nag-gigs,* 92, 20, 135.

38. Ibid., 92; Andersen, *Witch on the Wall,* 149.

39. Andersen, *Witch on the Wall,* 96.

40. Weir and Jerman, *Images of Lust,* 39.

41. Ibid., 102.

42. Ibid., 103.

43. Andersen, *Witch on the Wall,* 42.

44. Andersen, *Witch on the Wall,* 70; Thurlby, *Herefordshire School,* xii.

45. Thurlby, *Herefordshire School,* xi–xii.

46. Ibid., xi.

47. Ibid., 11.

48. Ibid., 10.

49. Michell, *Traveler's Key,* 215.

50. Ibid.

51. Bailey, *Parish Church,* 7.

52. Thurlby, *Herefordshire School,* ix.

53. Ibid.

CHAPTER 10.
THE POWER OF IMAGES

1. Austen, *Heart,* 118; "'Finest' Neolithic Stone."

2. Shaw, *Passionate Enlightenment,* 111.

3. Mookerjee, *Kali,* 22.

4. Sütterlin, "Universals," 72.

5. Mookerjee, *Kali,* 61.

6. Ibid., 11.

7. Ibid.

8. Ibid., 16.

9. Ibid., 21.

10. Dexter and Mair, *Sacred Display,* 53.

11. Mookerjee, *Kali,* 8.

12. Ibid., 61.

13. McDaniel, "Kali," 17.

14. Amazzone, "Durga," 81.

15. Ibid., 71.

16. Chamunda Devi Temple.

17. McDaniel, "Kali," 31.

18. Mookerjee, *Kali,* 61.

19. Bolon, *Forms,* 23.

20. Ibid., 13.

21. Donaldson, "Propitious-Apotropaic," 88.

22. Bolon, *Forms,* 14.

23. Kramrisch, "Image," 269.

24. Bolon, *Forms,* 25.

25. Dexter and Goode, "Sheela na gigs," note 55.

26. Andersen, *Witch on the Wall,* 131; Rawson, *Art,* 68.

27. Andersen, *Witch on the Wall,* 131.

28. Rawson, *Art,* 209.

29. Ibid., 70.

30. Ibid., 68.

31. Ibid.

32. Ibid.

33. Austen, *Heart,* 119.

34. Appiah and Gates, *Encyclopedia,* 128.

35. Austen, *Heart,* 119.

36. Barber, *Women's Work,* 155, 62.

37. Gimbutas, *Language,* 145.

38. Ibid.

39. Ibid.

40. Dashú, "Icons of the Matrix."

41. Barreiro, "Taino," 110–11.

42. "Taíno Gallery."

43. Mendieta, *Ana Mendieta,* 66.

44. Ibid., 11.

45. Ibid., 41.

46. Waldron, "Traditional."

47. Ibid.

48. Ibid.

49. Maestri, "Ancient."

50. Alamy Stock photos. This site shows a photo of the censured Atabey; compare her to figure 10.10 with the clearly marked vulva.

51. Fraser, "Heraldic Woman," 74.

52. Saville, *Antiquities,* 21.

53. Ibid., 8.

54. Fraser, "Heraldic Woman," 36, 74.

55. Saville, *Antiquities,* 61.

56. Ibid., 64.

57. Dockstader, *Indian Art,* 88.

58. Andersen, *Witch on the Wall,* 133.

59. McEwan and Delgado-Espinoza, "Late Pre-Hispanic Polities," 512.

60. Fraser, "Heraldic Woman," 76.

61. Ibid., 77.

62. Dashú, "Icons of the Matrix."

63. Saville, *Antiquities,* 23.

64. Fraser, "Heraldic Woman," 76.

65. *Cuenca News Digest* reported the repatriation plans on September 21,

2012. In an e-mail to the author on May 16, 2016, the NMAI said they are not working on such a repatriation.

66. Fraser, "Heraldic Woman," 60.

67. Ibid.

68. Nero, "Breadfruit Tree," 239.

69. Fraser, "Heraldic Woman," 62; Kleiner, *Gardner's Art,* 232.

70. Kleiner, *Gardner's Art,* 233.

71. "Yoni."

72. Fraser, "Heraldic Woman," 63.

73. Andersen, *Witch on the Wall,* 133.

74. Liston and Reich, "Palau's Petroglyphs," 408.

75. "Missionaries."

76. "Educational Tropical Island."

77. Rawson, foreword to *Primitive Erotic Art,* ix.

78. Ibid.

79. Ibid.

80. Ibid., x.

81. Plutarch, *Moralia* 248 A-B, translated by Miriam Robbins Dexter in Dexter and Mair, *Sacred Display,* 39–40.

82. Zegura, *Rabelais,* 182.

83. Blackledge, *Story,* 9.

84. Dashú, "Warding Off."

85. Andersen, *Witch on the Wall,* 134.

86. Dexter and Mair, *Sacred Display,* 113.

87. Ibid.

88. Sütterlin, "Universals," 73.

89. Blackledge, *Story,* 8.

90. Ibid.

91. Dexter and Mair, *Sacred Display,* 37.

92. Ibid.; Lubell, *Metamorphosis,* 178.

93. Monaghan, "Uzume," 353; Lindemans, "Uzume"; Blackledge, *Story,* 19.

94. Lubell, *Metamorphosis,* 176.

95. Ibid.

96. Ibid., 177; Dexter and Mair, *Sacred Display,* 36.

97. Chester Beatty Papyrus I, recto 4.2-4-3, translated by Miriam Robbins Dexter in Dexter and Mair, *Sacred Display,* 36.

98. Blackledge, *Story,* 11.

99. Ibid.

100. Gimbutas, *Language,* 141.

101. Blackledge, *Story,* 12.

102. Dexter and Mair, *Sacred Display,* 38.

103. Dexter and Mair, "Apotropaia," 113.

104. Dashú, "Warding Off"; see also Guangmin, *Women,* 12.

105. Dashú, "Warding Off."

106. "Curse of Nakedness."

107. Schlichter et al., "Nigeria"; Dashú, "Warding Off."

108. Lubell, *Metamorphosis,* 181.

109. Ibid.

110. Ibid., 182–83.

111. Caldecott, "Dance," 18.

112. Lubell, *Metamorphosis,* 183; Rodríguez, "Preserving."

113. Brown, "Lisa Brown."

114. Waddell, "Medea Benjamin."

115. Meier, "Vagina Costumes."

CHAPTER 11.
THE CREATIVE SOURCE

1. Fraser, "Heraldic Woman," 46, 51.

2. Ibid., 47.

3. Dashú, "Essentialism."

4. Fraser, "Heraldic Woman, 37; Sütterlin, "Universals," 66.

5. Sütterlin, "Universals," 65–66.

6. Fraser, "Heraldic Woman," 79.

7. Sütterlin, "Universals," 66.

8. Abt, *Introduction,* 15.

9. Jung, "Structure of the Psyche," 158.

10. Yeats, "Poetic Symbols," 906.

11. As quoted in Miller, "Everyman," 72.

12. Ibid., 72–73.

13. Jung, *Two Essays,* 299.

14. Ibid.

15. Jung, "Structure of the Psyche," 158.

16. Ibid., 152.

17. Abt, *Introduction,* 26.

18. Cheetham, *All the World,* 247.

19. Abt, *Introduction,* 33.

20. Mamet, *Three Uses,* 50.

21. Abt, *Introduction,* 16.

22. Balter, "Becoming Human."

23. Abt, *Introduction,* 15–16.

24. Ibid., 16.

25. Jean Clottes as cited in Soetens, "Source Goddess"; Ranyard, "Rock Art."

26. Rawson, *Art,* 68.

27. Gimbutas, *Goddesses and Gods,* 159.

28. Leroi-Gourhan, *Treasures,* 144; see also Baring and Cashford, *Myth,* 18.

29. Ibid.

30. Leroi-Gourhan, *Treasures,* 185.

31. Dexter and Mair, "Sacred Display: New Findings," 6.

32. Gimbutas, *Civilization,* 222.

33. Thurman, "First Impressions," 67.

34. Gimbutas, *Language,* xix.

35. Ibid.

CHAPTER 12.
THE RETURN OF THE GODDESS

1. Laude, "Imagination," 13.

2. Ibid.

3. Dashú, "Essentialism."

4. Abt, *Introduction,* 17.

5. Lacher, "Sunday Conversation," 3.

6. Ibid.

7. Miller, "Everyman," 74.

8. Ibid.

9. Ibid.

10. Jung, "Approaching," 94–95.

11. Campbell, *Goddesses,* xxiii.

12. Berry, "Ecozoic."

13. Carson.

14. Hedges, "Implosion."

15. Ibid.

16. Gurevich, "50 Shades."

17. Hedges, "Implosion"; Baring and Cashford, *Myth,* 638.

18. See Gurevich, "50 Shades," for a deeper investigation of the causes of our collective cultural "forgetting" of the past.

19. Gadon, "War," 245.

20. Hedges, "Implosion."

21. Turner, *Ritual Process,* 97.

22. Johnson, "Survival."

23. Darwin, *Descent,* 85.

24. Johnson, "Survival."

25. Ibid.

26. Rifkin, *Empathic.*

27. Marler, "Beginnings," 65.

28. Sanday, "Matriarchy."

29. Marler, "Beginnings," 65.

30. Gimbutas, *Civilization,* viii.

31. Ibid.

32. Marler, "Beginnings," 59–60.

33. Gimbutas, *Civilization,* viii.

34. Ibid., x.

35. Ibid.

36. Ibid., xi.

37. Dexter and Mair, "Sacred Display: New Findings," 8.

38. Baring and Cashford, *Myth,* 158.

39. Göttner-Abendroth, "Notes," 38.

40. Plath, *Ariel,* 49.

41. Sanday, "Matriarchy as a Sociocultural Form."

42. Sanday, "Trapped," 32.

43. Ibid.

44. Christ, "Patriarchy."

45. Dexter, *Whence,* 11.

46. De Beauvoir, *Second Sex,* 90.

47. Starhawk, *Spiral Dance,* 20.

48. De Beauvoir, *Second Sex,* 691.

49. Baker, "Violence."

50. Weir and Jerman, *Images of Lust,* 22.

51. Christ, "Why Women Need," 72.

52. Ibid., 75.

53. Sanday, "Antigone," 105–6.

54. Sanday, "Matriarchy."

55. Sanday, *Women,* xi.

56. Sanday, "Matriarchy."

57. Sanday, "Antigone," 96.

58. Sanday, "Matriarchy."

59. Sanday, "Antigone," 107.

60. Sanday, "Trapped."

61. Ibid.

62. Ibid.

63. Sanday, *Women,* 40, 34.

64. Sanday, "Trapped."

65. Ibid.

66. Ibid.

67. Dolmetsch, "Nashira."

68. Ibid.

69. Gimbutas, *Language,* 321.

70. Ibid.

71. Ibid., 320.

72. Ibid., 318.

73. Christ, "Why Women Need," 74.

74. Campbell, foreword to Gimbutas, *Language,* xiv.

75. Eisler, "Rediscovering," 336.

76. Meador, "Ripe Time," 587.

77. Ibid.

78. Gimbutas, *Language,* 321.

CHAPTER 13.
THE SECRET OF THE SHEELAS

1. Concannon, *Sacred Whore,* 164.

2. Ibid., 179.

3. Ibid., 164.

4. Rees, *Vagina,* 150.

5. Chicago, *Embroidering,* 9.

6. Gerhard, *Dinner Party,* 221.

7. Jones, "Sexual Politics," 93.

8. Gadon, *Once and Future,* 273.

9. Quoted in Christ, "Why Women Need," 75.

10. Lippard, *Overlay,* 176.

11. Edelson, "Success."

12. King, "Tricksters!," 22.

13. Edelson, "Success."

14. King, "Tricksters!," 20.

15. Friedman, "Humor."

16. Lippard, "Fire and Stone."

17. Edelson, "Success."

18. Gadon, *Once and Future,* 273.

19. Schwabsky, "No Images."

20. Hoban, "Spero's Heroes."

21. Saltresse, "Journey."

22. Isaak, *Feminism,* 25.

23. Gopnik, "What Is Feminist Art?"

24. Klein, "Goddess," 598.

25. Ibid.

26. Ibid., 579.

27. Ibid., 578.

28. Dashú, "Essentialism."

29. Klein, "Goddess," 592.

30. Westen, "Matriarchy," 7.

31. Booker, "Art as Solace."

32. Cotter, "Art of Feminism."

33. Michol Hebron's Facebook page. (Accessed May 2014.)

34. Ibid.

35. Aitkenhead, "Eve Ensler."

36. Ibid.

37. Ibid.

38. Hoggard, "Naming."

39. Ibid.

40. Mills, "'I Won't Go," 73.

41. Mullin, "Representations," 42.

42. Ibid.

43. Mills, "'I Won't Go,'" 74.

44. González-Arias, "Wide-open," 106.

45. Mullin, "Representations," 46.

46. Ibid., 31.

47. Ibid., 34.

48. Ibid., 38.

49. González-Arias, "Wide-open," 107.

50. Connolly, "Female Figure."

51. González-Arias, "Wide-open," 109.

52. Ibid., 115.

53. Connolly, "Sheela-na-gig."

54. González-Arias, "Beyond Categorisations," 94.

55. Ibid., 94.

56. Ibid., 95.

57. Ibid., 92.

58. González-Arias, "Wide-open," 110.

59. Marron, "Meetings."

60. Ibid.

61. Ibid.

62. Ibid.

63. Marron, "Nature."

64. Marron, "Meetings."

65. González-Arias, "Wide-open," 116.

66. Ibid., 107

67. Mullin, "Representations," 39.

68. Ocampo-Gooding, "Sheela-na-gig," 101.

Bibliography

Abt, Theodor. *Introduction to Picture Interpretation: According to C. G. Jung.* Zurich: Daimon Verlag, 2005.

Aitkenhead, Decca. "Eve Ensler: 'We Should Be Hysterical about Sexual Violence.'" *Guardian,* Feb. 7, 2014. www.theguardian.com/stage/2014 /feb/07/eve-ensler-vagina-monologues-one-billion-rising.

Alamy Stock photos. www.alamy.com/stock-photo-taino-indian-stone -carvings-at-indian-ceremonial-center-in-caguana-18209682.html.

"Amaterasu, Goddess of the Sun; Uzume, Goddess of Mirth and Dance." www.goddessgift.com/goddess-myths/japanese_goddess_Amaterasu .htm.

Amazzone, Laura. "Durga: Invincible Goddess of South Asia." In *Asia and Africa,* volume 1 of *Goddesses in World Culture,* edited by Patricia Monaghan, 71–84. Santa Barbara, Calif.: Praeger, 2011.

Andersen, Jørgen. *The Witch on the Wall: Medieval Erotic Sculpture in the British Isles.* Copenhagen: Rosenkilde and Bagger, 1977.

Appenzeller, Tim. "Art: Evolution or Revolution?" *Science* 282, no. 5393 (1998): 1451.

Appiah, Kwame Anthony, and Henry Louis Gates, Jr., eds. *Encyclopedia of Africa.* New York: Oxford University Press, 2010.

Archive for Research in Archetypal Symbolism (ARAS). *The Book of Symbols: Reflections on Archetypal Images.* Taschen, 2010.

Austen, Hallie Iglehart. *Heart of the Goddess: Art, Myth and Meditations of the World's Sacred Feminine.* Berkeley, Calif.: Wingbow Press, 1991.

Bailey, James. *The Parish Church of St. Mary and St. David at Kilpeck*. Self-published, 2000.

Baker, Monya. "Violence against Women at Epidemic Proportions." *Scientific American,* June 20, 2013. www.scientificamerican.com/article /violence-against-women-at-epidemic-proportions.

Balter, Michael. "Becoming Human: What Made Humans Modern?" *Science* 295, no. 5558 (2002): 1219–25.

———. "Engravings of Female Genitalia May Be World's Oldest Cave Art." *Science,* May 14, 2012. www.sciencemag.org/news/2012/05/engravings -female-genitalia-may-be-worlds-oldest-cave-art.

Barber, Elizabeth Wayland. *Women's Work: The First 20,000 Years: Women, Cloth, and Society in Early Times.* New York: W. W. Norton, 1994.

Baring, Anne, and Jules Cashford. *The Myth of the Goddess: Evolution of an Image.* London: Penguin, 1993.

Barreiro, José. "Taino." In *Infinity of Nations: Art and History in the Collections of the National,* edited by Cécile R. Ganteaume, 110–11. Smithsonian, 2010.

Battaglia, Frank. "Goddess Religion in the Early British Isles." In *Varia on the Indo-European Past: Papers in Memory of Marija Gimbutas,* edited by Miriam Robbins Dexter and E. C. Polomé, 48–82. Journal of Indo-European Studies Monograph 19. Washington, D.C.: Institute for the Study of Man, 1997.

Baxter, Holly, and Lucy Cosslett. *The Vagenda: A Zero Tolerance Guide to the Media.* Vintage Digital, 2014.

Berry, Thomas. "The Ecozoic Era." Schumacher Center for a New Economics, Oct. 1991. www.centerforneweconomics.org/publications/lectures/berry /thomas/the-ecozoic-era.

Bignall, Sophie. "Solving an Ancient Mystery." *Shropshire Star,* Jan. 21, 2009.

Blackledge, Catherine. *The Story of V: A Natural History of Female Sexuality.* New Brunswick, N.J.: Rutgers University Press, 2004.

Bolon, Carol Radcliffe. *Forms of the Goddess Lajjā Gaurī in Indian Art.* University Park, Pa.: Penn State Press, 1992.

Booker, Hylan. "Art as Solace: Pinaree Sanpitak." *Unframed,* Sept. 27, 2013. https://unframed.lacma.org/2013/09/27/art-as-solace-pinaree-sanpitak.

Branston, Brian. *The Lost Gods of England.* New York: Oxford University Press, 1974.

Brenneman, Walter, and Mary Brenneman. *Crossing the Circle at the Holy Wells of Ireland.* Charlottesville: University Press of Virginia, 1995.

Brown, Lisa. "Lisa Brown: Silenced for Saying (Shock!) 'Vagina.'" June 21, 2012. www.cnn.com/2012/06/21/opinion/brown-kicked-out-for-saying -vagina/.

Caldecott, Léonie. "The Dance of the Woman Warrior." In *Walking in Water: Women Talk about Spirituality,* edited by Jo Garcia and Sara Maitland, 6–19. London: Virago, 1983.

Campbell, Joseph. Foreword to Marija Gimbutas, *The Language of the Goddess,* xiii–xiv. San Francisco: Harper and Row, 1989.

———. *Goddesses: Mysteries of the Divine Feminine.* Novato, Calif.: New World Library, 2013.

Camphausen, Rufus C. *The Yoni: Sacred Symbol of Female Creative Power.* Rochester, Vt.: Inner Traditions, 1996.

Carson, Rachel. dailypeacequotes@livingcompassion.com.

"Çatalhöyük Excavations Reveal Gender Equality in Ancient Settled Life." *Hurriyet Daily News,* Oct. 2, 2014. www.hurriyetdailynews.com.

Cave of Forgotten Dreams. DVD. Directed by Werner Herzog. New York: Sundance Selects, 2011.

Chamunda Devi Temple. Cultural India. www.culturalindia.net/indian -temples/chamunda-devi-temple.html.

Chauvet, Jean-Marie, Eliette Brunel Deschamps, and Christian Hillaire. *Dawn of Art: Chauvet Cave, the Oldest Known Paintings in the World.* New York: Harry N. Abrams, 1996.

Cheetham, Tom. *All the World an Icon: Henry Corbin and the Angelic Function of Beings.* Berkeley, Calif.: North Atlantic Books, 2012.

Chevalier, Jean, and Alain Gheerbrant. *The Penguin Dictionary of Symbols.* Translated from the French by John Buchanan-Brown. London: Penguin, 1996.

Chicago, Judy. *Embroidering Our Heritage: The Dinner Party Needlework.* New York: Doubleday, 1980.

Christ, Carol P. "Patriarchy as a System of Male Dominance Created at the Intersection of the Control of Women, Private Property, and War: Part 1." Feb. 18, 2013. https://feminismandreligion.com/.

———. "Why Women Need the Goddess: Phenomenological, Psychological, and Political Reflections." In *The Politics of Women's Spirituality: Essays on the Rise of Spiritual Power within the Feminist Movement,* edited by Charlene Spretnak, 71–86. Garden City, N.Y.: Anchor Books, 1982.

Clibborn, E. "An Ancient Stone Image Presented to the Academy by Charles Halpin, M.D." *Proceedings of the Royal Irish Academy* 2 (1840–44): 565–76.

Codrington, K. de B. "Iconongraphy: Classical and Indian." *Man* 35, no. 70 (1935): 65–67.

Cohen, Jennie. "Prehistoric French Artistes Painted Earliest Wall Art." History.com, May 14, 2012. www.history.com/news/prehistoric-french -artistes-painted-earliest-wall-art.

Colchester Castle Museum souvenir guide, 1997.

Coles, Bryony. "Anthropomorphic Wooden Figures from Britain and Ireland." *Proceedings of the Prehistoric Society* 56 (1990): 315–33.

Concannon, Maureen. *The Sacred Whore: Sheela Goddess of the Celts.* Cork, Ireland: The Collins Press, 2004.

Condren, Mary. *The Serpent and the Goddess: Women, Religion, and Power in Celtic Ireland.* San Francisco: Harper San Francisco, 1989.

Connolly, Susan. "Female Figure." In *Forest Music,* 56–57. Exeter, United Kingdom: Shearsman Books, 2009.

———. "Sheela-na-gig." In *For the Stranger,* 51–53. Dublin, Ireland: Dedalus Press, 1993.

Cooke, R. "Kiltinane." *Journal of the Royal Society of Antiquaries of Ireland* 39 (1909): 278.

Cooper, J. C. *Dictionary of Symbolic and Mythological Animals.* London: Thorsons, 1992.

Costello, Thomas B. "A Co. Galway Sheela-na-gig." *Journal of the Royal Society of Antiquaries of Ireland* 66 (1936): 312.

Cotter, Holland. "The Art of Feminism as It First Took Shape." *New*

York Times, March 9, 2007. www.nytimes.com/2007/03/09/arts/design/09wack.html?_r=0.

"The Curse of Nakedness." International Museum of Women. http://exhibitions.globalfundforwomen.org/exhibitions/women-power-and-politics/biology/curse-of-nakedness.

Darwin, Charles. *The Descent of Man.* Digireads.com Publishing, 2009. Originally published in 1871 by John Murray.

Dashú, Max. "Another View of the Witch Hunts (Response to Jenny Gibbons)." *Pomegranate: A Journal of Pagan Studies* 13, no. 9 (2011): 30–43.

———. "Essentialism or Essence: Out from the Land of Theory." www.goddess-pages.co.uk/the-meanings-of-goddess-part-3-2/.

———. "Icons of the Matrix." Suppressed Histories Archives. www.suppressedhistories.net/articles/icons.html.

———. "Warding Off Danger: Protective Power of the Vulva." Suppressed Histories Archives. www.suppressedhistories.net/sacravulva/warding off.html.

De Beauvoir, Simone. *The Second Sex.* New York: Vintage, 1974.

Dexter, Miriam Robbins. "The Ferocious and the Erotic: 'Beautiful' Medusa and the Neolithic Bird and Snake." *Journal of Feminist Studies in Religion* 26, no. 1 (2010): 25–41.

———. *Whence the Goddesses: A Source Book.* New York: Pergamon Press, 1990.

Dexter, Miriam Robbins, and Starr Goode. "The Sheela na gigs, Sexuality, and the Goddess in Ancient Ireland." *Ireland Journal or Feminist Studies* 4, no. 2 (2002): 50–75.

Dexter, Miriam Robbins, and Victor H. Mair. "Apotropaia and Fecundity in Eurasian Myth and Iconography: Erotic Female Display Figures." *Journal of Indo-European Monograph Series* 50 (2004): 97–121. Available online at www.academia.edu.

———. *Sacred Display: Divine and Magical Female Figures of Eurasia.* Amherst, N.Y.: Cambria Press, 2010.

———. "Sacred Display: New Findings." *Sino-Platonic Papers* 240 (2013): 1–122. http://sino-platonic.org/complete/spp240_sacred_display.pdf.

Dinneen, Patrick S. *Foclóir Gaedilge agus Béarla: An Irish-English Dictionary.*

Dublin, Ireland: M. H. Gill, 1904. Revised and enlarged edition published for the Irish Texts Society in 1979.

Dockstader, Frederick J. *Indian Art in South America*. New York: Bobbs-Merrill, 1962.

Dolmetsch, Angela. "Nashira." Gift Economy. http://gift-economy.com/angela-dolmetsch-nashira/.

Donaldson, Thomas. "Propitious-Apotropaic Eroticism in the Art of Orissa." *Artibus Asiae* 37 (1975): 75–100.

Dunn, James H. "Síle-na-gGíoch." *Éire-Ireland, a Journal of Irish Studies* 12 (1977): 68–85.

"Early Christian Sites in Ireland." *Journal of the Royal Society of Antiquaries of Ireland* 66 (1936): 312–13.

"Ecuador to U.S. Museum: Stop Hiding Our Treasures." Fox News Latino website, May 15, 2012. http://latino.foxnews.com/latino/lifestyle/2012/05/15/ecuador-to-us-museum-stop-hiding-our-treasures/.

Edelson, Mary Beth. "Success Has 1,000 Mothers: Art and Activism." In *Women's Culture in a New Era: A Feminist Revolution?*, edited by Gayle Kimball. Scarecrow Press, 2005.

"Educational Tropical Island Right in the Heart of Downtown Long Beach." July 18, 2011. https://realmomtime.com/2011/07/18/pieam-long-beach/.

Eisler, Riane. "Rediscovering Our Past, Reclaiming Our Future toward a New Paradigm for History." In *From the Realm of the Ancestors: An Anthology in Honor of Marija Gimbutas*, edited by Joan Marler, 335–49. Manchester, Conn.: Knowledge, Ideas and Trends, 1997.

———. *Sacred Pleasure: Sex, Myth, and the Politics of the Body*. San Francisco: HarperSanFrancisco, 1996.

Elworthy, Frederick Thomas. *The Evil Eye: The Classic Account of an Ancient Superstition*. Mineola, N.Y.: Dover Publications, 2004.

Erlande-Brandenburg, Alain. *Cathedrals and Castles: Building in the Middle Ages*. New York: Harry N. Abrams, 1995.

Eshleman, Clayton. *Juniper Fuse: Upper Paleolithic Imagination and the Construction of the Underworld*. Middletown, Conn.: Wesleyan University Press, 2003.

Feehan, John, and George Cunningham. "An Undescribed Exhibitionist

Figure (Sheela-na-gig) from County Laois." *Journal of the Royal Society of Antiquaries of Ireland* 108 (1978): 117–18.

Fethard Historical Society. "A Short History of Fethard." http://fethard.com.

"'Finest' Neolithic Stone Discovered at Orkney's Ness of Brodgar." BBC News. www.bbc.com/news/uk-scotland-north-east-orkney-shetland- 23529871.

Ford, Patrick K. "Celtic Women: The Opposing Sex." *Viator* 19 (1988): 417–38.

Franz, Marie-Louise von. *The Feminine in Fairytales.* Boston, Mass.: Shambhala Publications, 1993.

Fraser, Douglas. "The Heraldic Woman: A Study in Diffusion." In *The Many Faces of Primitive Art,* edited by Douglas Fraser, 36–99. Englewood Cliffs, N. J.: Prentice Hall, 1966.

Freitag, Barbara. "A New Light on the Sheela-na-gig." *Éire* 24, no. 1 (1998): 33–34.

———. *Sheela-na-gigs: Unravelling an Enigma.* New York: Routledge, 2004.

Friedman, Alissa Rame. "Humor and Masquerade: The Transformative Art of Mary Beth Edelson." www.marybethedelson.com/essay _humor.html.

Frothingham, Arthur L. "Medusa, Apollo, and the Great Mother." *American Journal of Archaeology* 15, no. 3 (1911): 349–77.

———. "Medusa II. The Vegetation Gorgoneion." *American Journal of Archaeology* 19, no. 1 (1915): 13–23.

FRSAI (Fellow of the Royal Society of Antiquaries of Ireland). "Figures Known as Hags of the Castle, Sheelas, or Sheela na gigs." *Journal of the Royal Society of Antiquaries of Ireland* 24, no. 1 (1894): 77–81, 392–94.

"Gable Figure (*Dilukái*), 19th–early 20th Century Belauan People, Belau (Palau), Caroline Islands." *Heilbrunn Timeline of Art History.* The Metropolitan Museum of Art. www.metmuseum.org/toah/works-of -art/1978.412.1558a-d/.

Gadon, Elinor. *The Once and Future Goddess: A Sweeping Visual Chronicle of the Sacred Female and Her Reemergence in the Cultural Mythology of Our Time.* New York: HarperCollins, 1989.

———. "War Is Man's Business." In *The Rule of Mars: The History and*

Impact of Patriarchy, edited by Cristina Biaggi, 241–48. Manchester, Conn.: Knowledge, Ideas and Trends, 2006.

Gerhard, Jane F. *The Dinner Party: Judy Chicago and the Power of Popular Feminism, 1970–2007.* Athens: University of Georgia Press, 2013.

Gimbel, Lena Mackenzie. "Bawdy Badges and the Black Death: Late Medieval Apotropaic Devices against the Spread of the Plague." Master's thesis, University of Louisville, Kentucky, 2012.

Gimbutas, Marija. *Achilleion: A Neolithic Settlement in Thessaly, Greece, 6400–5600 BC.* Los Angeles: Institute of Archaeology, University of California, Los Angeles, 1989.

———. *The Civilization of the Goddess: The World of Old Europe.* San Francisco: Harper San Francisco, 1991.

———. Foreword to Winifred M. Lubell's *The Metamorphosis of Baubo: Myths of Woman's Sexual Energy.* Nashville, Tenn.: Vanderbilt University Press, 1994.

———. *The Goddesses and Gods of Old Europe: Myths and Cult Images.* New York: Thames and Hudson, 1982.

———. *The Language of the Goddess: Unearthing the Hidden Symbols of Western Civilization.* San Francisco: Harper and Row, 1989.

———. *The Living Goddesses.* Edited and supplemented by Miriam Robbins Dexter. Berkeley: University of California Press, 2001.

González-Arias, Luz Mar. "Beyond Categorisations: A Conversation with Carmel Benson." In *Making a Difference: Women and the Creative Arts,* volume 8 of *Women's Studies Review,* edited by Vivienne Batt et al., 91–95. Dublin, Ireland: Colour Books Ltd., 2002.

———. "Wide-open . . . to Mirth and Wonder: Twentieth-Century Sheela-na-Gigs as Multiple Signifiers of the Female Body." In *Opening the Field: Irish Women, Texts and Contexts,* edited by Patricia Boyle Haberstroh and Christine St. Peter, 102–18. Cork: Cork University Press, 2007.

Goode, Starr. "The Power of Display: Sheela na gigs and Folklore Customs." *About Place Journal* 2 (2013). http://aboutplacejournal.org/earth-spirit-society/starr-goode-ii-ii/.

———. "Sheela na gig: Dark Goddess of Europe." In *Goddesses in World*

Culture, volume 2, Edited by Patricia Monaghan, 209–23. Santa Barbara, Calif.: Praegar, 2011.

Goode, Starr, and Miriam Robbins Dexter. "Sexuality, the Sheela na gigs, and the Goddess in Ancient Ireland." *ReVision* 23, no.1 (2000): 38–48.

Gopnik, Blake. "What Is Feminist Art?" *Washington Post,* April 22, 2007. www.washingtonpost.com/wp-dyn/content/article/2007/04/20/AR2007042000400.html.

Göttner-Abendroth, Heide. "Notes on the Rise and Development of Patriarchy." In *The Rule of Mars: The History and Impact of Patriarchy,* edited by Cristina Biaggi, 27–42. Manchester, Conn.: Knowledge, Ideas and Trends, 2006.

Green, Miranda. *Celtic Goddesses: Warriors, Virgins, and Mothers.* London: George Brazilier, 1996.

———. *The Gods of the Celts.* Dublin: History Press Ireland, 2011.

Grove, Margaret. "Rock Goddesses: Australia's First Creator Beings." In *Goddesses in World Culture,* volume 3, edited by Patricia Monaghan, 13–26. Santa Barbara, Calif.: Praegar, 2011.

Guangmin, Yang. *Women Not to Be Blocked by Canyon: The Lisus.* Beijing: Yunnan Education Publishing House, 1995.

Guest, Edith. "Ballyvourney and Its Sheela-na-gig." *Folklore* 48 (1937): 374–84.

———. "Irish Sheela-na-gigs in 1935." *Journal of the Royal Society of Antiquaries of Ireland* 66, no. 1 (1936): 107–29.

Gurevich, Andrew. "50 Shades of Gaia: Climate Change Denial as Sadomasochistic 'Forgetting.'" www.pacificariptide.com/files/50-shades-of-gaia.pdf.

Harris, Stephan, and Gloria Platzner. *Classical Mythology: Images and Insights,* 5th ed. New York: McGraw-Hill, 2005.

Hedges, Chris. "The Implosion of Capitalism." *Truthout,* April 30, 2012.

Henry, Françoise. *Irish Art during the Viking Invasions, 800–1020 A.D.* London: Methuen Publishing, 1974.

———. *Irish Art in the Early Christian Period.* London: Methuen Publishing, 1965.

Henshilwood, Christopher S., Francesco d'Errico, Royden Yates, et al.

"Emergence of Modern Human Behavior: Middle Stone Age Engravings from South Africa." *Science* 295, no. 5558 (2002): 1278–80.

Hoban, Phoebe. "Spero's Heroes." *ARTnews,* June 1, 2009. www.artnews .com/2009/06/01/speros-heroes.

Hoggard, Liz. "The Naming of Parts: A New Frankness about Vaginas." *Evening Standard,* Aug. 25, 2011. www.standard.co.uk/lifestyle/the -naming-of-parts-a-new-frankness-about-vaginas-6436937.html.

Howe, Thalia Phillies. "The Origin and Function of the Gorgon-Head." *American Journal of Archaeology* 58, no. 3 (1954): 209–21.

Hughes, Virginia. "Were the First Artists Mostly Women?" *National Geographic,* Oct. 9, 2013. http://news.nationalgeographic.com/news/2013/ 10/131008-women-handprints-oldest-neolithic-cave-art/.

Ilieva, Anna, and Anna Shturbanova. "Some Zoomorphic Images in Bulgarian Women's Ritual Dances in the Context of Old European Symbolism." In *From the Realm of the Ancestors: An Anthology in Honor of Marija Gimbutas,* edited by Joan Marler, 309–21. Manchester, Conn.: Knowledge, Ideas, and Trends, 1997.

Isaak, Jo Anna. *Feminism and Contemporary Art: The Revolutionary Power of Women's Laughter.* New York: Routledge, 1996.

Jagadiswarananda, Swami. *Devi Māhātmyam.* English translation. Madras: Sri Ramkrishna Math, 1953.

Joan, Eahr Amelia. *Re-Genesis Encyclopedia.* http://library.ciis.edu /resources/regenesis/re-genesis_ency.pdf.

Johnson, Eric Michael. "Survival of the . . . Nicest? Check Out the Other Theory of Evolution." *Yes Magazine,* May 3, 2013. www.yesmagazine .org/issues/how-cooperatives-are-driving-the-new-economy/survival -of-the-nicest-the-other-theory-of-evolution.

Jones, Amelia. "'The Sexual Politics' of *The Dinner Party:* A Critical Context." In *Sexual Politics: Judy Chicago's Dinner Party in Feminist Art History,* edited by Amelia Jones and Laura Cottingham, 82–125. Los Angeles: Wight Art Gallery/University of California Press, 1996.

"Journeys through Grief—Part 3." March 31, 2012, www.diggingthedirt .com.

Jung, Carl Gustav. "Approaching the Unconscious." In *Man and His Symbols,* 18–103. New York: Doubleday, 1964.

———. *Archetypes and the Collective Unconscious*. Volume 9, part 1, of *The Collected Works of C. G. Jung*. Translated by R. F. C. Hull. Princeton, N.J.: Princeton University Press, 1981.

———. "The Structure of the Psyche." In *The Structure and Dynamics of the Psyche*. Volume 8 of *The Collected Works of C. G. Jung*, 139–58. Translated by R. F. C. Hull. Princeton, N.J.: Princeton University Press, 1972.

———. *Symbols of Transformation*. Volume 5 of *The Collected Works of C. G. Jung*, Translated by R. F. C. Hull. Princeton, N.J.: Princeton University Press, 1976.

———. *Two Essays on Analytical Psychology*. Translated by R. F. C. Hull. New York: Meridian Books, 1968.

Kelly, Eamonn P. "Irish Sheela-na-gigs: The Kerry Connection." In *Medieval Treasures of County Kerry*, edited by G. Murray, 73–81. Tralee, County Kerry, Ireland: County Museum, 2010. Also available online at www.academia.edu.

———. "Sheela-na-gig: A Brief Description of Their Origin and Function." In *Beyond the Pale: Art and Artists at the Edge of Consensus*, 43–59. Dublin: The Irish Museum of Modern Art, 1994.

———. *Sheela-na-gigs: Origins and Functions*. Dublin, Ireland: Country House, 1996.

Kenny, Niall. "The Irish Sheela-Na-Gig—Once Scorned but Now Revived and Celebrated." In *Proceedings of the Association of Young Irish Archaeologists Annual Conference 2007*, edited by Brian Dolan, Amy McQuillan, Emmett O'Keeffe, and Kim Rice, 11–30. Dublin, Ireland: University College Dublin, 2008.

King, Jonah. "Tricksters! Non-Oppositional Dissent in Contemporary Art." B.A. thesis, National College of Art and Design, Dublin, Ireland, Faculty of Fine Art Media, 2013.

Klein, Jennie. "Goddess: Feminist Art and Spirituality in the 1970s." *Feminist Studies* 35, no. 3 (2009): 575–602.

Kleiner, Fred S. *Gardner's Art through the Ages: Non-Western Perspectives*, 13th ed. Boston: Wadsworth, 2010.

Kramrisch, Stella. "An Image of Aditi-Uttānapad." *Artibus Asiae* 19, no. 3–4 (1956): 259–70.

Lacher, Irene. "The Sunday Conversation: Peter Sellars." *Los Angeles Times*, May 4, 2013.

Lamm, Robert C. *The Humanities in Western Culture*, 4th ed. Boston: McGraw Hill, 2004.

Laude, Patrick. "Imagination and the Void: To Be or Not To Be." *Parabola* 4, no. 1 (2009): 12–19.

Lawlor, H. C. "Two Typical Irish 'Sheela-na-gigs.'" *Man* 31, no. 4. (1931): 5–6.

Lee, Adrian. "Pagan Whodunnit Grips Village." *Times* (London), Dec. 20, 2004.

Le Guillou, Yanik. "Discoveries: The Pont-D'Arc Venus." *International Newsletter of Rock Art* 29 (2001): 1–5.

Leroi-Gourhan, André. *Treasures of Prehistoric Art*. New York: Harry A. Abrams, 1960.

Lethbridge, T. C. *Witches*. New York: Citadel Press, 1968.

Levack, Brian P. *The Witch-Hunt in Early Modern Europe*. New York: Routledge, 1987.

Lindemans, Micha F. "Uzume." Encyclopedia Mythica. www.pantheon.org.

Lippard, Lucy R. "Fire and Stone: Politics and Ritual." Introductory essay on Mary Beth Edelson's *Seven Cycles: Public Rituals* (1980). www.marybethedelson.com/essay_firestone.html.

———. *Overlay: Contemporary Art and the Art of Prehistory*. New York: Pantheon, 1983.

Liston, Jolie, and Timothy M. Reich. "Palau's Petroglyphs: Archaeology, Oral History and Iconography." *Journal of the Polynesian Society* 119, no. 4 (2010): 401–14.

Lubell, Winifred M. *The Metamorphosis of Baubo: Myths of Woman's Sexual Energy*. Nashville, Tenn.: Vanderbilt University Press, 1994.

Maestri, Nicoletta. "Ancient Mesoamerican Ball Game Origins and Gameplay." March 8, 2016. http://archaeology.about.com/od/mameterms/a/Mesoamerican_Ball_Game.htm.

Mamet, David. *Three Uses of the Knife: On the Nature and Purpose of Drama*. New York: Columbia University Press, 1998.

Mann, Charles C. "Göbekli Tepe." *National Geographic,* June 2011. http://ngm.nationalgeographic.com/2011/06/gobekli-tepe/mann-text.

Manning, Conleth. "A Sheela-na-Gig from Glanworth Castle, Co. Cork."

In *Figures from the Past: Studies in Figurative Art in Christian Ireland in Honor of Helen M. Roe,* edited by E. Rynne, 278–82. Dun Laoghaire: Glendale Press for the Royal Society of Antiquaries of Ireland, 1987.

Marler, Joan. "An Archaeomythological Investigation of the Gorgon." *ReVision* 25, no. 1 (2002): 15–23.

———. "The Beginnings of Patriarchy in Europe: Reflections on the Kurgan Theory of Marija Gimbutas." In *The Rule of Mars: The History and Impact of Patriarchy,* edited by Cristina Biaggi, 53–76. Manchester, Conn.: Knowledge, Ideas, and Trends, 2006.

Marron, Fiona. "Meetings with Remarkable Sheela-na-Gigs." *Goddess Alive! Goddess Celebration and Research,* Nov. 15, 2013. www.goddessalive.co .uk/?s=Meetings+with+Remarkable+Sheela-na-Gigs.

———. "The Nature of Things." *About Place Journal* 2, no. 2 (2013). http:// aboutplacejournal.org/earth-spirit-society/fiona-marron-ii-ii/.

Marshack, Alexander. *The Roots of Civilization.* Mount Kisco, N.Y.: Moyer Bell, 1991.

Martin, R. R. "The Sheela-na-gig at Oxford." *Man* (1929): 134–35.

McDaniel, June. "Kali: Goddess of Life, Death, and Transcendence." In *Asia and Africa,* volume 1 of *Goddesses in World Culture,* edited by Patricia Monaghan, 17–31. Santa Barbara, Calif.: Praegar, 2011.

McEwan, Colin, and Florencio Delgado-Espinoza. "Late Pre-Hispanic Polities of Coastal Ecuador." In *Handbook of South American Archaeology,* edited by Helaine Silverman and William Isbell, 505–26. New York: Springer, 2008.

McKee, Linda. "Fury over Plan to Relocate Historic Statue." *Belfast Telegraph,* April 17, 2007.

McMahon, Joanne, and Jack Roberts. *The Sheela-na-Gigs of Ireland and Britain: The Divine Hag of the Christian Celts—An Illustrated Guide.* Dublin, Ireland: Mercier Press, 2000.

Meador, Betty De Shong. "Ripe Time: An Inquiry into Gimbutas' Appeal." In *From the Realm of the Ancestors: An Anthology in Honor of Marija Gimbutas,* edited by Joan Marler, 587–92. Manchester, Conn.: Knowledge, Ideas and Trends, 1997.

Meier, Sam. "Vagina Costumes at the RNC: How CODEPINK Is Confronting the GOP's War on Women." PolicyMic, Aug. 28, 2012. https://mic.com/articles/13571/vagina-costumes-at-the-rnc-how-code-pink-is-confronting-the-gop-s-war-on-women.

Mellaart, James. *Çatal Hüyük: A Neolithic Town in Anatolia.* New York: McGraw Hill, 1967. Available at http://archive.org.

Mendieta, Ana. *Ana Mendieta: A Book of Works.* Edited by Bonnie Clearwater. Miami Beach, Fla.: Grassfield Press, 1993.

Mercier, Vivian. *The Irish Comic Tradition: The Key Book of Irish Literary Criticism.* London: Souvenir Press Ltd., 1991.

Michell, John. *The Traveler's Key to Sacred England.* New York: Alfred A. Knopf, 1988.

Miller, James, E. "Everyman with a Blue Guitar: Imagination, Creativity, Language." In *Landmark Essays on Rhetorical Invention in Writing,* edited by Richard E. Young and Yameng Liu, 69–78. New York: Routledge, 1995.

Mills, Lia. "'I Won't Go Back to It': Irish Women Poets and the Iconic Feminine." *Feminist Review* 50 (1995): 69–88.

"Missionaries." www.pacificworlds.com/palau/visitors/mission.cfm.

Monaghan, Patricia. *O Mother Sun! A New View of the Cosmic Feminine.* Freedom, Calif.: Crossing Press, 1994.

———. "Uzume." In *The Book of Goddesses and Heroines,* 353. St. Paul, Minn.: Llewellyn, 1993.

Mookerjee, Adit. *Kali: The Feminine Force.* New York: Destiny Books, 1988.

Mullin, Molly. "Representations of History, Irish Feminism, and the Politics of Difference." *Feminist Studies* 17, no. 1 (1991): 29–50.

Murray, Margaret A. "Female Fertility Figures." *Journal of the Royal Anthropological Institute* (Dublin) 64 (1934): 93–100.

Mylonas, George E. *Eleusis and the Eleusinian Mysteries.* Princeton, N.J.: Princeton University Press, 1961.

Nero, Karen L. "The Breadfruit Tree Story: Mythological Transformations in Palauan Politics." *Pacific Studies* 15, no. 4 (1992): 235–60.

"Nigerian Women Agree to End Peaceful Siege of Oil Facility." *Jet,* Aug. 5, 2002.

Oakley, Theresa C. *Lifting the Veil: A New Study of the Sheela-Na-Nigs of Britain and Ireland*. Oxford, England: British Archaeological Reports, 2009.

Ocampo-Gooding, Sonya Ines. "The Sheela-na-gig: An Inspirational Figure for Contemporary Irish Art." Master's thesis, Concordia University, Montreal, Canada, 2012.

O'Connor, James. *Sheela na gig*. Fethard, County Tipperary, Ireland: Fethard Historical Society, 1991.

O'Donovan, John. Ordnance Survey Letters: Tipperary (Dublin 1840) 1: 152–55.

"Places of Interest in Chamba." www.himachaltouristguide.com/index .php/chamba/chamba-town/places-of-interest.

Plath, Sylvia. *Ariel*. New York: Perennial Library, Harper and Row, 1961.

Perks, Anthony M., and Darlene Marie Bailey. "Stonehenge: A View from Medicine." *Journal of the Royal Society of Medicine* 96, no. 2 (2003): 94–97.

Ranyard, John. "Rock Art Research and Jungian Psychology." Lecture at Jung Institute, Los Angeles, Calif., Oct. 22, 2011.

Rawson, Philip S. *The Art of Tantra*. Greenwich, Conn.: New York Graphic Society, 1973.

———. "Early History of Sexual Art." In *Primitive Erotic Art,* edited by Philip Rawson, 1–76. New York: G. P. Putnam, 1973.

———, ed. *Primitive Erotic Art*. New York: G. P. Putnam, 1973.

Rees, Emma L. E. *The Vagina: A Literary and Cultural History*. New York: Bloomsbury Academic, 2013.

Reif, Jennifer. *The Mysteries of Demeter: Rebirth of the Pagan Way*. York Beach, Maine: Samuel Weiser, 1999.

Resonox, Albert. "Recalling the Sad Case of the Destruction of an Extremely Rare Sheela-na-gig." *Heritage Journal,* April 2, 2010. https:// heritageaction.wordpress.com.

Rifkin, Jeremy. *The Empathic Civilization: The Race to Global Consciousness in a World in Crisis*. New York: Jeremy P. Tarcher/Penguin, 2009.

Roberts, Jack. *The Sheela-na-gigs of Britain and Ireland: An Illustrated Guide*. Skibbereen, West Cork, Ireland: Key Books Publishing, 1993.

Roche, Richard. *The Norman Invasion of Ireland*. Dublin, Ireland: Anvil Books, 1995.

Rodríguez, Russell. "Preserving the Colors of My Skirt: Laga, Backstrap Weaving of the Kalinga of the Philippines." March 10, 2013. ACTA, www.actaonline.org/content/preserving-colors-my-skirt-laga-backstrap-weaving-kalinga-philippines.

Ross, Anne. "Celtic and Northern Art." In *Primitive Erotic Art,* edited by Philip Rawson, 77–106. Worthing, England: Littlehampton Book Services, 1973.

———. "The Divine Hag of the Pagan Celts." In *The Witch Figure: Folklore Essays by a Group of Scholars in England Honouring the 75th Birthday of Katharine M. Briggs,* edited by Venetia Newall, 139–64. Boston: Routledge and Kegan, 1973.

———. *Pagan Celtic Britain: Studies in Iconography and Tradition.* New York: Columbia University Press, 1967.

Rynne, Étienne. "A Pagan Background for Sheela-na-gigs." In *Figures from the Past: Studies in Figurative Art in Christian Ireland in Honor of Helen M. Roe,* edited by Étienne Rynne, 189–202. Ireland: Glendale Press, 1987.

"Salle du Fond Chamber: The Venus and the Sorcerer." The Cave Art Paintings of the Chauvet Cave. www.bradshawfoundation.com/chauvet/venus_sorcerer.php.

Saltresse, Danielle. "A Journey with Nancy Spero." *Artsy* 1 (2001). www.artsymag.com/2001/issue01/interviews/spero.html.

Sanday, Peggy Reeves. "Antigone in Sumatra: Matriarchal Values in a Patriarchal Context." In *The Rule of Mars: The History and Impact of Patriarchy,* edited by Cristina Biaggi, 95–110. Manchester, Conn.: Knowledge, Ideas and Trends, 2006.

———. "Matriarchy." https://feminismandreligion.com/2011/07/29/matriarchy-by-peggy-reeves-sanday/.

———. "Matriarchy as a Sociocultural Form: An Old Debate in a New Light." Paper presented at the 16th Congress of the Indo-Pacific Prehistory Association, Melaka, Malaysia, July 1–7, 1998. http://www.sas.upenn.edu/~psanday/matri.html.

———. "Trapped in a Metaphor." *Criminal Justice Ethics* 13, no. 2 (1994): 32–38.

———. *Women at the Center: Life in a Modern Matriarchy.* Ithaca, N.Y.: Cornell University Press, 2002.

Saville, Marshall H. *The Antiquities of Manabi, Ecuador: A Preliminary Report.* New York: Irving Press, 1907. Reprint ed. Andesite Press, 2015.

Schlichter, Sarah, Melissa Wimbrow, Elizabeth Brookbank, and Jennie Ruby. "Nigeria: Nigerian Women Occupy Chevrontexaco Facilities." *Off Our Backs* 32, no. 9/10 (Sept.–Oct. 2002): 4.

Schwabsky, Barry. "No Images of Man: On Nancy Spero." *Nation,* Nov. 29, 2010. www.thenation.com/article/no-images-man-nancy-spero.

Shakespeare, William. *Love's Labor Lost.* In *The Riverside Shakespeare,* 2nd ed., 208–50. Boston: Houghton Mifflin, 1997.

———. *Romeo and Juliet.* In *The Riverside Shakespeare,* 2nd ed., 1101–45. Boston: Houghton Mifflin, 1997.

Shaw, Miranda. *Passionate Enlightenment: Women in Tantric Buddhism.* Princeton, N.J.: Princeton University Press, 1994.

Sheela Na gig Project. "Copgrove." www.sheelanagig.org.

———. "Easthorpe." www.sheelanagig.org.

Siggins, Albert. "Heads and Tails of Stone." *County Roscommon Historical and Archeological Society Journal* 3 (1990): 45–46.

———. "Rahara." *County Roscommon Historical and Archeological Society Journal* 5 (1994): 111.

Smith, Jill. *Mother of the Isles.* Penzance, Cornwall, England: Dor Dama Press, 2003.

Soetens, Katinka. "The Source Goddess of the Chauvet Caves." *Goddess Alive: Goddess Celebration and Research,* Autumn/Winter 2008. www .goddessalive.co.uk/issue-14-home/the-source-goddess-of-the-chauvet -caves.

Solnit, Rebecca. *Men Explain Things to Me.* Chicago: Haymarket Books, 2014.

Srejović, Dragoslav. *Europe's First Monumental Sculpture: New Discoveries at Lepenski Vir.* New York: Stein and Day, 1972.

Starhawk. *The Spiral Dance: A Rebirth of the Ancient Religion of the Great Goddess*. San Francisco: HarperOne, 1989.

Stevens-Arroyo, Antonio M. *Cave of the Jagua: The Mythological World of the Tainos*. Scranton: University of Scranton Press, 2006.

Sütterlin, Christa. "Universals in Apotropaic Symbolism: A Behavioral and Comparative Approach to Some Medieval Sculptures." *Leonardo* 22, no. 1 (1989): 65–74.

"Taíno Gallery." Powhatan Museum of Indigenous Arts and Culture. www.powhatanmuseum.com/Taino_Gallery.html.

Thurlby, Malcolm. *The Herefordshire School of Romanesque Sculpture*. Little Logaston, Herefordshire, England: Logaston Press, 1999.

Thurman, Judith. "First Impressions: What Does the World's Oldest Art Say about Us?" *New Yorker,* June 23, 2008.

Turner, Victor. *The Ritual Process: Structure and Anti-Structure*. Chicago: Aldine Transaction, 1969.

Waddell, Lynn. "Medea Benjamin and Code Pink Protest the RNC in Tampa." *Daily Beast,* Aug. 28, 2012. www.thedailybeast.com.

Waldron, Lawrence. "Traditional Narratives and Religion." http://ancientantilles.com/traditionalnarrativesandreligion.html.

Watkins, Calvert. *How to Kill a Dragon: Aspects of Indo-European Poetics*. New York: Oxford University Press, 1995.

Weinbaum, Batya. "Madhubani Art: What Do Women Experience Painting Durga and Kali." *Femspec* 14, no. 1 (2014): 14–73.

Weir, Anthony. "Selected Monuments in County Fermanagh." Gazetteer of Irish Prehistoric Monuments, www.irishmegaliths.org.uk/antrim.htm.

Weir, Anthony, and James Jerman. *Images of Lust: Sexual Carvings on Medieval Churches*. New York: Routledge, 1999.

Westen, Mirjam. "Matriarchy, Spirituality and Utopia." In *Female Power,* edited by Mirjam Westen, 4–7. Catalog for the exhibition Female Power: Matriarchy, Spirituality and Utopia, March 2–May 20, 2013, Museum voor Moderne Kunst Arnhem, the Netherlands. Arnhem, 2013.

White, Randall, Romain Mensan, Raphaëlle Bourrillon, et al. "Context and Dating of Aurignacian Vulvar Representations from Abri Castanet,

France." *Proceedings of the National Academy of Science of the United States of America* 109, no. 22 (2012): 8450–55.

Widele, John. Top. Cork West and North-East (p. 710 Dunmanway). Manuscript in Royal Irish Academy, 1850s.

Wilkinson, Richard H. *The Complete Gods and Goddesses of Ancient Egypt.* London: Thames and Hudson, 2003.

Wright, Thomas. "The Worship of the Generative Powers during the Middle Ages of Western Europe." In *Sexual Symbolism: A History of Phallic Worship,* edited by Richard Payne Knight and Thomas Wright, 6–196. New York: Julian Press, 1957.

Yeats, William Butler. "Poetic Symbols." In *Literature: An Introduction to Fiction, Poetry, and Drama,* 10th ed, edited by X. J. Kennedy and Dana Gioia, 906–7. New York: Longman, 2007.

"Yoni." In *Encyclopedia of Religion,* vol. 15, edited by Mircea Eliade, 534. New York: Macmillan, 1986.

Zegura, Elizabeth C., ed. *The Rabelais Encyclopedia.* Westport, Conn.: Greenwood Press, 2004.

Index

Numbers in *italics* indicate illustrations.

Copgrove Sheela, 191–94, *192–93*
corbel tables, 16–21, *17, 20*
Corbin, Henry, 252–53
cosmological images, 256, 272–73
Cosslett, Lucy, 299
Cotter, Holland, 294
Counter-Reformation, 86–87, 159
County Roscommon, Four Sheelas,
    157–62, *158–59*
creation, 90, 143
Croft-on-Tees Sheela, 59
Cromwell, Oliver, 43, 45
Crone, The, 314
Crouching Sheelagh, 310–11, *311*
Cú Chulainn, 85, 105, 237
Cullahill Castle, 10
Cullahill Castle Sheela, *11, 64*
Cup Stone, 35, *35*
Curtis, J. P., 75

Da Derga's hostel, 45–46
Dagenham Idol, 52, *54,* 183
Daily Beast, 248
Danube River, 113
Dark Goddess, 78, 81, 89, 101, 120,
    127–30, *129,* 264, 281
Darwin, Charles, 269
Dashú, Max, 231, 236, 249, 265,
    292–93
da Vinci, Leonardo, 133–34
death, 76, 78, 130, 142
Delgado-Espinoza, Florencio, 230
Delporte, Henri, 133
Demeter, 91–92, 94–95, 105, 240
Descent of Man, The, 269

destruction, 90, 143
"Destruction of Da Derga's Hostel,
    The," 45–46
Devī-Māhātmyam, 215–18
Dexter, Miriam Robbins, 31, 215, 241
Diels, Hermann Alexander, 90
Dilukái, 231–36, *231–32, 235*
Dinner Party, The, 283
Diodorus, 97
display, power of, 78–85, *82–83,* 105,
    236–48, *239, 243–45, 247,* 259
divine hag of the Celts, 43
Divine Mother, 275
Dockstader, Frederick J., 229–30
Dolmetsch, Angela, 278
domination, 292–93
doorways. *See* entrances, guardian of
Dornan, Robert K., 283–84
Dowth Old Church, 74
dragons, 31
Dribble, Harold, 142
duality, 43
Dublin Millennium, 305
Dublin Penny Review, 83
Dunn, James H., 14, 46–47
Durgā, 213, 215, 217

Earth Mother, 52, 230, 256, 310
Easthorpe Sheela, 182–85, *184*
Ecuador, 229–31, *230*
Edelson, Mary Beth, 284–87,
    288–90, *288–90,* 293
Eisen, Charles, 239
Eisler, Riane, 133, 268–69
El Castillo cave vulvas, *134,* 136

About the Author

Starr Goode, MA, teaches writing and literature at Santa Monica College. She is producer and moderator for the cable TV series *The Goddess in Art* (available on YouTube). An award-winning writer, she has been profiled for her work as a cultural commentator in such publications as the *L.A. Weekly,* the *Los Angeles Times,* the *Wall Street Journal,* and the *New Yorker.* Her previous work on the Sheelas was published in *ReVision: A Journal of Consciousness and Transformation,* the *Irish Journal of Feminist Studies,* the three-volume encyclopedia *Goddesses in World Culture,* and *About Place Journal.* She is also the author of *The Art of Living: Falstaff, the Fool, and Dino* (Acacia Books Press, 2015).

Books of Related Interest

Norse Goddess Magic
Trancework, Mythology, and Ritual
by Alice Karlsdóttir

The Celts
Uncovering the Mythic and Historic Origins of Western Culture
by Jean Markale

Women of the Celts
by Jean Markale

The Druids
Celtic Priests of Nature
by Jean Markale

The Norse Shaman
Ancient Spiritual Practices of the Northern Tradition
by Evelyn C. Rysdyk

King Arthur and the Goddess of the Land
The Divine Feminine in the *Mabinogion*
by Caitlín Matthews

Ogam: The Celtic Oracle of the Trees
Understanding, Casting, and Interpreting the Ancient Druidic Alphabet
by Paul Rhys Mountfort

The Making of a Druid
Hidden Teachings from the Colloquy of Two Sages
by Christian J. Guyonvarc'h

INNER TRADITIONS • BEAR & COMPANY
P.O. Box 388
Rochester, VT 05767
1-800-246-8648
www.InnerTraditions.com

Or contact your local bookseller